Investing in Japan

Investing in Japan

The Nomura Research Institute, Tokyo

Foreword by Brian Reading

WOODHEAD-FAULKNER
in association with
NOMURA EUROPE NV

Published by Woodhead-Faulkner Limited
8 Market Passage, Cambridge CB2 3PF

Published in association with Nomura Europe NV
Sarphatistraat 33–35, Amsterdam
(London Office: Barber-Surgeons Hall, Monkwell Square,
London Wall, EC2Y 5BL)

ISBN 0 85941 067 6

Designed by Ron Jones

Production services by Book Production Consultants

Typeset in Monotype Imprint by Bedford Typesetters Ltd

Printed and bound in Great Britain by J. W. Arrowsmith Ltd, Bristol

FOREWORD

by Brian Reading

This book is a veritable treasure trove of facts and figures about Japan. While they won't answer *all* the potential investor's questions, they will answer many. More important, they will prompt other questions. But facts alone are dull and indigestible: they need to be used to support a thesis, make a case or answer a problem. Here they do so. The question at issue is basically whether Japan can adjust to the changed, more hostile, world economic environment of the 1970s and 1980s.

The Japanese system was astonishingly successful over the first quarter-century following the end of the Second World War. In pre-war days Japanese growth averaged 5% a year, itself no mean feat. Over the period 1945–70 the growth rate doubled to 10% a year and Japan leapfrogged into the position of being the world's third largest economy. Much has been written of this Japanese economic miracle. It can be explained by the very different social, political, economic, industrial and financial system in Japan compared with that of other advanced industrial countries. But whereas "groupism", lifetime employment, promotion by seniority, growth before profit, highly geared corporate finance, enormous investment in capital-intensive mass-production industry regardless of pollution and the environment, a total dependence upon cheap imported energy and natural resources, and the blitzkrieg upon the markets for manufactured goods in other developed economies were the ingredients for success before the oil crisis and the world slump, these factors could now be a recipe for disaster.

Japan must change its ways. But can it? Outwardly, the omens are ill. Japanese exports have continued to surge ahead. Growth has slowed. Imports have been restrained both by slow growth and by the break in commodity prices since the spring of 1977. Japan has run up a massive merchandise trade surplus and, together with West Germany, has become the whipping boy of the international community. It is being pressurised to open up its domestic markets to the manufactured goods of other competitive economies. It is being told to reflate home demand. Increasingly barriers are being erected elsewhere against imports from Japan. It is being forced to limit its exports "voluntarily". The tide seems to have turned against Japan. What were strengths in a growing economy – lifetime employment, "groupism", heavy investment, manufacturing efficiency – have become weaknesses.

It is all very well for foreigners to carp at and criticise Japan for its industrial success. This misunderstands the nature of the Japanese problem. The salient facts are simple enough. By population size, with 110 million people, Japan is the world's sixth largest country; by land area it comes 56th. But only 15% of Japan's land is habitable. This gives a population density of 2,000 per square kilometre of habitable land – not far short of the population density in the suburbs of many big cities. With the shortage of land comes a scarcity of natural resources. Japan imports all its oil, iron ore, nickel, cotton, wool and bauxite, three-quarters of its coal, half its food. It is short on resources and long on labour, a gigantic Hong Kong or Singapore. Yet Japanese living standards have reached the level of a second-rank developed country, on a par statistically with Britain and Italy. To enjoy the life-style of a modern developed economy, with the sixth largest population in the world, it must perforce import huge quantities of energy and raw materials. To pay for its imports it has no alternative but to export manufactured goods on a massive scale. That is a necessary fact of Japanese life which cannot be changed without impoverishing the nation as a whole: the Japanese have nothing to export but their work. It is to this reality that the Japanese economy is geared, even distorted.

Textbook theories of international trade explain Japan's predicament. A country specialises in producing and exporting those things in which it has a comparative advantage. The comparative advantage is determined by comparing the relative productivity of resources between different domestic uses. Japan originally did not have to be very good at producing manufactured goods, nor was it. All that was required was that resources were better employed relatively within Japan on manufacturing activities than elsewhere and that this gradient in productivity, so to speak, was steeper in Japan than in competitor countries. Because of Japan's lack of natural resources this condition was easily satisfied. Once Japan specialised in manufacturing production, however, its sheer inefficiency in other sectors meant that resources were concentrated disproportionately in this one advanced sector. The result was lop-sided growth. In 1973, the last "normal" year before the oil crisis, Japan had a gross domestic product per head of $3,752 (at current price and exchange rates) compared with $3,138 for Great Britain. But output per worker (and thus overall productivity) was very similar: $7,642 for the $44\frac{1}{2}\%$ of workers in Britain's 56 million population, compared with $7,428 for the $50\frac{1}{2}\%$ in Japan. In Britain manufacturing accounted for

31% of GDP and 31.3% of employment. GDP per worker in manufacturing was similar to that in other occupations and much lower than in agriculture, which contributed 4% to GDP with only 3% of the working population. In Japan manufacturing accounted for 28% of GDP and 24% of employment. Productivity in manufacturing was one-fifth higher in than in all other activities. When compared with agriculture the differential was much greater; some 17% of Japanese worked in agriculture but produduded only 7% of GDP – thus Japan's manufacturing workers were three times more productive than the agricultural workers.

Moreover, broad sectorial comparisons of this sort understate the disparity between the most advanced and the most backward elements within the Japanese economy. Basically, some 20% of Japan's economy is highly developed, efficient and capable of competing with the best in the world. The remaining 80% is backward and inefficient. Growth has been concentrated hitherto on the advanced element; resources must now be redirected to raising the standard within the other four-fifths of the economy. This requires institutional changes – a move towards state pensions or health insurance, better roads and housing, reorganisation of distribution and service industries and the reform of the banking system.

All these changes take time. Meanwhile industry does what it can to survive. That means it continues to export, and at a rate geared to meet an import bill which was expected to be swollen by fast growth and high commodity prices. The investment necessary for this has already been made, the workers are already employed and cannot be laid off, the money has been borrowed from the banks and must be repaid. This industrial momentum is the cause of the present export surplus.

In time resources will be shifted. The less developed sectors must be brought forward. Production in industry will switch from low added-value, high energy- and resource-consuming industries like shipbuilding, steel, textiles and cars to technologically advanced, high added-value manufacture. The Japanese must continue to export their labour but, instead of applying a small amount of labour to a large volume of raw material to produce things which anybody can make (and most do), they must combine a large amount of labour with limited materials to create what others can't or don't make.

This shift in and broadening of Japan's economic base will provide new investment opportunities. Here is a country for investors to watch, and to help them watch it this book, rare among reference books in its readability, can be strongly recommended.

Acknowledgements

The Nomura Research Institute, Tokyo, wishes to express gratitude for help in the production of this book to: Mr J. Sakamoto and Miss K. Iwasawa of the Japanese Information Centre in London for providing maps of Japan; Mr K. J. Clarke and Miss A. Denise Coupé of European Public Relations Ltd for editing and indexing; Mr Brian Reading, broadcaster, journalist and international economics commentator, for writing the Foreword.

CONTENTS

		Page
Foreword by Brian Reading		v
Acknowledgements		viii
List of tables		xi
List of figures		xiii
Map		xiv
1	**Japan – the Background**	1
1.1	Geography and Climate	1
1.2	History	1
1.3	Natural Resources	9
1.4	Food	15
1.5	Population	15
1.6	Politics	19
1.7	National Income and Expenditure	30
1.8	Prices	35
1.9	The Labour Market	37
1.10	Foreign Trade and the Balance of Payments	40
1.11	The Industrial Structure	44
1.12	Japan's Macro-economic Policy	45
1.13	Japan's Industrial Policy	48
2	**The Structure of Japanese Companies**	51
2.1	Brief History and Recent Development	51
2.2	The Organization of Japanese Companies	52
2.3	Major Characteristics of Japanese Companies	54
2.4	Fundamental Differences between Japanese and Western Companies	58
2.5	Joint Ventures	62

Page

3   Japanese Industry   67
3.1   The Outlook for Major Japanese Industries in 1980   67
3.2   Iron and Steel   77
3.3   Shipbuilding   82
3.4   Construction   86
3.5   Automobiles   89
3.6   Consumer Electronic and Electrical Products   93
3.7   Audio Equipment   99
3.8   Synthetic Fibres   103
3.9   Trading Companies   107
3.10 Department Stores and Chain Stores   112

4   The Japanese Financial System   118
4.1   The Structure of the Financial Market   118
4.2   Monetary Policy and its Instruments   132
4.3   The Money Market   135
4.4   Changes in the Structure of the Financial Market   139

5   The Japanese Securities Market   144
5.1   History and Development   144
5.2   Stocks and Bonds in Japan   148
5.3   The Structure of the Stock Exchange   152
5.4   Listing Requirements of the Tokyo Stock Exchange   155
5.5   The Dealing System   161
5.6   Indices of the Tokyo Stock Exchange   163
5.7   The Over-the-counter Market   165
5.8   Commission Rates   166
5.9   Securities Companies   167
5.10 Unit Trusts   170
5.11 Rules Governing Foreign Investment   173
5.12 The Japanese Accounting System   176

6   Reforming the Japanese Economy   178
6.1   Adaptation to Changes in the International Environment   178
6.2   Economic Reformation Using Market Mechanisms   179
6.3   The Medium-term Outlook for the Japanese Economy   183
6.4   The Rapid Growth of the Capital Market   185
6.5   Conclusion   188

Index   189

Tables

(Tables refer to Japan except where stated otherwise)   *Page*

1. Import dependence ratios for major natural resources   10
2. Effect of energy conservation measures and shifts in the composition
    of demand for energy, classified by sectors   12
3. Dependence on imports of primary commodities in major countries
    (1974)   14
4. Labour supply and demand   16
5. Population, by age groups   17
6. New employees, by level of education   18
7. Breakdown of further education statistics   19
8. Number of Diet members, by party (25 January 1978)   20
9. Composition of the workforce, by occupation   22
10. Per capita gross domestic product of OECD countries   31
11. Gross national expenditure   33
12. Amounts and rates of spring wage increases   39
13. Composition of exports and imports in 1976   41
14. Balance of payments   42
15. Proportion of total industrial output, by industry   44
16. Examples of stimulative fiscal and monetary policy   47
17. Rates of growth of corporate sales in major countries   59
18. Rate of earnings on total capital in major countries   59
19. Ratio of profits to sales in major countries   60
20. Financial ratios in major countries (1973)   61
21. Performance ratios of foreign-capital and domestic firms in Japan   63
22. Ratios of main costs to sales in foreign-capital and domestic firms in
    Japan (1973)   64
23. Financial safety ratios of foreign-capital and domestic firms in Japan
    (1973)   65

		Page
24.	Average annual growth rates of 50 industries	68
25.	Changes in annual growth rates of 50 industries	71
26.	Factors affecting growth in 50 industries	74
27.	Export levels of the main exporting industries	76
28.	Steel production and supply in Japan	79
29.	Steel production capacities of the world	80
30.	Major shipbuilding nations' shares of the world market	82
31.	Trend and projection of orders received by the shipbuilding industry	84
32.	Orders received and revenue of the construction industry	88
33.	World automobile industries in 1975	90
34.	Growth of the automobile industry	91
35.	Changes in exports of consumer electronic and electrical products	96
36.	Growth pattern of consumer electronic and electrical products	96
37.	Changes in production of consumer electronic and electrical products	97
38.	Production and exports of audio equipment	102
39.	Composition of domestic demand for fibres, by type of fibre	104
40.	Demand for synthetic fibres	106
41.	Synthetic fibre production capacities in South-East Asia (end of 1975)	107
42.	Changes in trade volume of nine major trading companies	110
43.	Japan's top 20 retailers	113
44.	Sales volume of department and chain stores	117
45.	Balance sheet of city banks (31 March 1977)	120
46.	Current state of financial institutions (30 September 1976)	122
47.	Balance of deposits, by banking groups	126
48.	Balance of outstanding loans, by banking groups	127
49.	Changes in the reserve ratio of all Japanese banks	134
50.	Changes in the flow of credits to city banks through regulation at the discount window (1973–)	134
51.	Changes in the volume of the short-term money market	136
52.	Recent highs and lows of the short-term money rate	138
53.	Structure of the repurchase market (31 March 1977)	139
54.	Changes in investment preferences	140
55.	Securities issued in Japan	149
56.	Stock trade volume, by stock exchange (1976)	152
57.	Current stock exchange commission rates	166
58.	Classification of securities companies	169
59.	Status of major securities firms (September 1976 term)	170
60.	Taxes applicable to acquired securities	174
61.	Japan's trade liberalization	180
62.	Japan's liberalization of capital transactions	181

Figures

(Figures illustrate information relating to Japan except where otherwise stated)   *Page*

1. International comparison of demographic structure   21
2. Lifestyle satisfaction breakdown   24
3. Rates of increase in consumer and wholesale price indices 37
4. Structure of the financial market   119
5. Mechanism of Treasury investment and loans   130
6. Process of the ripple effect of a tight money policy   132
7. Short-term and long-term rates   137
8. Ratio of funds of long-term financial institutions to those of commercial banks   142
9. The development of the world's modern industrial civilization   179
10. The growth trend of the Japanese economy   182
11. Changes in interest rates   184

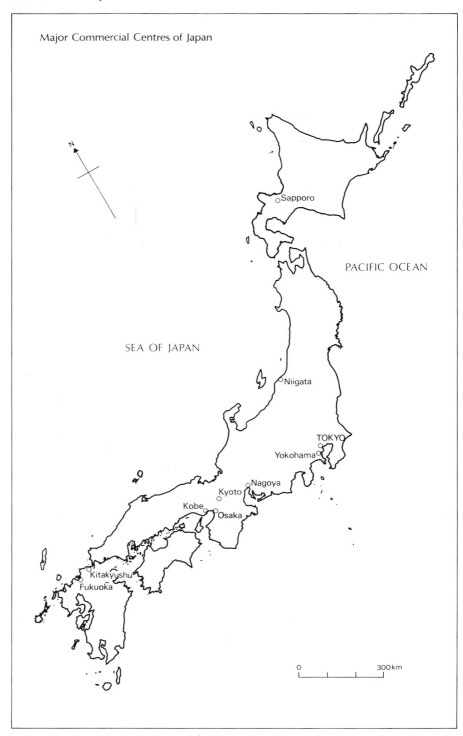

Major Commercial Centres of Japan

N

Sapporo

PACIFIC OCEAN

SEA OF JAPAN

Niigata

TOKYO

Yokohama

Nagoya

Kyoto

Kobe

Osaka

Kitakyushu

Fukuoka

0   300 km

1 JAPAN-THE BACKGROUND

1.1 Geography and Climate

The Japanese archipelago consists of four major islands and hundreds of smaller islands. Located in the Western Pacific, it is separated from the Asian continent by the Sea of Japan and the Korean Strait. Although it has a land area of 143,000 square miles (372,000 km^2), or 1·5 times that of West Germany, the country's landscape is dominated by mountains, and only 15% of the land is habitable.

Mountain ranges divide the narrow main island, Honshu, into the Pacific coast side and the Sea of Japan side. They also function as climatic modifiers by sheltering the Pacific side in winter from the severe cold that comes from the Asian continent. Because of this and its more favourable topography, the Pacific coast region is highly industrialized. All of Japan's major cities are located on the western Pacific coastline, which forms a giant industrial belt.

Since Japan has a latitude span of 15 degrees, there are significant regional differences in temperature and precipitation between north and south. With the exception of Hokkaido, the northernmost of the four major islands, the country has a rainy season that lasts from mid-June to the end of July. The rainy season, followed by a hot summer, is good for growing rice, the major staple food and the nation's main crop. During late summer and early autumn, the country is visited by destructive typhoons of tropical origin. The autumn is crisply pleasant and the foliage turns red and golden in the mountains. In winter, snow falls on most of Japan, although the amount and duration vary greatly from region to region.

1.2 History

1.2.1 THE TOKUGAWA PERIOD (1603–1867)
Japan began to shape itself into a modern state with the Meiji Restoration of 1868. However, before that Japan was under the powerful centralized rule

of the Tokugawa military government for some 250 years. Many of the political and economic institutions which facilitated the transformation of Japan into a modern state were developed during the Tokugawa period.

Following a tradition dating back to the thirteenth century, the Tokugawa government received its legitimacy from the Emperor. However, to maintain its superiority over other Daimyo (feudal lords), early in the seventeenth century the Tokugawa family instituted a system of alternate residence for the Daimyo. Under this system, all Daimyo were required to spend alternate years in the Shogunate* capital, Edo, and when they returned to their domains they left their wives and eldest sons behind. This system effectively controlled the power of the Daimyo, as the trips between their domains and Edo and the need to maintain two residences kept their expenses high. At the same time, the periodic absences from their domains prevented the Daimyo from plotting against the Tokugawa family. The Shogunate government also carried out various construction projects, such as road construction, the building of castles, etc., to siphon off the wealth of the Daimyo's coffers.

The Tokugawa administration was a skilful combination of central control and local autonomy. Although the Shogun presided over the Daimyo, his government only had direct control over about a quarter of the country. The remaining three-quarters of the country was parcelled out among 260 Daimyo. The domains were autonomous except for some broad requirements set by the Shogunate government. The Tokugawa period was characterized by the growth of bureaucracy and commerce. The periodic absences of Daimyo from their domains gave rise to government by councils early in the seventeenth century. The routine administration of each domain was carried out by a small number of officials under the general control of the council. Eventually, there was an over-abundance of officials in the system but bureaucracy provided the nation with the elementary political disciplines of law and order. Local autonomy also allowed useful initiative and, since the size of the population remained stable throughout the Tokugawa period, there was a slow but persistent rise in mass living standards. Since the rural population in various regions tended to specialize in the production of specific goods, trade was carried out on a nationwide level, which unified the country as an economic entity.

Early in the seventeenth century, the Tokugawa government took a series of measures to close the country to foreign intercourse, except for a limited amount of trade with the Dutch at a designated port in southern Japan. Despite this ban on foreign trade, marine transport developed for the domestic commerce of rice, marine products and other goods. By the late seventeenth century, Edo had a population of nearly 1 million and Osaka, the commercial centre, nearly 400,000. There were more than 300 Daimyo capitals across the

---

* The Shogun was the most senior of the feudal lords.

entire country, each serving as the administrative as well as commercial centre for a domain. Helped by the development of communication, transportation and a money economy, Osaka merchants developed a system for the distribution of goods and also began to play a role as moneylenders. In some provinces, revenues from the sale of rice to Osaka merchants amounted to 60–70% of the official revenue. Merchants were given special privileges and, although their official social status was low, they began to have considerable social and economic influence.

The continuing peace and the development of bureaucracy and commerce contributed to widespread interest in education from the second half of the eighteenth century. By 1800 the warrior class had long been literate. Sons of the warrior class attended colleges run by the domain government, while daughters received their education on a tutorial basis. The education of the warrior class mostly consisted of Chinese studies and training in the martial arts. Commoners' educational needs were met by local community schools, often run by Buddhist temples. These taught children how to read and write in Japanese, simple mathematics and the basics of filial piety and loyalty. By the first half of the nineteenth century, 11,000 temple schools were scattered throughout the country. At the end of the Tokugawa era the literacy rate for the total population was over 30%, whilst the rate for men was about 50%. This exceptionally high level of education and discipline proved to be a great asset when Japan began its modernization after the Meiji Restoration.

1.2.2 MODERN INDUSTRIAL DEVELOPMENT

1868–1945

Although the policy of isolation effectively protected the Shogunate government, it also cut Japan off from the development of science. Therefore, when the Shogunate government was overthrown at the time of the Meiji Restoration, Japan was technologically behind the advanced countries of Europe and America.

In 1868 the Emperor Meiji ascended the throne of Japan and appointed the ministers who were to set up Japan's first modern political system. During the Emperor Meiji's reign from 1868 to 1912 (known as the Meiji era), Japan attempted to learn about all aspects of modern society – political, legal, social, military and economic – from the advanced countries of the West, especially Britain, France, Germany and the United States. The basic policy of the Japanese government of the Meiji era was that of "enriching the country and strengthening the military", a policy aimed at catching up with the advanced nations of the West.

In the early years of the Meiji era, there was not enough accumulated private capital to establish modern industries, and so the Meiji government took the initiative in establishing enterprises in fields such as mining, shipbuilding, cement, glass, spinning and weaving. Most of the plant and equipment necessary for these enterprises was imported and foreign engineers

were hired to run it. Since the primary purpose of these government enterprises was to start modern industries in Japan, little attention was paid to
costs. A decade or so into the Meiji era, these public industries were sold to
the private sector at nominal prices. Thus, the quest to catch up with western
countries has been the main feature of modern Japan's history.

The second feature has been the important role played by the military
until the end of the Second World War and the subsequent dissolution of
that role. The military involvement deeply affected the nature and character
of the development of Japan's economic structure and technology. Its
influence was at times favourable and at others unfavourable to technological
progress, but its presence was always evident.

One assessment of how far behind in technology Japan was at the start
of the Meiji era is illustrated by the lack of steam engines, which were present
in various countries at that time. Although there was a big spurt in industrial
production at the time of the Sino-Japanese War of 1894–95, Japan's capacity
was still only equal to that of France or Germany in the 1840s. The gap
between Japan, which had not yet experienced even its first industrial
revolution, and the advanced countries of the West, which had already experienced both their first and second industrial revolutions, cannot be
over-stressed.

Japan's first industrial revolution really matured between the turn of the
century and the outbreak of the First World War. One basic characteristic
of this period was the sale of government enterprises to private businesses
at a nominal price, since they had been operated with little consideration of
cost and had not been making good profits. After these acquisitions, private
enterprises ran more efficiently and accumulated technical experience. The
textile industry took the best advantage of these circumstances. A few years
after the introduction of ring spinning machines, domestic production of
cotton yarn exceeded imports. During this period the textile industry firmly
established itself as a modern industry.

The second feature of the period before the First World War was the rapid
development of the defence industry. In addition to the industries directly
concerned with defence, there were many private industries which had close
ties with them through supplying steel, non-ferrous metals, metal-working
machinery and ships. The shipbuilding industry was one of the industries
which reaped the greatest profits from doing business with the military. As
the industry made considerable progress in size and technology, the Navy
Ministry began to place large orders and further support the development
of the industry by providing funds and technical assistance. Two other
factors speeded the development of the shipbuilding industry. One legal
factor was the enactment of the Navigation Promotion Act of 1896 and the
Foreign Liners Assistance Act of 1909, which replaced the 1896 Act. These
statutes helped domestic ship operators switch from foreign suppliers to

domestic suppliers of ships. The other factor was diplomatic. In the 1890s the government finally succeeded in its quest for revision of the "unequal treaties"* between the Shogunate government and such Western powers as Britain, the United States, Germany, France and Russia. As a result of the treaty revision, the duty rate for ships was raised from 5% to 15%, which promptly caused a switch from the use of imported ships to those domestically built.

The third important characteristic of Japan's first industrial revolution, joint ventures with foreign firms, is exemplified by the experience of the electrical machinery industry. Although Japan's electrical machinery industry was not ready for manufacturing large-capacity equipment in the first industrial revolution, as at the time Japanese firms lacked the necessary technology, it more than doubled its output within a few years, based on the demand for small-capacity equipment.

Japan's electrical machinery industry had begun operation at about the same time as that of the United States. However, because of low domestic demand and lack of funds for research and development, after only ten years the Japanese industry had begun to lag considerably behind that of the rest of the world. To compensate, many Japanese firms had to enter into often unfavourable joint ventures with giant foreign companies.

Labour conditions in Japan also hampered the modern machinery industry's development into a mass production operation. Generally, the techniques of machinery building during this time were the product of imported technology, non-mechanized manpower and the experience of a few skilled people. Uniformity and the interchangeability of parts required for mass production could not be guaranteed under these conditions. The first attempt to overcome these constraints came in the field of textile machinery with the invention of the Toyota automatic loom and its production which began in 1907.

The second surge of industrial development came with the outbreak of the First World War in Europe. With the Western countries busy in Europe, Japan was given respite from their drive to export machinery. The cessation of machinery imports posed a great challenge to Japan, and it was given the chance to pursue industrial development for itself. Imports of electrical machinery, metal-working machinery, spinning and weaving machinery, and railway equipment dropped sharply, and the private capital accumulated during the Russo-Japanese war of 1904–5 went into these fields.

The shipbuilding industry developed rapidly as a result of the Navy's

---

* After the Meiji restoration Japan had announced its intention of renegotiating its existing treaties with the Western powers. These treaties had given them consular jurisdiction in civil and criminal cases and had fixed the import duty rate at 5%. For the next 25 years the revision of these treaties was a major political and diplomatic problem for the Japanese.

contracts for heavy warships. However, the concentration on warship building came to a halt at the conclusion of the Washington Naval Disarmament Conference in 1921. The Washington Treaty sharply curtailed the Navy's orders for new ships. Therefore, the shipbuilding industry searched for new areas of opportunity and entered other industries related to shipbuilding. Shipbuilders went into such diversified fields as diesel engines, automobiles, aircraft, building and construction, steel pipes, railway carriages and electrical machinery. Expertise in shipbuilding contributed greatly to technological advancement in these industries.

In the United States there were many industries that had achieved economies of scale, and the automobile industry was supported by the related fields of machinery and materials. The Japanese automobile industry lacked this kind of support, especially in the metal-working machinery industry and the metal materials industry. This difference in the production environment made it impossible for the Japanese automobile industry to be as successful as the shipbuilding industry which had given birth to it.

Under these conditions, the Japanese government tried to protect the domestic automobile industry by imposing a duty rate of as high as 35% on imported cars. However, American automobile companies counteracted this measure by a policy of direct investment in Japan. The few Japanese automobile companies that survived did so through military contracts. Another limiting factor on the Japanese automobile industry was that the living standard of the Japanese people in general was not high enough to guarantee a large market for private cars.

In spite of the decline in shipbuilding, and the difficulties of the automobile and metal-working industries, the period after the First World War was one of great progress for Japanese industry as a whole, especially the textile industry.

In the field of chemicals, there were not many noticeable advances during this period, except in the production of explosives by the military plants and in the production of *Ajinomoto* (monosodium glutamate, a chemical which enhances the taste of food). When imports from Europe ceased, Japanese companies entered new fields such as synthetic dyes and optical glass.

Between the Great Depression and the Second World War Japanese industrial production was directed predominantly towards military ends. So much effort was put into war production that Japan's economic structure was disproportionately geared toward the defence industry at the expense of other industries. About half of the military budget was used to produce machinery. Much of this production was carried out in civilian factories, since in the late 1930s these comprised well over 90% of the total machinery production capacity in the country. The effects of the civilian production of military equipment were seen in the decline of the production of cotton spindles and of spinning machines.

This period provided many firms with their first experience in using the techniques of mass production, even though much of the production was military in nature. Many plants expanded during this time. However, much of the expansion was accomplished not by further mechanization or increasing the number of machines per worker, but rather by putting more workers into the production process.

The industries which had established their foundations before the Depression, such as shipbuilding, railway carriages and electrical machinery, matured and polished their technology. The electrical machinery industry raised its technical level by absorbing the newest developments from its partners in joint ventures and grew to the stage where it could produce large-capacity electrical equipment. From 1932 onwards, domestic products began to replace imports.

The chemical industry also achieved large production increases; Japan's dyestuffs and soda industries had been held back by the European export drive of the 1920s, but the beginning of the new decade altered the situation favourably for Japan. The renewed ban on gold exports resulted in the price of Japanese exports being lower than that of imports.

Production of consumer durables such as sewing machines, radios and automobiles also increased in the 1930s. The present-day Nissan and Toyota companies started their operations in 1934 and 1937 respectively. Unfortunately, however, the quality of these consumer durables was very poor. Consumer durables industries had not achieved economies of scale from mass production.

Some of the technology developed in connection with military projects flowered in the form of precision machinery, aircraft, shipbuilding and sewing machines. However, these young buds, which might have led to production of goods in the most advanced, technology-intensive industries, were not cared for during the Second World War. Moreover, after Japan's demilitarization, following the end of the war, excellent project leaders, managers and the research atmosphere were lost as military research facilities were disbanded.

The Post-war Period

Reconstruction As a result of the war, Japan's productive capacity was reduced to less than half the peak of the pre-war period. Industrial production in 1946 was one-fifth of the war-time high. The direction of Japan's rapid growth in the catching-up process declined at the end of the war, as most of its economic strength was lost. Japan started a remarkable process of reconstruction in the post-war period. There were different market conditions in this period which can be attributed to two factors. One was the role of the US policy towards Japan, and the other was the switch from the military to the civilian economy. Immediately after the war, US policy seemed to be aimed at making Japan a repair shop for the US military. The outbreak of the Korean War in 1950 fully achieved this objective. The Korean War also served as a catalyst to restore Japan's industrial production to the 1934–36 average, as a result of special US war demands.

Another objective of US policy was the creation in Japan of American-style capitalism. The United States not only regarded Japan as a military base from which to guard against Communism but knew that it would profit by helping Japan pursue capitalistic development in the American way. Efforts were made to modernize and rationalize the Japanese industrial structure by introducing new techniques in management. Low productivity sectors such as small businesses and agriculture were also reviewed.

The Dodge Mission, named after the president of the Bank of Detroit who headed it, and the policy adopted as a result of its recommendations were undeniably epoch-making in the economic history of modern Japan. The Mission's main objective was to control post-war hyperinflation. Government subsidies to large firms were ended, labour's wage rate was pegged at a low level and a unique foreign exchange rate was established. Both labour and management were urged to pursue the rationalization of their organizations and increase their efficiency.

Coupled with the "Dodge Line" policies, the US Government lifted its production control policy in Japan. In 1950 the shipbuilding industry was returned to private hands. The ceiling on the number of cotton spindles, which had been set at 4 million, was lifted. The regulation against the use of foreign coal was discontinued, as was the regulation against C petroleum, the residual oil used in industry.

The outbreak of the Korean War boosted certain Japanese industries which were having difficulty in taking off economically. The capital required for rationalizing the internal organization of these firms was accumulated throughout this period. The steel industry, for instance, which started in the 1890s as a government enterprise and had already been transferred to private business, began its first rationalization plan. It studied the American steel industry and adopted the most recent developments available in steel production technology. The year 1955 was the starting point of a nationwide productivity promotion campaign.

Economic Independence The years 1955 and 1956 were international boom years. This boom gave Japan a chance to expand domestic and export markets. Textiles, ships and steel were exported in growing amounts. Japan's heavy industrialization proceeded at a rapid pace. After the Korean War, consumer durables began to be mass produced, again contributing to the high rate of economic growth. The primary reason for re-emphasis on consumer durables was the switch in the industrial structure and capital flow from the military sector to the civilian. The post-war change in the demand structure also helped the consumer durables industry. Land reform contributed to the equalization of income and the boom in the world economy advanced Japan's national income at a fast pace. For the first time, the income with which to purchase consumer durables was within the reach of the average Japanese.

Another important factor in Japan's rapid growth after the war was the introduction of foreign technology. Between 1950 and 1960, for instance, Japanese companies signed nearly 2000 agreements with foreign concerns for the use of technology. Of these, 70% were with US firms. Japan had to reduce the gap between the technical level of advanced Western countries and its own. This served as an incentive for large investments in modern plant and equipment by Japanese firms.

Industries which had high growth rates can be classified in two groups. The first group included automobiles, oil products, precision machines and machine tools, which already were on a mass-production basis in advanced countries such as the United States in the early decades of this century. These industries brought prosperity to their countries in the 1920s. In Japan, however, these industries were not put on a mass-production basis until the 1950s. The second group of high growth rate industries included synthetic resins, synthetic fibres and transistors. These developed simultaneously in the United States, Japan and other countries after the war. In Japan, the simultaneous development of both groups of industries in the 1950s created boom conditions.

Advanced Industrialization In 1960, the government formulated the National Income Doubling Plan, aimed at doubling the national income at an annual rate of 7·2% in the ten years from 1961. This was the highest goal ever set by the government, but the actual growth of the economy far outpaced it. Japanese industry made an enormous capital investment to expand modern facilities and raise productivity. By the mid-1960s, Japan solved the problem of persistent deficits in its international balance of payments. Domestic consumer demand also expanded with the emergence of a vast middle class.

As the growth during the 1960s was based largely on heavy consumption of energy and other resources, the oil crisis caused the Japanese government and industry to change the structure of the economy to one that was more knowledge-intensive and less resource-consuming. This goal, along with minimizing social and economic friction as the Japanese economy shifts from a high growth to a lower growth, forms the core of Japan's economic policy extending over the next decade.

1.3 Natural Resources

1.3.1 HIGH IMPORT DEPENDENCE RATIO

Japan's past high economic growth was supported by the availability of abundant imported natural resources. Although there are practically no domestic resource supplies, Japan was able to develop high resource-consuming chemical and heavy industries due to the relatively low international resource prices in the 1960s. As indicated in Table 1, the ratio of imports to domestic consumption of most major natural resources rose sharply during this decade. In 1970, Japan imported all the bauxite and nickel ore it consumed, nearly 90% of iron ore, 75% of copper ore and coking coal, and a little over 50% of the lead and zinc supply. Japan's share in the world demand for these materials has risen dramatically, but the pace is expected to slow down during the 1970s, owing to changes in technology and the structure of the nation's industry. Nevertheless, in 1980 Japan is expected to account for nearly one-fifth of world trade in bauxite and petroleum and probably one-half of the world transactions in iron ore.

TABLE 1 *Import dependence ratios for major natural resources*

	FY 1960	FY 1965	FY 1970
	%	%	%
Copper	50·6	57·6	75·6
Lead	54·6	51·7	54·6
Zinc	26·3	38·1	54·5
Bauxite	100·0	100·0	100·0
Nickel (including ferronickel)	100·0	100·0	100·0
Iron ore	68·0	80·7	87·9
Coking coal	35·8	54·9	78·5

1.3.2 CHARACTERISTICS OF JAPAN'S RESOURCE IMPORTS

Japan's resource imports are characterized by a number of features. The country tends to import natural resources in crude forms rather than after some processing in the country of origin. In 1969, 46% of world aluminium imports, 88% of copper and 24% of petroleum imports were processed or semi-processed, but Japan's import ratios of processed or semi-processed goods were considerably below these figures.

In the future, due to the desire of developing countries to step up the local processing needed to create jobs, the ratio of processed or semi-processed material imports is expected to increase. However, the rise is expected to be faster for Japan than the rest of the world because of the country's difficult domestic industrial siting.

The uneven world distribution of natural resources means that Japan's heavy dependence on two or three major producing countries has intensified for some raw materials, including copper ore, bauxite and petroleum, which has resulted in a sharp increase in Japan's share of certain exports from these countries. Although the concentration of purchases in a few countries is economical for Japan, as it reduces costs of transportation and information-gathering, it makes Japan's resource supply vulnerable to sudden political or economic changes. It also tends to provoke nationalist sentiments in the producing countries. Therefore, diversification of sources is an important task for Japanese industry.

One effective means of such diversification is to accelerate Japan's overseas development investment. In the past, Japan purchased more than 90% of its natural resource supply without any long-term commitment to the producing countries. The system had its merits when there was a glut of raw materials, but it became less and less acceptable with the tightening of the world resource supply–demand balance. During the 1970s, Japan's overseas direct investment in resources is projected to increase more than tenfold, from $2·7 billion in 1972 to $30 billion in 1980. This investment must be made in such a way that it will contribute to the orderly development of the international economy, as well as industrialization of the resource-producing countries.

1.3.3 ENERGY

Japan is heavily dependent on imports for its energy supply, especially on petroleum. In 1960, when Japan's high economic growth had just begun, indigenous energy, consisting of coal and hydraulic power, accounted for 60% of the total supply. The self-sufficiency rate then declined sharply as demand expanded and imported petroleum replaced domestic coal as a more desirable energy source. In fiscal year 1973, the self-sufficiency rate declined to 9·5% and imported petroleum accounted for 77% of the country's energy supply. Japan's dependence on petroleum is much higher than that in the United States (47% in 1972) or the European Community (61% in 1973).

Although Japan's energy demand through the early 1970s grew more than twice as fast as the world energy demand, its energy consumption per capita is still only one-third that of the United States and 60% of that of Britain and West Germany. This may be attributed to low consumption of energy by the household and commercial sector. This sector accounts for 35–36% of the total energy consumption in both the United States and West Germany, but only 17–18% of the total in Japan. Cutting back energy consumption in this sector would be difficult in Japan because it is already low. Furthermore, the rising standard of living will boost energy consumption in this sector, as demonstrated by the increasing use of air-conditioners in the past few years.

The industrial sector accounts for about 60% of the total energy consumption in Japan as compared with 30% in the United States and 40% in West Germany. The iron and steel industry alone accounts for 20% of the total consumption and the chemical industry for 14%. Even with the gradual restructuring of Japanese industry and extensive conservation efforts, these industries are expected to account for nearly 30% of the total consumption in 1985 (*see* Table 2).

TABLE 2 Effect of energy conservation measures and shifts in the composition of demand for energy, classified by sectors

(Demand expressed in 10^{13} k cal)

	FY 1965		FY 1973		FY 1985 (before conservation)		FY 1985 (after conservation)		Energy conservation rates for FY 1985 (%)	Average annual growth rates of demand for energy		
	Demand	%	Demand	%	Demand	%	Demand	%		FY1965–FY1973	FY1973–FY1985 (before conservation)	FY1973–FY1985 (after conservation)
										%	%	%
Paper and pulp	5·1	3·1	9·9	2·6	21·1	2·7	20·0	2·8	4·9	8·6	6·5	6·0
Chemical	21·1	12·7	52·3	13·7	101·9	13·0	94·0	13·2	7·8	12·0	5·7	5·0
Ceramics and cement	7·9	4·8	15·1	4·0	32·5	4·1	28·6	4·0	12·2	8·4	6·6	5·4
Iron and steel	27·5	16·6	75·5	19·7	129·1	16·1	114·8	16·2	11·1	13·5	4·6	3·5
Non-ferrous metal	2·1	1·3	6·4	1·7	12·2	1·6	11·5	1·6	6·6	15·0	5·6	5·0
(Total for industries consuming larger amount of energy)	(63·7)	(38·5)	(159·3)	(41·7)	(296·9)	(37·9)	(268·9)	(37·8)	(9·4)	(12·2)	(5·3)	(4·5)
Other industries (ii)	27·8	16·8	64·0	16·7	137·7	17·6	135·8	19·1	1·4	7·2	6·6	6·5
(Other manufacturing industries)	(23·4)	(14·1)	(50·0)	(13·1)	(112·5)	(14·3)	(110·5)	(15·6)	(1·7)	(10·0)	(7·0)	(6·8)
Total for industrial sector	91·5	55·3	223·3	58·4	434·6	55·4	404·6	57·0	6·9	7·7	5·7	5·1

(Demand expressed in 10^{13} k cal)

	FY 1965		FY 1973		FY 1985 (before conservation)		FY 1985 (after conservation)		Energy conservation rates for FY1985 (%)	Average annual growth rates of demand for energy		
	Demand	%	Demand	%	Demand	%	Demand	%		FY1965–FY1973	FY1973–FY1985 (before conservation)	FY1973–FY1985 (after conservation)
Transport sector (iii)	20.0	12.1	45.3	11.8	96.6	12.3	78.9	11.1	18.4	10.8	6.5	4.7
Household and commercial sector	24.4	14.8	64.8	16.9	155.4	19.8	134.3	18.9	13.5	13.0	7.6	6.3
Household	—	—	30.1	7.8	72.1	9.2	61.3	8.6	14.9	—	7.5	6.1
Commercial	—	—	34.7	9.1	83.3	10.6	73.0	10.3	12.3	—	7.6	6.4
Others (iv)	29.7	17.8	49.2	12.9	97.7	12.5	92.4	13.0	5.4	4.3	5.9	5.4
Supply of primary energy	165.6	100.0	382.6	100.0	784.3	100.0	710.2	100.0	9.4	11.0	6.2	5.3

Notes (i) Total may not tally because of rounding up or because calculation is made on the basis of figures before rounding up.
(ii) Includes agriculture-forestry-fishery, mining, and construction, in addition to "other manufacturing industries".
(iii) Includes passenger cars for private use.
(iv) Energy sector, export, and loss of energy.
Source: Ministry of International Trade and Industry, *Japan's New Energy Policy* (Tokyo, 1976)

The goals of Japan's energy policy for the next decade are:

(a) reduction of dependence on petroleum through development of other energy sources;
(b) securing a stable petroleum supply by diversifying sources, including development investments in areas other than the Middle East;
(c) acceleration of energy conservation through the development of energy-saving technology.

TABLE 3 *Dependence on imports of primary commodities in major countries (1974)*

	USA	West Germany	France	UK	Italy	Japan
			(%)			
Beef	4·2	10·2	0	17·1	32·0	15·7
Wheat	0	13·9	0	32·2	20·7	95·9
Corn	0	85·7	0	100·0	45·0	99·6
Greasy wool	10·3	90·0	82·0	53·2	82·4	100·0
Cotton	0	100·0	100·0	100·0	99·6	100·0
Lumber	0·3	12·7	3·1	77·6	43·9	41·2
Copper	26·1	99·8	99·9	100·0	99·7	90·1
Lead	41·5	88·5	88·2	98·5	88·9	80·3
Zinc	61·8	70·1	95·3	98·9	61·6	64·5
Bauxite	60·9	99·8	0	100·0	91·0	100·0
Tin	100·0	100·0	98·2	80·8	100·0	98·5
Nickel	93·5	100·0	100·0	100·0	100·0	100·0
Iron ore	34·1	94·1	8·8	80·3	97·9	99·4
Coal (including raw coal)	0	0	37·2	0	93·5	72·2
Crude oil	26·2	94·3	99·1	99·9	99·2	99·7

Notes
(i) Dependence on overseas has been derived using this formula.

$$\frac{imports - exports}{production + imports - exports}$$

In the case of copper, lead, zinc, bauxite, tin and nickel, it has been derived from the following:

$$1 - \frac{production\ (ore)}{consumption\ (ore,\ seat\ metals)}$$

(ii) 1973 figures were used for lumber, coal and crude oil, the others are 1974 figures.
Sources: FAO Statistics, Metal Statistics, World Energy Supplies, Summary of Steel Statistics, *in* MITI, *White Paper on the International Trade 1976* (Tokyo, 1976).

According to the Ministry of International Trade and Industry, by 1985 nuclear energy and liquefied natural gas (LNG) should be increased to 5·5–7·5% and 5·0–6·5% of the total supply from their respective shares of 1·7% and 1·8%.

1.4 Food

Japan's food supply is also characterized by a high dependence on imports. Although in 1960 Japan was 80% self-sufficient (on an original calorie basis) in food, the self-sufficiency rate declined steadily to 53% in 1973. The ratios of imports to the total supply are particularly high for soya beans (97%), wheat (96%), oats and barley (90%), sugar (80%) and concentrated animal feed (70%). Despite a sharp increase in consumption of meat and dairy products by the Japanese since the Second World War, due to the lack of pasture land the combined number of heads of cattle and horses in Japan has increased by only 20% during the past 40 years to the present 3·7 million.

Japan's annual rice output now exceeds demand because of the government rice price support system. The development of new strains, fertilizers and insecticides in addition to mechanization has greatly reduced the labour required for rice production. This has made it possible for farmers to take industrial jobs, leaving the farming to their wives and parents. In the fore-seeable future rice will maintain its central position in Japan's agriculture.

1.5 Population

Japan, with a population of 110 million, is the world's sixth most populous country following the People's Republic of China, India, the USSR, the United States and Indonesia. Despite the size of their population, the Japanese have maintained a remarkable degree of cohesiveness, as they all belong to one ethnic group, speak one language and share a common history. Their major religions are Shintoism (an indigenous religion based on nature and ancestor worship) and Buddhism, which have been practised side by side for centuries by most Japanese.

One of the major factors in Japan's rapid economic growth since the Second World War has been the availability of labour. As indicated in Table 4, Japan's labour force grew between 1955 and 1970 by more than 1% a year. However, the rate of growth has diminished considerably, due to a sharp decline in the birth rate since the mid-1950s and the rising level of education.

At the same time, the nation's expanding industries have been able to absorb young people from the agricultural sector. This sector's share of the total labour force declined from 45·2% in 1950 to 30·2% in 1960 and 12·3% in 1975. The share of the secondary industries, on the other hand, expanded steadily from 24·4% in 1955 to 36·4% in 1975.

The shift of population from the agricultural to the industrial sector has been accompanied by extensive urbanization. According to a survey by the Prime Minister's Office published in 1977, nearly 60% of the total population live in urban areas, which account for only 2% of Japan's total land mass. Furthermore, 60% of the people living in urban areas are concentrated in and around the three major cities, Tokyo, Osaka and Nagoya. The large disparity in population density between the major cities and the rest of the country can be attributed to the uneven distribution of job opportunities and cultural and educational facilities.

TABLE 4 *Labour supply and demand*

(Million persons) (% *annual growth rate*)							
	1955	1960	1965	1970	1975	1980	1985
Productive population	59·3	65·2	72·9	78·9	83·9	88·7	93·6
(15 years +)	*1·9*	*2·2*	*1·6*	*1·1*	*1·1*	*1·1*	—
Labour force	41·9	45·1	47·9	51·5	52·8	54·9	56·8
population	*1·5*	*1·2*	*1·5*	*0·4*	*0·8*	*0·7*	—
Labour force as percentage of productive population	70·8	69·2	65·7	65·4	62·9	61·9	60·7
Employees:							
Total	40·9	44·4	47·3	50·9	51·8	54·2	56·1
	1·6	*1·3*	*1·5*	*0·3*	*0·9*	*0·7*	—
Primary industries	15·4	13·4	11·1	8·9	6·6	5·8	5·0
	−2·7	*−3·7*	*−4·5*	*−5·8*	*−2·7*	*−3·0*	—
Secondary industries	9·9	12·4	15·1	17·9	18·2	20·2	21·1
	4·5	*3·9*	*3·5*	*0·3*	*2·1*	*0·8*	—
Tertiary industries	15·6	18·5	21·1	24·1	26·9	28·2	30·1
	3·6	*2·6*	*2·7*	*2·2*	*1·0*	*1·3*	—
Unemployment rate (%)	2·5	1·7	1·2	1·2	1·9	1·4	1·2

Sources: Figures for 1955–75 from the Labour Force Survey, Prime Minister's Office. 1980 and 1985 figures estimated by the Industrial Structure Council.

Tokyo, in addition to being the political and economic centre, is the academic and cultural heart of the nation. All the major newspapers and TV and radio broadcasting networks have their headquarters in Tokyo. Although the city occupies only 1% of Japan's total land area and contains 11% of the population, it accounts for approximately 25% of the country's purchasing power, 33% of its college graduates and 60% of its top businessmen.

Other major characteristics of Japan's population are its youthfulness and its high educational level. In 1970, 24% of the population were under 15 years old, 69% 15–64 years old and only 7% 65 plus. The number of people 65 and over was less than one-third that of people under 15, whereas the ratio was more than 1:2 in Sweden, West Germany and Britain.

The youthfulness of the population as a whole is reflected in the composition of the nation's work force. Growth industries which hired a large number
of new school graduates during the 1960s and the early 1970s have a larger

TABLE 5 *Population, by age groups*

Age group	1955	1960	1965	1970	1975	1985
	(000 persons) (% *of total population*)					
0–14	29,798	28,067	25,166	24,751	27,187	29,727
	33·4	*30·0*	*25·6*	*23·9*	*24·3*	*24·1*
15–64	54,727	60,002	66,928	71,269	75,843	81,735
	61·3	*64·2*	*68·1*	*69·0*	*67·8*	*66·3*
65+	4,747	5,350	6,181	7,335	8,858	11,851
	5·3	*5·7*	*6·3*	*7·1*	*7·9*	*9·6*
Sub-total:						
15+	59,474	65,352	73,109	78,604	84,701	93,586
	66·6	*69·7*	*74·4*	*75·1*	*75·7*	*75·9*
Total	89,276	93,419	98,275	103,356	111,934	123,312
	100·0	*100·0*	*100·0*	*100·0*	*100·0*	*100·0*

Source: Census statistics. 1985 figures estimated by the Industrial Structure Council.

share of young workers. For example, approximately 33% of the male workers
in the manufacturing industries are in their twenties, but this age bracket
accounts for only 23% of the workers in France and the United States. On
the other hand, those in the 45–64 age bracket account for only 21% of male
manufacturing workers in Japan, compared with 36% in the United States,
30% in France and 38% in Britain. Young workers are a great advantage to
companies because the seniority-based wage structure pays older workers
more for the same job. Young workers are also generally more adaptable to
innovations in both management and technology.

The average age of the Japanese, however, is rapidly increasing, due to
the sharp post-war decline in the birth and death rates. As indicated in
Table 5, the number of people 65 years or older is projected to increase by
3 million between 1975 and 1985, and its proportion of the total population
will rise from 7·9% to 9·6%.

Consequently, the proportion of the nation's labour force in the 45–64 age
bracket, which has remained around 25% since the 1920s, is estimated to
rise to 34% in 1980 and 37% in 1985. Japan will be faced with the task of
coping with a population aging three or four times faster than in other advanced countries.

The educational level has risen rapidly during the past two decades: the
ratio of junior high school graduates (with only nine years of compulsory

education) to all the school graduates entering the labour force dropped from 62% in 1955 to 7% in 1975, as indicated in Table 6. The proportion of senior high school graduates (with 12 years education) rose from 30% to 61% in the same period. As a result, more senior high school graduates have been engaged in "blue-collar" work instead of traditional clerical jobs. The quality of production workers is probably better in Japan than elsewhere due to their high morale and conscientious attitude to work. Their high morale is a result of identification with the company rather than with the individual job. Some college graduates are also taking blue-collar jobs. They now account for approximately three out of every ten youths entering the labour market, compared with only one out of every twelve in 1955.

TABLE 6 *New employees, by level of education*

		Composition (%)			
Year	Numbers of new graduates (000s)	Junior high school	Senior high school	Junior college	Four-year college
1955	1,120	62·0	30·3	1·4	6·2
1960	1,380	49·8	41·7	1·2	7·3
1965	1,500	41·8	46·8	2·3	9·1
1970	1,360	19·9	60·1	6·1	13·8
1972	1,180	15·0	59·0	6·9	18·9
1975	1,040	7·0	61·4	8·9	22·7
1980 (estimated)	1,110	4·8	61·9	11·1	22·2
1985 (projected)	1,280	4·3	59·1	18·9	23·7

The rapid increase in the college attendance ratio, now second only to the United States, can be attributed to the absence of a rigid class system in Japan as well as the sharp drop in the birth rate. The spread of higher education, however, has raised the value of graduates from the handful of prestigious universities. This has resulted in intensified competition to be admitted to "better" lower schools with better records of admittance to higher schools. Competition now extends down to the kindergarten level and, although it is often criticised for its severity, it makes the Japanese probably the most educationally-aware people in the world.

In addition to formal education, education and training is carried out extensively by employers. As Japanese companies generally recruit directly from schools and can assume that the new recruits will stay with them throughout their entire careers, employee education is a good investment. Such education ranges from on-the-job training to selecting a few employees each year for advanced studies overseas at the company's expense. The practice of lifetime employment also allows employers to use their work force flexibly, since there is little opposition to retraining and reassignment of employees. Thus the availability of continuing education by employers, coupled with the excellent school attendance ratio, accounts for the high productivity of Japanese workers.

TABLE 7 *Breakdown of further education statistics*

Year	Senior high school		Higher education	
	Male	Female	Male	Female
	%	%	%	%
1970	81·6	82·7	30·8	19·4
1973	84·8	85·3	33·2	24·7
1975	92·2	94·7	37·3	28·1
1980 (estimated)	95·0	95·0	47·2	36·5
1985 (estimated)	95·0	95·0	50·5	42·8

1.6 Politics

1.6.1 INTRODUCTION

In 1890 Japan adopted a British type of bicameral system composed of the House of Peers and the House of Representatives. Under the New Constitution proclaimed immediately after the Second World War, the House of Peers was replaced by the House of Councillors, commonly called the upper house. With a tenure of six years, one half of the upper house members come up for election every three years. The term of office is four years for the House of Representatives' members, but this is often cut short by dissolution. The House of Councillors cannot be dissolved and thus each member of the House serves out his full six-year term.

Under a system unique to Japan, upper house candidates run either in the national constituency or in local (prefectural) constituencies, and a voter can vote for two candidates, one each from the former and the latter constituencies. The upper house provides both local as well as national representation (the members being elected from either local or nationwide constituencies, based on the strength of trade unions, religious groups, etc.), whereas the lower house provides proportional representation. As in Britain, but not in the United States, the Japanese lower house – the House of Representatives – takes precedence over the upper house. For instance, the most important bills concerning the budget and treaty ratification which have passed the lower house automatically become law after they are sent to the upper house unless they are defeated within 30 working days.

One significant post-war feature of Japanese politics has been the almost uninterrupted conservative dominance of the government. Since 1955, when two conservative parties merged to form the Liberal Democratic Party (LDP), the opposition parties failed to increase their popularity and lacked the strength to capture power. Recently, as in many Western nations, the tide in the Diet (the Japanese parliament) has been turning against the ruling party. The LDP has already lost its comfortable majority in the Diet (*see* Table 8). In the upper house, it retains a paper-thin majority, while in the lower house it has been gradually losing the margin necessary for controlling all the standing committees. An era of multi-party politics seems to be developing. In 1976, for the first time in 21 years, the LDP saw a defection by some young dissidents, who formed the New Liberal Club. In 1977, the Japan Socialist Party also faced the desertion of many members to form a new political party.

TABLE 8 *Number of Diet members, by party* (*25 January 1978*)

	House of Representatives	House of Councillors
Liberal Democratic	256	123
Japan Socialist	120	53
Komeito	56	28
Democratic Socialist	28	11
Japan Communist	19	16
New Liberal Club	17	5
Others	10	12
Vacancies	5	5
Total	511	253

1.6.2 CHANGES IN THE SOCIAL STRUCTURE

Multi-party politics is a direct result of major changes in the Japanese social structure. Although some of these changes cannot be quantitatively analysed, most can be explained statistically and can serve to predict future trends. Social conditions will be reviewed in terms of demographic changes, economic changes concerning income and industrial structure and the resulting changes in people's consciousness. Demographic changes come from an aging and increasingly highly educated population and economic changes dervice from the development of tertiary industries and equalization of income. Changes in consciousness arise from a growing trend toward regarding oneself as belonging to the middle class, a growing sense of contentment with one's life and a trend toward new conservatism.

In the year 2000, Japan's demographic structure will be similar to that of Britain in 1960 (*see* Fig. 1). According to *People and Land in the 21st Century*, by the National Land Agency, the number of people between 45 and 64 years of age will surpass that of those aged from 25 to 44 by the year 2000. Over the past 20 years more and more people have been receiving higher education. Of all the young people in their twenties in 1955, 16·8% were graduates from universities and colleges, and the percentage rose to 27·5% in 1975.

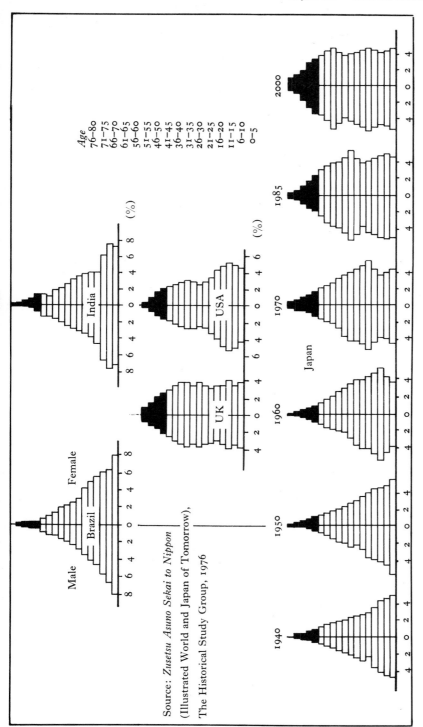

Fig. 1 International comparison of demographic structure

TABLE 9 *Composition of the workforce, by occupation*

	1955		1960		1965		1970		1975	
	(000s)	%	(000s)	%	(000s)	%	(000s)	%	(000s)	%
Professional	1,910	4.9	2,137	4.9	2,490	5.2	3,428	6.6	4,127	7.8
Managerial	841	2.1	1,017	2.3	1,295	2.7	2,052	3.9	2,294	4.3
Clerical	3,416	8.7	4,556	10.4	6,058	12.8	7,280	14.0	8,917	16.8
Salespeople	4,182	10.6	4,613	10.6	5,706	12.0	6,253	12.0	7,008	13.2
Agriculture, forestry and fisheries	15,874	40.4	14,253	32.6	11,654	24.5	10,009	19.2	7,317	13.8
Mining	348	0.9	368	0.8	206	0.4	139	0.3	81	0.1
Transportation	856	2.2	1,424	3.3	2,051	4.3	2,325	4.5	2,386	4.5
Production process	9,451	24.1	12,485	28.6	14,743	31.0	16,592	31.8	16,408	30.9
Services and safety	2,383	6.1	2,827	6.5	3,390	7.1	4,013	7.7	4,433	8.3
Unclassifiable	0	0	11	0	17	0	19	0	170	0.3
Total	39,261	100.0	43,691	100.0	47,610	100.0	52,110	100.0	53,141	100.0

Source: National Census. The 1975 figures are based on a 1% sampling survey.

The growth of the service industries has been partly at the expense of the drastic decrease in the people engaged in agriculture and fisheries, from 40·4% of the total population in 1955 to 13·8% in 1975. In the 1970s the percentage of both white- and blue-collar workers has been declining, while that of transportation and communication workers has been levelling off. Three types of vocation are expected to grow in the future: services, sales, and professionals and specialists. Currently, professionals and specialists in Japan account for a smaller proportion of the total working population than in other advanced nations, but the proportion will increase rapidly in the future as the general level of education rises (*see* Table 9).

The trend toward income equality is noted in the report released by OECD in October 1976 under the title *Income Distribution in OECD Countries.* Although the survey deals with income only in terms of flow, it shows that Japan is now among the countries where income is most equal. The most striking finding of the survey is that the proportion of national income in the lowest bracket is the largest in the world, 2·1 times that of France. This trend has continued over the past 20 years and contrasts with the increasing inequality of income in the United States and West Germany.

These changes have altered people's assessment of their social standing and in all public opinion polls conducted over the past seven to eight years, those who regard themselves as members of the middle class have accounted for 90%. Of particular interest is the fact that, according to a survey conducted by the Prime Minister's Office in November 1976, people who regard themselves as "middle of the middle class" have increased from 50% to 60% over the past ten years. In contrast, people who regard themselves as lower-middle class members have decreased to 22%. This trend is observed in white-collar and blue-collar workers, in management and labour, and in urban and rural areas. In other words, most Japanese think that they are enjoying an average or above-average life unless there is a serious domestic problem or a chronic illness in the family.

All this points to a high degree of satisfaction with the current lifestyle. In the *Survey of Lifestyle Preference* conducted by the Economic Planning Agency in June–July 1975 (*see* Fig. 2), many survey items were scored at 50% satisfied. Another survey conducted by the Prime Minister's Office, on the sense of solidarity among young people, also showed that 73·6% of young people aged between 15 and 24 are satisfied with their life. What is common to all surveys is that the living environment, including housing, medical treatment and public services such as transportation, have scored relatively low rates of satisfaction, whereas consumer durables such as automobiles have given rise to generally high rates of satisfaction. This contrast may indicate the future nature of political problems. The less satisfactory items all require vast amounts of investment in the social infrastructure. Since the period of high economic growth is now over, it will take many

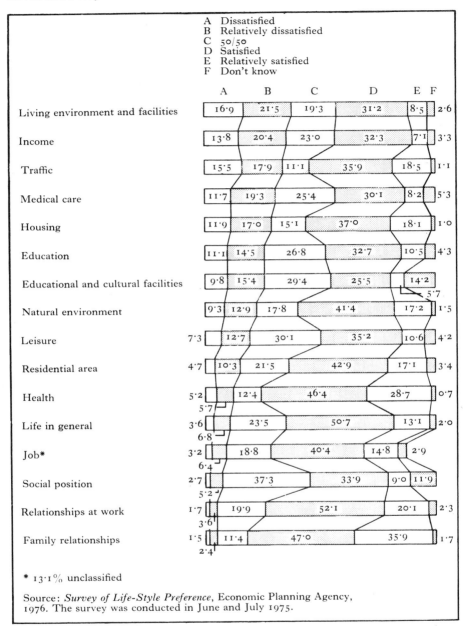

	A	B	C	D	E	F
	Dissatisfied	Relatively dissatisfied	50/50	Satisfied	Relatively satisfied	Don't know

A Dissatisfied
B Relatively dissatisfied
C 50/50
D Satisfied
E Relatively satisfied
F Don't know

	A	B	C	D	E	F
Living environment and facilities	16·9	21·5	19·3	31·2	8·5	2·6
Income	13·8	20·4	23·0	32·3	7·1	3·3
Traffic	15·5	17·9	11·1	35·9	18·5	1·1
Medical care	11·7	19·3	25·4	30·1	8·2	5·3
Housing	11·9	17·0	15·1	37·0	18·1	1·0
Education	11·1	14·5	26·8	32·7	10·5	4·3
Educational and cultural facilities	9·8	15·4	29·4	25·5	14·2	5·7
Natural environment	9·3	12·9	17·8	41·4	17·2	1·5
Leisure	7·3	12·7	30·1	35·2	10·6	4·2
Residential area	4·7	10·3	21·5	42·9	17·1	3·4
Health	5·2 / 5·7	12·4	46·4	28·7		0·7
Life in general	3·6 / 6·8	23·5	50·7	13·1		2·0
Job*	3·2 / 6·4	18·8	40·4	14·8	2·9	
Social position	2·7 / 5·2	37·3	33·9	9·0	11·9	
Relationships at work	1·7 / 3·6	19·9	52·1	20·1		2·3
Family relationships	1·5 / 2·4	11·4	47·0	35·9		1·7

* 13·1% unclassified

Source: *Survey of Life-Style Preference*, Economic Planning Agency, 1976. The survey was conducted in June and July 1975.

Fig. 2   Lifestyle satisfaction breakdown

years for this massive investment to materialize.

The move toward new conservatism is conspicuous as a short-term phenomenon but, in the medium or long term, we cannot expect the move to continue. The findings of many surveys point to the marked progress of egalitarianism through income equalization, growing "middle-class" aware-ness and stronger satisfaction with life. The burgeoning middle class is what some pundits call the new intermediate class and is identical to what the French President Giscard d'Estaing calls "un immense groupe central".

However, we must not overlook the fact that as many as 70–90% of the Japanese people gain their satisfaction not from their accumulated wealth but from the flow of income. Should they be forced to lose all or part of their present income, how many of them would be able to continue the present lifestyle with their assets? Probably no more than 10% of the total population could do so, because only about 1% believe that they belong to the upper class and about 8% to the upper-middle class. In other words, even if they believe they belong to the middle class, they do not have the assets of pre-war Japanese middle-class families, still less of European middle-class families.

Apparently, when the new middle-class people enjoy their life, they base their satisfaction not on their present assets, but rather on the assumption that their present income flow will continue. This assumption takes for granted the continued stability of the present social system. If the social system breaks down, there is no way to ensure the present level of income. Naturally people want the present social order to continue and this means an inclination to conservatism.

1.6.3 THE DIRECTION OF POLITICAL CHANGE

The present conservative trend has nothing to do with ideology. Rather it indicates that many Japanese, having realized that the era of high economic growth has ended, have begun to take steps to safeguard their future life style. In urban public opinion polls, more and more people say that they don't have any political parties to support. This indicates their uncertainty as to whether the political parties can meet their demands and also the rapidly expanding gap between the Liberal Democratic Party and the new con-servatives.

It seems to be widely accepted that the conflict between conservatives and progressives over the issue of the socio-economic system is diminishing. The people of middle-class outlook account for the majority of the population and will find few reasons to support a socialist system. For them the liberal economy is relatively, if not absolutely, the best system. This has almost become a consensus. Even the Communists do not agree with nationalization of big business. Nationalization of industry is advocated in a small way; of coal by the Japan Socialist Party and Komeito and of the energy industry by the Japan Communist Party. Their moderate attitude toward nationalization undeniably seems to reflect the fact that the Socialist countries such as the Soviet Union, East European countries, China and North Korea have displayed an economic inefficiency which has no attraction for Japan.

The formation of such a consensus has provided the impetus toward multi-party politics. Since sympathy with new conservatism has spread far outside the traditional supporters of the LDP, and since the difference between conservatives and progressives has become very ambiguous, voters now have many alternatives. With these recent developments in mind, the present situation of each of Japan's major political parties will now be reviewed.

Liberal Democratic Party

The new conservatives are being alienated from the Liberal Democratic Party. The party experienced a 6% decrease in the share of votes won in the 1967 election and a 5% drop in the 1976 election, in which the Komeito and the New Liberal Club registered marked gains. This demonstrates that the attraction of the LDP may be eroded by a political party which can appeal to a wider range of conservative people. Another growing trend is that the LDP support is concentrated more and more in rural areas. Indeed, the LDP's share of total votes has dropped to less than 30% in big cities, while it is about 30% in other cities and nearly 50% in semi-urban and semi-rural areas. Only in rural areas is it more than 50%.

This trend may prevail for the next five to ten years. Moreover, following the lead of the New Liberal Club, other factions may also break with the LDP. In the immediate future, the LDP seems likely to maintain its old conservative organizations, supported mainly by its Diet members with solid rural backing and those people who win elections through their occupational and religious connections. If this continues, the LDP will lose more and more of its supporters in an accelerating spiral, and its members from the urban electorates will drop out to join urban conservative parties such as the New Liberal Club.

New Liberal Club

Undoubtedly the New Liberal Club will grow at the expense of the established parties, but it remains to be seen how far it will expand and what role it will play in Japan's parliamentary politics. The party is popular among the new conservatives in large cities, but its assessment in polls is not constant, indicating that its image is not sufficiently established at present. As the Club is not yet well organized, its popularity has fluctuated since its foundation. It scored a major advance in the 1976 general election and only a minor advance in the 1977 upper house election. In the latter, the Club tentatively sponsored candidates in rural areas and they won significant support, indicating the possibility of nationwide expansion. There is no sign that the voters with "no party to support", who account for nearly 40% of the total voters, will rally round. They have misgivings as to whether the Club will prove a genuine party or not. These floating voters are considered to be the new conservatives. Therefore, if the NLC is successful, it will significantly reorganize Japan's political community.

In the next general election, the NLC plans to put up candidates on a nationwide scale. If the Club's organization proves successful, then a two- or threefold expansion of its representation may be possible. If there is a second or third block desertion from the LDP, its growth may be held down or it may be virtually incorporated into the other new parties. Alternatively, it may merge with others on an equal basis, or it may expand its force by incorporating all other newly formed new parties.

Japan Socialist Party

The Japan Socialist Party's popularity trend is similar to that of the LDP. The left and right socialist parties merged in 1955, the same year the two conservative parties united to form the present LDP. Its support in the poll has continued to fall over the years and in the 1976 general election its popular vote was down to almost 20%. It is uniformly supported in all parts of the country but, like the LDP, the JSP has suffered setbacks in urban areas and fared well in rural areas. The JSP's strength was eroded in cities by new conservative parties like the NLC, while continuing to attract non-LDP supporters in rural areas where the new conservative parties have not sponsored candidates. As the waves of new conservatism spread to rural areas, the JSP will probably suffer a severe setback.

The JSP also faces desertions. The late Mr Saburo Eda, former acting chairman, left the party and formed the Social Citizen's Union. Whether the SCU will make as much headway as the NLC and grow at the expense of the JSP is uncertain. Unlike the case of the LDP, most of the Diet members from the JSP could not be elected without the support of the labour unions within the General Council of Trade Unions of Japan, which is internationally known as Sohyo. If the SCU is capable of sending its members to the Diet without relying on Mr Eda's name, the JSP will be divided. It is difficult to predict how labour unions will adapt themselves to the multi-party phenomenon. The relation between the deserting right wing and the Democratic Socialist Party also depends on labour unions. The JSP may split into a right wing acceptable to the new conservatives and a relatively minor group that seeks a Socialist–Communist coalition.

Komeito

The Komeito came into being 15 years ago as the political arm of the militant Buddhist Sokagakkai. Supported by a cohesive group of people, the party will not expand or shrink to any significant degree. With the Sokagakkai members as its core, the party attracts some floating voters. These floating voters may be lured to other parties, at the expense of the Komeito. With about 50 safe Diet seats, so to speak, the party will maintain its political character. Its future will depend on changes in leadership of both the Sokagakkai and the Komeito, and how the generation gap among its members will affect its behaviour as a political party.

Democratic Socialist Party

In 1959 the right wing of the Japan Socialist Party withdrew to form the Democratic Socialist Party. Like the Komeito, the DSP has a stable group of supporters. However, since they consist only of the supporters of the

Japanese Confederation of Labour, known as Domei, plus some of the new floating conservative voters, the DSP cannot be expected to expand rapidly. In the future, the party's support will be eroded by other city-based parties like the NLC and the SCU. Clashes with the Komeito over the issue of religion also create difficulties. Although the DSP enjoys strong support from the anti-Sokagakkai Buddhist circle, its way ahead is indeed thorny.

Japan Communist Party

The Japan Communist Party has found it increasingly difficult to pick up floating votes in cities. Its results in the past three general elections have been reciprocal to those of the Komeito and the Democratic Socialist Party, indicating keen competition with these two parties. In the 1976 general election, the JCP lost votes even to the NLC. An increase in its rural votes was more than offset by the sharp decrease in urban votes and the party's overall polling results have levelled off compared with the 1972 election.

To cope with the voters' recent inclination toward conservatism, the JCP is striving to soften its image, in a way reminiscent of the Western European "White Communism", by denying as a goal "dictatorship of the proletariat". The fact that there are more political parties appealing to new conservatives than before and that according to opinion polls as many as 30–40% of the population "don't like" the JCP indicates that its future is not rosy. In the past, voters, especially young ones in the cities, voted for the JCP as a gesture of criticism against the LDP, while assuming the LDP administration would continue. However, as the LDP's control declines and new political parties are available, no sharp increase in support for the JCP is expected.

Possible Coalitions

This review of the major political parties indicates their future prospects. Both the Komeito and the JCP will strengthen their organizations, whereas the LDP and the JSP will lose factions to new parties. After two or three more general elections and two more upper house elections, the parties will consist of the LDP and one or two of its offshoots, the JSP and one or two of its offshoots, the DSP, Komeito and the JCP. The LDP may lose the majority in both houses. In that event, it will have to seek a coalition with opposition parties or continue a minority single-party rule. The most probable partner for LDP coalition is the Komeito. If the Komeito relies on its organized supporters instead of on floating votes, then participation in a coalition with the LDP is within reach.

The possibility of an opposition coalition without the LDP is quite remote, because both the LDP and the JSP will have to lose a large number of their present forces if the so-called new conservative parties are to secure the majority. Antagonism among labour unions and conflict between the Komeito and the DSP makes possibility of a coalition very slim. A JSP and JCP coalition is far more remote because of the trend towards new conservatism.

More probable courses of action are a coalition between the LDP and the Komeito, a loosely committed policy agreement between the LDP and new conservative oppositions or minority single-party rule by the LDP. In the short run, the most likely is an LDP single-party rule. This eventuality could have a great impact on the decision-making capability of the nation's policy-makers.

1.6.4 POLICY-MAKING CAPACITY

What would become of national policy in the midst of the establishment of new conservatism, emergence of a multi-party system and LDP minority single-party rule? No drastic changes are foreseen. The emergence of a multi-party system and the setback of the LDP are the result of a new conservatism, and not of the expansion of the Communists as in Italy. In addition, the firmly established bureaucracy is a key component of decision-making in Japan.

If the LDP lost its majority, the opposition parties would have the opportunity to participate in the government. They would be unable to continue to oppose the government party or advocate a utopian policy as they did during the LDP's unchallenged rule. They would have to present realistic policies that would win the support of the new conservatives. For example, during the deliberation of the 1977 budget bill, for the first time the opposition strength in the House of Representatives almost equalled that of the ruling party. All opposition parties demanded a sharp tax reduction, resulting in an amicable compromise by both government and opposition parties, surprising even experienced political observers. The opposition parties showed an unprecedented degree of willingness to enter into the discussion.

The strength of the bureaucracy has previously compensated for the political parties' lack of policy-making capability. It will be some time before the party bureaucrats are capable of policy-making (with the exception of the JCP). Many observers believe such a time will never arrive. Since planning and execution of national policies is currently undertaken by five million central and local government officials, the job seems beyond the scope of a political party with a 50,000 or even 100,000 membership. The drafting of a bill cannot possibly be done without the help of the specialists in the appropriate ministry or the Cabinet Legislation Bureau. The political parties will then be almost at the mercy of bureaucrats, and there should be little concern over the decision-making stalemate. Or at the very least, the government would be able to set up the parameters of its policies on its own. Along with France, Japan is one of the most advanced countries in the world in terms of administrative capability. The future will see fewer sharp distinctions between parties, as they cautiously avoid impairing their public images. They will refrain from behaviour that might invite popular criticism. They will provide checks on each other, and more bureaucrats will participate in political activities by joining the new conservative parties. In fact, this has already begun to occur. It will mean the political neutralization of bureaucrats and the formation of a real technocracy.

These relatively short-range observations are based on the assumption that the LDP will form a minority single-party government. There would be no significant difference even if a coalition or policy agreement situation arose. A drastic change in the decision-making process would be quite exceptional. In the present "trial and error" process, the LDP can pass many bills through the Diet with the support of the DSP and of the NLC. This phenomenon indicates the direction of political manoeuvring and decision-making in the immediate future.

1.7 National Income and Expenditure

1.7.1 THE SECOND LARGEST ECONOMY IN THE FREE WORLD

Since her gross national product outpaced that of West Germany in 1968, Japan's economy has been the largest in the free world next to that of the United States. Japan's GNP in 1976 stood at $560 billion, or one-third that of the United States. The magnitude of the Japanese economy can be attributed to her large population and high per capita productivity. The country has a population of more than 110 million, with a gross domestic product per capita of $4,900 (1976). This is larger than the per capita GDP of Britain and is approximately 60% of that of the United States (*see* Table 10).

In many ways the characteristics of the Japanese economy are a result of its size. The Japanese economy has a large domestic market. Its export dependence ratio, though greater than that of the United States, is much smaller than that of Western European countries. While exports account for 25–35% of gross national expenditure in Western European countries, even after a recent rise they account for only 14–15% in Japan.

With a large domestic market, Japanese enterprises can take advantage of economies of scale, first in the domestic market and then by moving to overseas markets after they have strengthened their international competitiveness.

Despite its low export dependence ratio, Japan ranks third in the world after the United States and West Germany in the volume of exports. Conversely, the volume of Japanese imports has a large impact on the international market. This is especially so for natural resources, as Japan depends on a variety of such imports.

1.7.2 NATIONAL INCOME AND HIGH PERSONAL SAVINGS RATE

Japan's per capita national income has been rising along with increased productivity; the 1976 per capita national income was estimated at approximately $4,200. This represents a sharp increase from the $1,000 ten years earlier and $300 twenty years earlier. Doubtless, some of the increase is due to inflation, but the rise of Japan's per capita national income from less than

TABLE 10 *Per capita gross domestic product
of OECD countries*

	US $		
	1974	1975	1976
1. Sweden	6,880	8,470	8,940
2. Switzerland	7,350	8,460	8,910
3. Canada	6,630	6,990	8,200
4. USA	6,630	7,080	7,830
5. Norway	5,840	7,060	7,560
6. Denmark	5,980	7.010	7,500
7. West Germany	6,210	6,870	7,260
8. Australia	5,940	6,230	6,890
9. Belgium	5,460	6,350	6,800
10. Luxembourg	6,160	6,120	6,630
11. France	5,060	6,360	6,550
12. Iceland	6,510	5,960	6,330
13. The Netherlands	5,130	5,940	6,330
14. Finland	4,770	5,640	5,980
15. Austria	4,340	4,990	5,320
16. Japan	4,120	4,390	4,900
17. New Zealand	4,380	4,270	3,980
18. Britain	3,400	4,060	3,850
19. Italy	2,750	3,080	2,920
20. Spain	2,440	2,860	2,900
21. Ireland	2,160	2,490	2,500
22. Greece	2,120	2,310	2,450
23. Portugal	1,490	1,540	—
24. Turkey	740	880	950

20% to approximately 60% of that of the United States speaks of an exceptionally high growth rate of the economy and productivity.

A major characteristic of Japan's national economy is an unusually high rate of savings by private individuals relative to that of Western countries. The proportion of disposable income set aside as savings has risen since around the time of the oil crisis to 24–25%. Various reasons are cited for this high savings rate. It is attributed to the need to save for the purchase of homes and education for children. Others attribute it to a relatively small ratio of regular income to total remuneration, because bonuses and overtime payments account for a large proportion of total income.

Until several years ago, the high savings rate was a major force behind Japan's sustained economic growth. The funds supplied by the individual sector through savings were absorbed primarily by the corporate sector to be used for active plant and equipment investment and played an important role in equipment modernization and productivity increases. However, during the last few years, the high sustained savings rate coupled with stagnant plant and equipment investment has delayed economic recovery.

1.7.3 GROSS NATIONAL EXPENDITURE AND HIGH RATE OF FIXED CAPITAL FORMATION

Reflecting the high personal savings rate, fixed capital formation accounts for a large share of gross national expenditure. In 1976, despite the prolonged sluggishness in private plant and equipment investment during the last few years, gross fixed capital formation – including private plant and equipment investment, government fixed capital formation and private residential investment – accounted for 30% of gross national expenditure. This is substantially higher than the rate in the United States and Western Europe. While private plant and equipment investment occupies a large share of gross national expenditure, government fixed capital formation for building social infrastructure and private residential investment are both very active. However, the sluggish private plant and equipment investment on the one hand and growing budget deficits on the other hand are creating various problems.

Characteristics of expenditure components and points to be noted are as follows:

Personal Consumption

Although personal consumption accounts for a slightly smaller proportion of gross national expenditure in Japan than in other advanced countries, it is still the largest component of aggregate demand, accounting for nearly 57% of gross national expenditure in 1976. Movement of personal consumption expenditure depends on real disposable income and the propensity to consume. Real disposable income, in turn, is determined by the movement of nominal income and consumer prices. In order to forecast income, one must take into account the margin of wage increases agreed to in the spring wage negotiations and the prospects for overtime and bonuses. Generally, when the economy is on an upswing, the rate of increase in income is higher than the rate of wage rises, as there are increases in overtime working hours as well as in bonus payments; the converse is true during a downturn of the economy.

The propensity to consume tends to decline when the share of bonuses and other variable payments in total compensation rises, and vice versa. As a result, personal consumption tends to mitigate cyclical fluctuations of the economy by rising less rapidly than income when the economy is expanding and by rising faster than income when the economy is contracting. Since the oil crisis, however, this pattern has not been so evident.

Consumers have become much more cautious about their spending than they were before the oil crisis. In order to make up for the erosion of their financial assets by inflation, they have increased their savings. The resultant drop in the propensity to consume has deepened the recession. At the same time, the cancelling of tax cuts in fiscal year 1976 meant a tax increase in real terms due to the progressive taxation system. It slowed the growth of

TABLE 11 *Gross national expenditure*

(current prices)	1975			1976		
	Amount (¥ billion)	Change (%)	Proportion of total (%)	Amount (¥ billion)	Change (%)	Proportion of total (%)
Personal consumption expenditure	82,306·7	+17·8	56·6	93,054·4	+13·1	56·6
Private residential investment	10,521·4	+7·6	7·2	12,532·2	+19·1	7·6
Private plant and equipment investment	20,649·7	−12·1	14·2	21,825·0	+5·7	13·3
Private inventory investment	1,806·0	−63·7	1·2	2,572·9	+42·5	1·6
Government consumption expenditure	16,203·7	+22·8	11·1	18,147·6	+12·0	11·0
Government fixed capital formation	13,640·8	+13·9	9·4	14,837·9	+8·8	9·0
Government inventory investment	413·3	+88·4	0·3	314·8	−23·8	0·2
National surplus on current account	−95·1	−92·4	0	1,185·5	−	0·7
Exports	20,255·3	+4·1	13·9	23,838·2	17·7	14·5
Imports	20,350·4	−1·7	14·0	22,652·7	11·3	13·8
Gross national expenditure	145,446·4	10·0	100·0	164,470·3	13·1	100·0

disposable income and sharply depressed personal consumption.
Private Residential Investment
In forecasting the performance of the economy, it is essential to take into account movement of private residential investment. Since the beginning of the 1970s, this area has become very sensitive to the economic situation.

Throughout the 1960s, the goal of housing construction was primarily quantitative expansion of supply to satisfy a real shortage of housing. This shortage had disappeared by the turn of the decade, and since then new housing construction has been geared to the upgrading of homes. Sharp increases in land prices and construction costs boosted the cost per unit, making residential investment very sensitive to the availability of housing loans and their interest rates. The rate of increase in the income of the prospective customer also had a direct effect. Recently, the monetary situation has had an especially large impact on residential investment.
Private Plant and Equipment Investment
Of all the demand components, private plant and equipment investment has the largest impact on the economic situation. Although personal consumption

accounts for the largest share of gross national expenditure and is heavily influenced by the movement of real disposable income, it is a dependent demand component. On the other hand, private plant and equipment investment is an independent demand component and, along with exports, has a large impact on the movement of the economy.

The economy often appears to be recovering, aided by a rise in the propensity to consume, or a recovery in personal consumption. However, unless the rise in the propensity to consume is sustained, the recovery of the economy is destined to be short-lived; without a corresponding recovery in private plant and equipment investment and exports, it is doomed. An accurate projection of plant and equipment investment, although extremely difficult, is the most vital information for economic forecasting.

Major factors which influence private plant and equipment investment are the capacity utilization ratio, corporate profits and the monetary situation. The capacity utilization ratio indicates the balance of supply and demand, corporate profits the availability of internal funds and the monetary situation the availability of funds as well as financial costs. At the same time, plant and equipment investment is greatly influenced by management's expectations for the future, since such investment generally requires a lead time of between several months to four or five years.

Since the oil crisis, Japanese businessmen have lost some of their optimism. This is one of the reasons why private plant and equipment investment has been slow to pick up during the present recovery.

The 1976 Economic White Paper states that some of the changes now under way in the environment of private plant and equipment investment are as follows:

(a) pollution and the difficulties of industrial siting are becoming medium- to long-term constraints on private plant and equipment investment;
(b) emphasis in plant and equipment investment is shifting from the addition of new capacity to repair and maintenance, and research and development;
(c) management policy is shifting from quantitative expansion to strengthening of the corporate structure.

Government Expenditure
Government expenditure, consisting of consumption and fixed capital formation, accounts for 20% of gross national expenditure and is the second largest demand component following personal consumption. It is characterized largely by investment expenditure, with fixed capital formation being only slightly smaller than consumption. Since Japan's military outlay is smaller than that of other advanced countries, the Japanese government is directing a larger share of its expenditure to investments in social infrastructure. Government spending takes place within an annual budget authorized before

34

the start of the fiscal year; the budget's size is a fairly good indicator of the scale of government expenditure. However, by accelerating or decelerating actual payments, the government can pursue stimulative or contractive policies even within the same budget. Sometimes, the budget is revised in both directions during the fiscal year.

In measuring the effect of treasury outlay, it is important to take price movement into account. Since the budget is made in nominal terms, any price increases larger than the original expectation will diminish real demand created by government expenditure.

Exports and Factor Income Received from Abroad

Although Japan's export dependence is smaller than that of Western European countries, exports and factor income from abroad constitute the second largest single expenditure component after personal consumption, accounting for 14·5% of gross national expenditure in 1976. Along with private plant and equipment investment, it plays a leading role in determining the business climate.

Growth in foreign economies can stimulate the Japanese economy through increased exports, while their decline can have the opposite effect. Occasionally, however, export increases or declines are caused by domestic rather than external factors: the emergence of an export drive during a domestic recession or a lull in exports caused by a tight domestic market. In such instances, exports function to stabilize the domestic economy, although they can create problems in the balance of payments by producing excessive surpluses or deficits.

In the absence of a significant upturn in domestic demand, the present recovery has been supported primarily by exports, creating a heavy trade surplus which has given rise to international friction.

1.8 Prices

1.8.1 SIGNALS FOR TIGHTENING POLICY

The main factors which determine economic policy are prices, the balance of payments and unemployment. Inflation and deterioration of the balance of payments cause a tighter policy, while an increase in unemployment, price stability and an improvement of the balance of payments allow an expansionary trend.

Throughout the mid-1960s, Japan's economic policy was determined primarily by the balance of payments, but payments deficits have ceased to be a problem. Unemployment is a relatively minor problem in Japan, owing to the country's unique lifetime employment system. Therefore, price movement is now the chief determining factor in economic policy. Tighter policy, in particular, is brought on by prices. When consumer prices continue to register double digit increases, it is safe to assume that economic policy will be tightened.

1.8.2 PRICE INCREASE PATTERNS

Before 1973, price increases in Japan were characterized by wholesale prices rising 1–2% a year, always less steeply than consumer prices at 5–6% a year. This phenomenon may be explained by "productivity gaps" within Japanese industry: a large number of items included in the calculation of wholesale prices consist of goods produced by large enterprises, which enjoy high productivity increases, while items making up consumer prices include services and products of small- and medium-sized firms, whose productivity does not rise so rapidly.

As a result of price inflation of the world's natural resources, including the quadrupling of oil prices, the price movement deviated from the conventional pattern. The inflation rate accelerated and wholesale prices rose faster than consumer prices. During 1973 and 1974, wholesale prices rose by 15·9% and 31·3% respectively, outpacing even the annual increases in consumer prices of 11·8% and 24·3%. The rate of wholesale price increases has declined sharply due to the recession and the stagnant pace of the recovery, and the previous pattern has returned, with consumer prices rising faster than wholesale prices.

This demonstrates the price movement characteristics in Japan, namely that wholesale prices are sensitive to the economic situation and the prices of resources, while consumer prices tend to be determined by the rate of increase in unit wage cost (but see also the next two sections).

1.8.3 CONSUMER PRICES

Consumer prices are influenced by factors other than unit wage cost. The first is the movement of wholesale prices. This is natural, as some of the items included in the calculation of the consumer price index are also used for obtaining the wholesale price index. Other items included in the wholesale price index are raw materials or intermediate goods for products or services used for the compilation of the consumer price index.

The impact of wholesale on consumer prices is felt after a lapse of time. Even in the case of items included in both indices, it usually takes some time for changes in wholesale prices to affect consumer prices. The lag depends on a number of factors, including the economic situation, but it usually runs at between three months and a year. The second factor is the price movement of perishable goods, such as fresh fish, vegetables and fruits, where prices fluctuate sharply due to extraneous factors such as the weather. Since they account for a little over 10% of the consumer price index, their influence is considerable.

The third factor is a change in publicly-regulated prices, such as private and national railway fares, charges for utilities such as electricity, and rice and tobacco prices. These prices are approved or set by the government after consideration of applications giving reasons such as increased costs, but decisions are often political and are not subject to the ordinary price

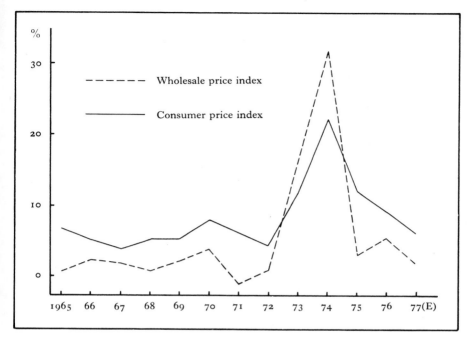

Fig. 3   Rates of increase in consumer and wholesale price indices

mechanisms. Their weight in the consumer price index is also slightly more than 10%, but careful attention should be paid to their movement, as they have a large secondary and tertiary impact.

1.8.4 WHOLESALE PRICES

As mentioned earlier, wholesale prices are sensitive to resource prices and the economic situation, but they are also greatly influenced by wage costs. As Japan imports most of the natural resources it consumes, import prices generally reflect the movement of resource prices. A good indicator of the economic situation is the balance of supply and demand. Thus, wholesale prices can be said to be determined by import prices, wage costs and the supply–demand balance. In addition to being a leading indicator of consumer prices, wholesale prices are a reliable indicator of the overheating or cooling of the economy.

1.9 The Labour Market

1.9.1 LOW UNEMPLOYMENT RATE

Prior to the oil crisis, the Japanese economy had a very high level of employment, accompanied by a severe labour shortage. While the rapid economic growth increased the demand for labour, supply grew slowly, due to a lower population growth and the rising level of education. In this tight labour market, the unemployment rate was at an extremely low 1·1–1·4%.

The oil crisis and the subsequent slowing down of the economy have radically changed this situation. Since 1975, the unemployment rate has risen to around 2% and in many months the number of completely unemployed persons exceeded 1 million. Many companies faced the problem of redundant workers. The problem of overmanning was particularly great among large companies which had taken on many new graduates in anticipation of a continuing high-growth economy. Many firms have reduced or completely dropped the recruiting of people in their mid-career, ceased extending the employment contracts of temporary workers, or simply discharged some workers. They have also reduced or called off employment of additional new graduates. Since 1975, the hiring of new school graduates by large companies, in particular, has declined sharply. What had been a sellers' market turned into a buyers' market, giving enterprises a wider range of choice in accepting new recruits.

The unemployment rate has risen sharply, although it is still well below that in other advanced countries. However, the low jobless rate can be attributed partly to technical and national characteristics. In the first place, while Western firms generally lay off workers during a business slowdown, Japanese companies give their workers temporary leave of absence. In the West, laid-off workers are defined as jobless, but workers in Japan on temporary leave remain on the employer's payroll at a reduced wage and are not included in the unemployed totals. In June 1975, workers on temporary leave numbered 440,000. Including them among the jobless would raise the unemployment rate by 0.8%. Secondly, there is a national tendency for housewives who have left or lost their jobs to respond to labour surveys by saying that they do not intend to work. This removes them from the labour force and so from inclusion in the unemployment figures.

Even after taking these elements into account, the low Japanese unemployment rate is due largely to the practice of lifetime employment. Under this system, companies seldom fire their employees except for serious misdemeanours or mistakes. If the company sustains heavy losses and is heading for bankruptcy, the management may ask workers to retire voluntarily or leave the company. In principle, employees' wishes are respected at all times. Consequently, regular employees are forced to go jobless only when their company becomes insolvent.

The practice of not reducing the workforce, even when production and sales fall sharply during a recession, keeps the unemployment rate low, but creates for employers such problems as redundant workers. Heavy personnel costs can drastically reduce corporate profits. At present, however, enterprises' complaints about redundant workers have decreased, due to the gradual but sustained recovery of the economy following the oil crisis recession. Unemployment is a less severe problem in Japan than in other advanced countries.

1.9.2 FLEXIBLE RATE OF WAGE INCREASES

As the 1973 inflationary trend continued strongly, the annual rate of increase in basic wages accelerated to reach a high point of 32·9% in the spring of 1974. Although the direct causes of this increase were the global trend of rising resource prices and sharp oil price increases, there were fears that the high rate of increase would lead to a wage–price spiral. However, the rate of wage increases slowed to 13·1% in 1975 and to a single-digit 8% in 1976, indicating wage flexibility (*see* Table 12).

TABLE 12 *Amounts and rates of spring wage increases*

	Amount of increase	Rate of increase
	¥	%
1965	3,150	10·6
1966	3,403	10·6
1967	4,371	12·5
1968	5,296	13·6
1969	6,865	15·8
1970	9,166	18·5
1971	9,727	16·9
1972	10,138	15·3
1973	15,159	20·1
1974	28,981	32·9
1975	15,279	13·1
1976	11,596	8·8

Source: Ministry of Labour

Japanese employment practices are characterized by seniority-based wage structures and intra-enterprise unions as well as lifetime employment. These practices are based on the assumption of the continued presence and growth of the company. Unions cannot make wage demands which may threaten the survival of the company. Most companies raise their employees' wages at the beginning of a fiscal year. Unions press for higher wages at this time of the year (hence wage negotiations are called "spring labour offensives"), but unions which resort to tactics such as strikes are limited to those of the national railways and other public corporations. Unions of private enterprises seldom resort to tough measures, because they are organized within the company and share common interests with the management.

Historically, the rate of spring wage rises has been determined by the rate of consumer price increases, the labour supply–demand balance and the enterprise's ability to pay. Unions seldom use sheer force to win a large settlement. The inclusion of the enterprise's ability to pay as a major factor in determining the size of pay rises indicates that the employer's financial ability has some bearing on wage increases. The low rate of unemployment in Japan may be attributed to this flexibility in wage negotiations, although pay increases are occasionally influenced by the balance of power between management and union or by political circumstances.

Since the rate of pay increases has an extensive impact on prices and other aspects of the economy, the outcome of the spring wage negotiations is important to watch in viewing the Japanese economy.

1.10 Foreign Trade and the Balance of Payments

1.10.1 VERTICAL TRADE STRUCTURE

Foreign trade is extremely important for Japan, although her trade dependence rate is low compared with other advanced countries. Exports are an important demand component. Previously, exports, along with plant and equipment investment, had led Japan's economic growth. Creation of demand by exports has become even more important since the oil crisis resulted in a prolonged sluggishness of domestic plant and equipment investment. In 1976, exports and factor income received from abroad accounted for 14·5% of gross national expenditure, a share slightly larger than that of private plant and equipment investment.

Trade is important in order to secure natural resources. Japan depends on imports for most of its crude oil supply as well as iron ores, coking coal, lumber and many other natural resources. Had Japan not been able to import these raw materials, its economic growth would never have been possible. Exports are essential because they not only create demand but earn the foreign exchange needed to import raw materials. In this sense, trade is perhaps more important for Japan than it is for the advanced Western countries.

The need to import raw materials inevitably tilts Japan's trade structure towards imports of raw materials and exports of manufactured goods (*see* Table 13). Heavy industrial products constitute the predominant share of the exports, occupying 84·1% of the total value in 1976. The share of machinery and equipment is particularly large and, in 1976, accounted for 58·9% of the total. Metals and metal products accounted for 19·6% in the same year. In short, Japan's exports can be said to consist largely of machinery and steel.

Imports, on the other hand, consist primarily of raw materials and fuels. In 1976, 72·9% of the imports consisted of industrial raw materials, with fossil fuels, mainly petroleum, accounting for 43·6% of this figure.

This lop-sided trade structure is the main source of trade imbalances with various countries. Japan's trade balances with such resource producers as the Middle Eastern countries, Canada and Australia are always deficits, while those with the United States and the European Community countries are in Japan's favour. The trade balances with South-East Asian countries, with the exception of Indonesia, are all in Japan's favour.

The United States and South-East Asia each purchase a large share of

TABLE 13 *Composition of exports and imports in 1976*

Exports	Proportion of total	Imports	Proportion of total
	%		%
Foodstuffs	1·3	Foodstuffs	14·5
Textiles and textile products	6·3	Textile raw materials	2·8
Chemicals	5·6	Metal raw materials	7·1
Non-metallic minerals	1·4	Other raw materials	10·5
Metals and metal products	19·6	Mineral fuels	43·6
Machinery and equipment	58·9	Chemicals	4·1
Others	6·9	Machinery and equipment	7·1
		Others	10·3

Japan's exports, but exports to the European Community and the Middle East are on the increase, indicating diversification of Japan's export markets. In 1976, exports to the United States accounted for 23·3%, South-East Asia 20·9%, the European Community 16·3%, and the Middle East 10·8% of the total.

I.10.2 TRADE BALANCE

Japan's vertical trade structure has affected the balance of payments. The large share of machinery, equipment and metals in exports has greatly contributed to rapid export growth. Since the income elasticities of these products are high in all countries, their demand has grown faster than the average growth rate of world economies. By strengthening product competitiveness in areas other than price, which is particularly important for machinery and equipment, Japan has been able to increase exports of these products despite a rise in the yen's exchange value. Cars and colour television sets provide good examples. Japanese cars have a high fuel economy and have been very competitive in this age of energy conservation. Among colour television sets, Sony models are in heavy demand, because of their quality, even though they are priced higher than American models.

There are other elements which have short-term influences on exports. Japanese exports are vulnerable to changes in the world economic situation, especially that of the United States, but they are also influenced by the domestic economy. Strong domestic demand tends to slow export increases, while sluggishness tends to accelerate export growth. Export drive does not entail price reductions but efforts in other aspects which are usually quite successful.

An outstanding feature of Japan's imports is their unusually low price elasticity, *i.e.*, a decline in import prices seldom results in an increase in imports, while price increases seldom reduce their volume. Imports consist primarily of industrial raw materials which have no practical domestic substitutes. In short, Japan is importing whatever it needs without regard to

TABLE 14 *Balance of payments*

(IMF basis, US $ million)

Year	Exports	Change from the previous year	Imports	Change from the previous year	Trade balance	Invisibles balance	Transfers	Current balance
		%		%				
1970	18,969	21·0	15,006	25·3	3·963	−1,785	−208	1,970
1971	23,566	24·2	15,779	5·2	7,787	−1,738	−252	5,797
1972	28,032	19·0	19,061	20·8	8,971	−1,883	−464	6,624
1973	36,264	29·4	32,576	70·9	3,688	−3,510	−314	−136
1974	54,480	50·2	53,044	62·8	1,436	−5,842	−287	−4,693
1975	54,734	0·5	49,706	−6·3	5,028	−5,354	−356	−682
1976*	66,018	20·6	56,088	12·8	9,930	−5,887	−344	3,699

* Preliminary figures.

prices, but it does not have to import beyond its needs. The 1972 situation illustrates this point. Although the yen had been revalued by about 17% in December 1971, imports in 1972 increased by only 5·2% over a year before, although there had been a 25·3% increase in the previous year.

Therefore, the factors having the most impact on imports are the level of production activity in Japan and international resource prices. When domestic industrial production is brisk, imports rise with the increase in volume, while international resource price increases push up the value of imports. The typical example of the latter instance was provided in the wake of oil price increases when there was a sharp increase in Japan's imports. The trade balance depends on the international economic situation, especially that of the United States, the state of the domestic economy and international resource prices. In fact, it has fluctuated sharply due to changes in these factors.

1.10.3 DEFICITS IN THE INVISIBLES ACCOUNT

During the last ten years, the trade balance has always been in the black, although the size of the surplus has varied from year to year. This does not mean that Japan has been recording a chronic surplus in the overall balance of payments. Unlike the trade balance, the invisibles account has always been in the red, with the deficit growing year by year to reach $5·9 billion in 1976.

The presence of a permanent deficit in the invisibles account is closely related to the structure of Japan's foreign trade. Although exports, centring on machinery and equipment, exceed imports in value, they fall far short of imports in volume. Consequently, the amount of freight and charter costs paid for foreign vessels is always larger than the freight income received by Japanese shipping companies.

Another reason is a large imbalance caused by tourism. The number of foreign tourists who visit Japan is limited by the large distances that separate Japan from the other advanced countries, yet the volume of Japanese tourism abroad has increased sharply, due to curiosity about other people and cultures, a rising level of income and the lifting of foreign exchange controls on overseas travel. There are no longer restrictions on the amount of foreign currency a Japanese can take out of the country and the level of income is such that even young office girls can visit Europe on one of their half-yearly bonuses.

In order to offset the ever-present deficits in the invisibles account, Japan must earn a surplus in the trade account. Japan's payments position should be judged by the current account balance, which has varied between deficits and surpluses, depending on the balance of trade. However, a survey of results for the last ten years shows that the current balance has closed with a surplus more often than it has with a deficit. Consequently, the level of the gold and foreign exchange reserves has remained high and has generated a rising pressure on the value of the yen.

1.11 The Industrial Structure

The Japanese economy has experienced remarkable development since the Second World War and has successfully shifted the emphasis of its industrial structure during this progress. The changes consisted of a contraction of the primary industries to make room for rapid expansion of the secondary industries and fast development of chemical and heavy industries among the latter group. When industries are classified into the three categories developed by Professor Colin Grant Clark of the Institute of Economic Affairs, in 1974 the primary industries accounted for only 3·9% of the total, the secondary industries 58·8% and the tertiary industries 37·3%. (This is based on Table 15, which applies for the rest of this section.) In the same year, manufacturing industries – 60% of which were chemical or heavy industries –

TABLE 15 *Proportion of total industrial output, by industry*

(1974 Input–Output Table)	
	%
1. Agriculture, forestry and fishery	3·9
2. Mining	0·6
3. Foodstuffs	5·6
4. Textiles	3·1
5. Paper and pulp	1·8
6. Chemicals	3·7
7. Petroleum and coal products	2·7
8. Stone, clay and ceramics	1·7
9. Primary metals	7·8
10. Metal products	2·4
11. General machinery	4·6
12. Electric machinery	3·8
13. Transport equipment	5·3
14. Precision machinery	0·6
15. Other manufacturing	5·0
16. Construction	10·2
17. Public works	1·8
18. Transportation and communication	3·5
19. Commerce	9·5
20. Finance, insurance and real estate	7·0
21. Services	11·7
22. Public services	1·6
23. Classification unknown	2·1
Total	100·0

accounted for more than 80% of the secondary industries. The sharp decline in the proportion of the primary industries in the overall economy and the development of the heavy industries, including chemicals, have made Japan, along with the United States and West Germany, one of the world's leading industrial countries.

In the heavy industries, Japan is particularly strong in steel and machinery, including general machinery, electrical machinery, transport machinery and precision machinery. These two categories accounted for 80% of the heavy industries in 1974.

Japan's large heavy industrial sector, with the steel and machinery industries occupying the central position, is the result of industry's successive building of new facilities, embodying the latest technology. On the other hand, it can be said that this process of structural upgrading of industry has created a demand which has contributed to high growth.

At the same time, the upgrading of the industrial structure has created various problems. The most serious are those of pollution and the availability of resources, both of which have been receiving increasing attention since the oil crisis of 1973. It has been argued that Japan must change its industrial structure into one which is both pollution-free and energy-saving. This concept formed the basis of *A Long-Range Vision of Japan's Industrial Structure*, prepared in 1974 by the Industrial Structure Council attached to the Ministry of International Trade and Industry.

The basic premises of the report are as follows:

(a) National welfare must be expanded to realize qualitative improvement of national life.

(b) In view of the limited, unstable supply of resources and energy, the industrial structure must be converted into one which is resource- and energy-saving to enable sustained, stable growth, leading to true enrichment of people's lives.

(c) In order to realize stable development, the level of sophistication of the industrial structure must be raised by developing superior technology-intensive industries.

(d) Japan's industrial structure must be such that it accelerates international co-operation and is adaptable to the changes in the international economy.

The report recommends development of "knowledge-intensive" industries to fulfill these premises. Knowledge-intensive industries are those which require sophisticated technology and create high value-added products in which knowledge is a major component. Examples of such industries are electronic computers and computer software, aircraft and systems machinery and equipment.

1.12 Japan's Macro-economic Policy

1.12.1 STIMULUS FOR POLITICAL CHANGE

Nations adopt aggregate demand management policies when changes in the economic situation create problems with prices, the international balance of payments or employment. However, factors which prompt government to adopt a particular policy, as well as policy mechanisms, vary from country to country.

As mentioned earlier, in Japan contractionary policy is triggered chiefly by inflation, especially inflation of consumer prices. The immediate causes of expansionary policy, however, are not easily identifiable. This is because the unemployment rate, which in other countries forces the government to adopt stimulative policies, remains low in Japan for structural reasons, even during recessions, and is not an effective indicator. Provided prices are stable, economic policy makers switch to stimulative policy according to a picture of the whole economy determined by analyses of the deterioration of corporate profits, increases in business failures and other indicators. As a result, stimulative policy in Japan often starts too late. Frequently the government adopts a reflationary policy only after lengthy argument with the business community, which calls for such policy in the face of repeated government refusals.

1.12.2 FISCAL AND MONETARY POLICY

The economy is restrained or boosted through fiscal and monetary measures (*see* Table 16 below). The most frequently used means, and the pillars of fiscal policy, are increases or cutbacks in public works expenditure. When the economy is in need of stimulation, such investments as construction of roads, public school facilities and others by the central and local governments are stepped up to expand directly effective demand.

Since the public works allocation for a fiscal year beginning in April is usually determined by early January, increases in the allocation at a later date to stimulate the economy are not easily accomplished. Consequently, while the allocation remains unchanged, contracting and disbursement of public works outlay can be accelerated to expand effective demand for a while and induce recovery.

When this proves inadequate, the amount of the year's public works budget is increased by the adoption of an autumn supplementary budget. Under a contractionary policy, public works expenditure is reduced by carrying over part of the budget to the following fiscal year. Reduction of the public works budget through a supplementary budget is not usually feasible.

Tax cuts, the major tool of economic stimulation in the United States and Western Europe, are sometimes used, but they are not a principal tool. The predominant view has been that, while tax cuts have only indirect impact on demand creation, public works create direct effective demand and are more effective in buoying up the economy. Japan also has many potential social infrastructure projects and does not lack places and facilities which require public works. Adjustment of the amount of public works can be done with relative ease, since a large portion of such investment is financed directly

TABLE 16 *Examples of stimulative fiscal and monetary policy*

Principal Fiscal Measures

First Package (*Authorized on 14 February 1975*)
1. Acceleration of public works contracting for the fourth quarter of fiscal year 1974.
2. Acceleration of fiscal year 1974 fourth quarter activities of agencies benefiting from Treasury investment and loans.

Second Package (*Authorized on 24 March 1975*)
1. Smooth execution of public works during the first half of fiscal year 1975.
2. Request to local public bodies for smooth execution of public works.
3. Authorization of a supplementary quota (¥177·1 billion) for fiscal year 1974 local government bond issues and orderly local government bond issues for fiscal year 1975.

Third Package (*Authorized on 16 June 1975*)
1. Promotion of residential construction (advancing from the second half to the first half of fiscal year 1975 loans by the Housing Loan Public Corporation and the Okinawa Development Finance Corporation for 50,000 units).
2. Promotion of pollution-control works and safety measures. (An addition of ¥50 billion to the Japan Development Bank's lending quota for pollution controls and safety measures and acceleration of lending procedures by the Environmental Pollution Control Service Corporation.)
3. Smooth execution of public works during the first half of fiscal year 1975. (70% of the year's public works budget is to be contracted during the first half.)

Fourth Package (*Authorized on 17 September 1975*)
1. Acceleration of public works (a supplementary budget of ¥867·2 billion for public works and a ¥206·6 billion supplementary quota for local government bond issues to finance additional public works).
2. Promotion of residential construction (a supplementary allocation of ¥260·0 billion to the Housing Loan Public Corporation and others to finance construction of 70,000 units with total outlay of ¥560·0 billion).
3. A supplementary budget of ¥95·0 billion to promote pollution controls and other private plant and equipment investment worth ¥160·0 billion.

Monetary Measures		
1975	16 April	Reduction of the official discount rate by 0·5% from 9·0% to 8·5%
	6 June	Reduction of the official discount rate by 0·5% from 8·5% to 8·0%
	13 August	Reduction of the official discount rate by 0·5% from 8·0% to 7·5%
	24 October	Reduction of the official discount rate by 1·0% from 7·5% to 6·5%
	16 November	Lowering of reserve requirements on commercial banks
1976	1 February	Lowering of reserve requirements on commercial banks

by central government. However, there has been new interest in tax reductions for economic stimulation. In 1977, for the first time in its history, the

Japanese government made an American-style tax rebate designed to stimulate the economy.

Other countercyclical fiscal measures include controls exercised through government financial activities. The government lends funds collected from the private sector, through such instruments as postal savings accounts, to its related agencies for their activities, which it can control. For example, one frequently used method of economic stimulation is to increase lendings to the government-affiliated Housing Loan Public Corporation, which in turn increases loans for private residential construction. The central government can also raise its purchase of local government bonds with public funds to aid indirectly expansion of public works by local governments.

The principal instruments of monetary policy are the official discount rate and "window regulations" (the central bank's restrictions on the volume of bank loans). Reserve requirements changes are also used to supplement these two measures but, since the level of reserve requirements in Japan is low, their net effect is minor. Changes in the official discount rate are also used in the United States and Western European countries, but window regulations are unique to Japan. They impose quotas on increases in bank lendings and are used primarily to tighten credit. When the economy is overheated, the quotas on bank lending increases are reduced to below the actual increase during the same period of the previous year to restrain private investment activity.

The Bank of Japan can impose window regulations on commercial banks because, almost without exception, major Japanese banks have become dependent on it, through borrowing more than they deposit with it. They are obliged to follow its guidance.

1.13 Japan's Industrial Policy

Economic policy at the semi-micro and micro-levels is called industrial policy and is distinct from macro-level demand management policy carried out through fiscal and monetary measures.

The most important aspect of the micro-level economic policy is the promotion of competition, enforced by the Fair Trade Commission under the Antimonopoly Law (Act Concerning Prohibition of Private Monopoly and Maintenance of Fair Trade). The Act rests on three pillars, the first being "prohibition of private monopoly". It prohibits such monopolistic behaviour as price restriction, bans holding companies, and restricts stockholding by a financial institution. It also restricts outside employment of corporate directors, corporate mergers and transfers of part of a company's business.

The second pillar is "prohibition of unfair restrictive business practices or cartels", banning such practices as price fixing and restrictions on production and shipment volumes, technology, products and production facilities and market allocation.

The third pillar is "prohibition of unfair trading methods", banning dumping, boycotts, restrictive contracts, exclusive business contracts and discriminatory pricing. The typical application of this provision is the prohibition of resale price maintenance contracts, which, with the exception of a few specified cases, forbids manufacturers to set wholesale and retail prices.

The Antimonopoly Law was written in 1947 under American guidance and its spirit has been rather alien to the Japanese. As a result, the law has been repeatedly amended to relax the restrictions. For example, expansion of the scale of enterprises through mergers and other means has been actively pursued on the grounds that it strengthens the enterprise's ability to compete in the international market. Although the law originally stipulated splitting of enterprises under certain circumstances, this provision has been scrapped. There has been an increase in permissible exceptions to the ban on cartels, such as "recession cartels" and "rationalization cartels".

However, the acceleration of inflation in the wake of the oil crisis added to the awareness that the reduction of competition contributed to inflation, and calls to strengthen the Antimonopoly Law have increased. Consequently, the law was revised in 1977. The revised law accomplished the following:

(a) it revived the provision for splitting of corporations, including partial divestiture,
(b) stipulated fines for formation of illegal cartels,
(c) made it mandatory to report reasons for price increases when more than one company in the same industry raised their product prices, and
(d) strengthened restrictions on stockholding by enterprises.

While the Antimonopoly Law typifies policies used to ensure competition in the market place, measures designed to protect or provide relief to a number of designated industries constitute the industrial structure policy. This is aimed at structurally depressed industries, which, unlike other, more responsive, industries, do not react to an upturn in the macro-economy. This policy provides for

(a) formation of recession cartels as well as scrapping of production facilities;
(b) government mediation for adjusting interests of various groups within the industry in order to reorganize it; and
(c) allocation of funds for industrial reorganization.

From 1977, the Ministry of International Trade and Industry has been applying industrial structure policy to the textile, open-hearth steel producing, chemical fertilizer and other industries, designated as structurally depressed. The structural policies are executed according to laws applied to specific industries or through administrative guidance. Since they generally restrict competition, they stand in opposition to the Antimonopoly Law. Opinion is divided even within the government as to how to adjust these two policies.

If protection and reorganization of chronically depressed industries constitute "backward-looking" industrial structure policy, policies designed to guide selected industries to desirable directions are "forward-looking". Energy policy is the major example in the latter category.

2 THE STRUCTURE OF JAPANESE COMPANIES

2.1 Brief History and Recent Development

From about 30 years after the Meiji Restoration of 1868 through to the 1920s, modern joint stock companies were developed. Japan's industrialization was achieved through concerted efforts on the part of government and business to absorb foreign technology and through the introduction of foreign capital without participation in management. During these years the *seisho* entrepreneurs with political affiliations formed the *zaibatsu* such as Mitsui, Mitsubishi and Sumitomo. The *zaibatsu* were literally "family-concerns" under the control of a holding company which was owned by the family. These had established themselves as leading merchants with a sense of business administration and a degree of capital.

Apart from these *zaibatsu* companies, many new businesses were launched, but most of them went bankrupt or were merged with *zaibatsu* during the recession of 1920 and the Great Depression of 1927–31. The *zaibatsu* giants successfully survived many recessions and expanded their positions in the business community for the following reasons:

(a) They adopted modern corporate organization, employed capable people from outside their groups and entrusted them with management of the companies within their groups.

(b) The big banks within their groups gave them an advantage in raising funds.

(c) The holding companies made important decisions concerning personnel and the launching of new businesses, assuring them of good management.

During industrialization, from 1895 to the 1920s, it was relatively easy to secure unskilled labour from the farming villages which accounted for 80% of the population, but there was a chronic shortage of skilled labour. To retain their skilled workers, companies resorted to paternalistic management and adopted the lifetime employment practice, seniority wages and bonuses. However, these systems were open only to skilled male white-collar workers. Thus, the systems which characterize Japanese management were established in part at this early stage of industrialization.

From 1937 until the Second World War ended, Japan was a controlled economy, with many companies producing munitions. When the war ended, the *zaibatsu* groups were disbanded and their management was purged from public office. As a result, the overwhelmingly powerful *zaibatsu* entirely disappeared and the companies within those groups became independent entities. This drastic rejuvenation of management made it possible to pursue active management strategies during the post-war period of reconstruction, helping to achieve high economic growth thereafter.

Although holding companies were not revived, the *zaibatsu* companies have reunited themselves in groups such as Mitsui, Mitsubishi and Sumitomo, which enjoy the advantage of mutual cooperation, while maintaining equality among themselves.

Japan's rapid economic growth, particularly from 1956 to 1973, can be attributed to a particular set of conditions and factors. With the separation of capital from management, following the dissolution of the *zaibatsu*, and the revision of the commercial law, management employed, in many cases, the group leadership system, which enabled them to take bold measures for rationalization and expansion of operations. These expansionary measures, which depended on bank loans, served as an effective leverage. The technological vacuum of the war was quickly filled with technologies introduced from Europe and the United States. Successful industrialization based on these imported technologies was possible because Japan had the potential to absorb them. Post-war extension of the lifetime employment, seniority and bonus systems to all employees enhanced workers' morale and loyalty. Both management and labour were encouraged to make concerted efforts for corporate growth.

With the oil crisis of October 1973, the Japanese economy slowed down. Equipment investments made with borrowed capital presented a heavy burden and so did the excess workers employed in anticipation of further high growth. However, it is difficult to drastically alter the lifetime employment system, which is rooted deeply in Japanese management practice. Therefore, companies are taking modest measures by reducing the number of new recruits below that of those retiring and by repaying borrowed money.

2.2 The Organization of Japanese Companies

2.2.1 COMPOSITION OF THE BOARD OF DIRECTORS

Boards of directors are composed of between 7 and 35 members, with an average of 16. A larger company generally has more directors. Of the average

16, permanent directors account for 14·3 (89·8%) and part-time directors 1·7 (10·1%) with 80% drawn from within the company. The composition of the directors suggests that management is based on "groupism"* and that promotion is achieved within the framework of the lifetime employment and seniority systems. About 90% of Japanese companies utilize a managing director's meeting, composed of the chairman, president, vice-president, executive director and managing director. Since the important decisions are made in this *de facto* central organ of the company, the board of directors is a mere formality.

2.2.2 THE RINGI SYSTEM

The *ringi* system – the process of obtaining approval of a plan by circulating a draft prepared by a person in charge – is employed by about 90% of Japanese companies, for the following four reasons:

(*a*) The system entrusts power to the initiator, providing the same effect as the division of management.
(*b*) The system functions as intra-company communication.
(*c*) The system performs a reporting function between ranks.
(*d*) The system includes both planning and confirmation of the plan.

However, there is sometimes a gap between the principle and putting it into practice. Since the proposer of a plan is often lower than a section chief, for his specific proposal he should be given the power of implementation. However, under the *ringi* system, many persons are involved in making the decisions and they have power and responsibility as a group. No specific individual is given the power or responsibility and thus it is not clear where the power and responsibility for implementation lie. The system also has the disadvantage of being a slow decision-making process.

Decisions made during a period of high economic growth often proved successful, and there were few problems, even if the source of responsibility was unspecified. However, during a period of slow economic growth, decisions with serious consequences carry a greater risk, and the disadvantages of the *ringi* system come to the fore. These disadvantages should be corrected to make the process effective.

2.2.3 THE DIVISIONAL PROFIT CENTRE SYSTEM

It is estimated that 20% of Japanese companies are organized along major product lines. Although this system differs from industry to industry, it is

---

* In Japanese society, "group" importance and belonging to a group are more significant than in the West. The family group, the school group, the company group are all seen to exist for the benefit of their individual members. On marriage a girl is handed over from one family to another, and the new family accepts responsibility for her; in the same way, a company accepts responsibility for its employee, and he in turn thinks of himself as a Mitsui man or a Hitachi man, for example, rather than as an electrician or a plumber.

employed more frequently by industries where products tend to diversify, such as electrical appliances and electronic products, textiles and chemicals. This is designed to divide power and to establish the source of responsibility where operations are expanding and products diversifying.

However, the system does not usually give to the head of department the actual power and responsibility which the proprietor of an independent enterprise would have. In most companies, the system is partially employed. Only one-third of the companies using it provide their divisions with performance incentives. Moreover, major decisions are made not by divisional heads but by meetings of the managing directors. Decisions entrusted to a head of division include those on selling price and construction and renewal of equipment and facilities within a prescribed budgetary range. Unless the characteristic decision-making process is changed, it will be impossible to give substantial power to the head of a division.

2.3 Major Characteristics of Japanese Companies

2.3.1 GROUPISM AND THE CONSENSUS SYSTEM

Japanese companies are characterized by "groupism", in which both management and labour share a common fate, so to speak. Groupism is a result of Japan's being a homogenous society originating in agricultural paternalistic village communities. This was strongly reflected in the formation of the *zaibatsu* corporate groups in the Meiji period. Although family management has declined, groupism as a paternalistic management system has prevailed, even within the democratic institutions introduced to Japan after the Second World War.

Groupism has four important characteristics. First, by definition, it places priority on the group rather than on individuals. Thus, one important qualification of the president of a Japanese company is the capability to maintain harmony in his corporation and coordinate the balance of the departments.

Second, important decisions are made on the basis of consensus. The responsibility for the results of decisions is taken by the group and not by specific individuals. In a sense, the *ringi* system symbolizes group decision-making. Even if a wrong decision is made about a project, it is rare for any specific executive to take responsibility and resign. In many cases directors resign *en masse* only when their company is on the verge of bankruptcy and must be reconstructed by its bankers or other third parties.

Third, a corporate group forms a community whose members share each other's lives as well as their success or failure. Both management and labour share the same results while living in the same group. Labour unions in Japan are formed within the enterprise, not within the industry as is often the case with other countries. Annual wage negotiations are conducted within an enterprise between management and labour. Aware of the situation of their companies, labour unions know that they would lose everything if they made unrealistic demands which ruined their company. This makes co-operation between management and labour easy to achieve.

Fourth, group-oriented Japanese companies are closed to the outside. Workers move within the same corporate group, rarely from one enterprise to another. Employment begins at time of school graduation.

Japanese groupism has advantages and disadvantages. Decision-making based on consensus assures a strong feeling of unity in an enterprise. This is greatest when the business environment is favourable and high corporate growth is possible; then all members of the company devote themselves to high performance and can expect rewards for their efforts.

A critical disadvantage of groupism, however, is that individual power and responsibility are obscured. A group decision may cause a grave loss to a company, but the person responsible is not identified. Responsibility rests with all the directors, and all of them cannot resign if a project turns out unsuccessfully. Executives can and do decline their bonuses for a certain period as a gesture of taking responsibility. In the present era of slow economic growth any mistake in decision-making can lead to an irrevocable loss, more so than at other times.

2.3.2 LIFETIME EMPLOYMENT

We have seen that the Japanese lifetime employment system, established between 1868 and 1911 for skilled male workers and white-collar employees, was a result of competition for skilled workers in short supply and the need for systematic training of employees. However, a shortage of skilled manpower is common to many countries of the world, particularly at the early stage of industrialization. This system was employed by Japan and not by other countries because of Japan's closed groupism. Hiring new recruits fresh from school, who would work in one company until they retire, is a long-established practice. The lifetime employment system guarantees employment not by a legal contract between the company and the employee at the time of employment, but by social convention. In this unique practice, an employee is not discharged unless he commits a grave antisocial act or a crime.

When a company is threatened with insolvency due to continued deficits, it will resort to discharge, or, if there is little voluntary retirement, to "dismissal by designation". In such cases, it is necessary to obtain the unions' understanding. However, since they are formed within the enterprise, they usually consent to dismissal even if they at first oppose it.

Since Japanese companies are guided by closed groupism, capable employees in a group are rarely "poached" by other groups. A move to one's rival company for higher wages means betrayal of the group and an end to social life in one's business community.

When a Japanese enters a company fresh from school, he is prepared to join a community united by a common future and way of life, and to tie his career to the company. The lifetime employment system, therefore, has the following advantages:

(a) The system gives employees a sense of unity with their companies and enhances their corporate loyalty.
(b) The system enables companies to conduct planned employee education and the training programmes best suited to them. The time and money thus spent are rarely lost to poaching by other companies.
(c) Big companies with little risk of bankruptcy can secure quality manpower, because, as the Japanese saying goes, "people look for a big tree when they seek shelter".

For the workers, the advantage of the lifetime employment system is job security, even during recession. Thus, they can devote themselves to their office duties and know that they are assured of a certain standard of living at least until retiring. Nevertheless, the system has some disadvantages for both management and labour. Disadvantages for management are:

(a) Because of the difficulty in laying off surplus labour during a recession, wages become fixed costs, making recovery more difficult.
(b) It is difficult to prevent some employees from leaning on a "big tree" once they are hired, and not pulling their weight.
(c) It is difficult to promote capable personnel by merit only because it may cause dissatisfaction among employees.

The lifetime employment system has the following disadvantages for workers:

(a) Since most other companies operate under a lifetime employment system, a worker cannot move to another company.
(b) After an employee enters a company upon graduation, if he finds his job unfitted to him, it is difficult to move to another company.

Although the lifetime employment system was advantageous during the period of high economic growth, its disadvantages came to the fore during the recession. In an effort to rid themselves of surplus labour, some Japanese companies have recently retired employees at 45 instead of the ordinary retirement age of 55, in exchange for an extra allowance. However, the lifetime employment system will not break down in the foreseeable future.

2.3.3 THE SENIORITY SYSTEM

The seniority system is closely connected with the lifetime employment system. Japanese companies tend to emphasize "harmony", rather than promotion according to the assessment of an individual's capability; therefore, the general practice is to promote employees by seniority, rather than dissatisfy many by promoting a few. Although assessment is based on a combination of seniority and merit, the average distribution is 80% for seniority and 20% for merit.

The seniority system is based on educational background and the number of years of employment. Promotion is determined entirely by seniority for the first ten years and thereafter differs increasingly with ability. In contrast to US practice, promotion to manager at the age of 30 is quite rare and a junior employee rarely overtakes his seniors.

The seniority system also has its advantages and disadvantages. The advantages amount to these:

(a) With years of service as the basis of promotion, the system helps minimize complaints, dissatisfaction and friction among employees, and maintains harmony.
(b) It gives a sense of stability to employees.
(c) It discourages resignation and rewards continued service.

The disadvantages of the seniority system are:

(a) It greatly hampers promotion of capable young people. The average age of the presidents of 777 companies listed on the Tokyo Stock Exchange is 63·6.
(b) Since promotion is made on the basis of human relations rather than on ability, the system weakens fair competition.
(c) The "peace at any cost" principle tends to prevail and affects corporate vitality.

At one time both the seniority system and the lifetime employment system worked together during the era of high economic growth. However, during the slow growth since the oil crisis, the disadvantages of the seniority and lifetime employment systems have become more apparent. The greatest problem with the seniority system is the shortage of senior and management positions. For instance, 40% of those employed in 1960–65 upon graduation can expect to become section chiefs, whereas only 13% of those employed in and after 1970 can do so.

During a slowing economy, the lifetime employment system may prevail but the seniority system will have to undergo some changes. Many large companies hired a great number of graduates every year during the period of high economic growth but in recent years they have reduced the number of new recruits. As a result, the percentage of older employees is increasing and the middle management reserves are also on the increase. As long as the traditional seniority system continues, it will be difficult to promote an increasing number of middle management candidates without causing discontent and the deterioration of morale. To solve this problem, companies are slowly switching from the seniority system to the merit system by separating title from qualifications and by setting up management and professional courses.

In the past, promotion to management was often considered a symbol of success for employees. Unless this is altered, personnel administration under the lifetime employment system will come to a standstill. Because of a trend towards diversified values, an increasing number of employees desire professional rather than management status. As long as the lifetime employment system is used, it will be difficult to switch to an American personnel system based on merit, but seniority wages will gradually give way to pay according to ability.

Because of the deep-rooted groupism, assessment of performance is made more on the basis of sub-groups of an enterprise than on that of individuals. Since the power and responsibility of an individual employee are not clearly defined, fair assessment of individual performance is often difficult to make. Therefore, it will be necessary to clarify individual power and responsibility in the gradual process of switching from the seniority system to the merit system.

2.4 Fundamental Differences between Japanese and Western Companies

2.4.1 PHILOSOPHY ON CORPORATE GROWTH

During the period of high economic growth after the Second World War, Japanese business managers pursued a policy of "catching up with and outrunning" European and American companies. As a result, they pursued economies of scale by increasing sales and expanding to the size of the large European and American companies.

From such a philosophy came the consideration of sales growth and the increase of market share over everything else. In contrast, European and American companies have pursued net earnings per share. Japanese companies do not readily withdraw from an unprofitable product line, hoping that it will begin to yield profits in the long run and fearing that it might be supplanted by its competitors if it withdraws. Mindful more of profit increase than of sales increase, companies in Europe and the United States withdraw from a product line at an early stage if return is much below average and shows no sign of improvement. These differences in management strategy reflect the difference in corporate growth philosophy.

Between 1968 and 1973, 104 representative Japanese companies increased their sales 2·09 times, or at an annual rate of 15·9%. During the same period, 27 representative West German companies grew faster: their sales expanded 2·2 times, or at an annual rate of 17·1%. The average growth rates of 188 American companies, 12 Canadian companies and 33 British companies during the same period were much below the Japanese average (see Table 17).

Despite rapid growth, the Japanese ratio of earnings to total capital was about half that of American companies and much below that of Canadian and British companies (see Table 18). West German companies have many points in common with Japanese companies, but American, Canadian and British companies are basically different. The latter aim to secure profits, especially profit increase by improved management efficiency, while Japanese companies prefer expansion of sales.

TABLE 17 *Rates of growth of corporate sales in major countries*

Country and no. of companies analysed	Average per company, ¥ billion						Five-year growth (as a multiple)	Average annual growth rate (%)
	1968	1969	1970	1971	1972	1973		
Japan (104)	113·6	137·2	161·2	170·8	189·7	237·7	2·09	15·9
USA (188)	574·2	619·3	643·8	601·5	659·5	723·7	1·26	4·8
Canada (12)	202·5	221·0	242·7	248·1	251·7	291·4	1·44	7·6
UK (33)	520·7	588·2	617·3	635·9	521·1	603·6	1·16	3·0
West Germany (27)	276·9	344·3	431·7	457·7	546·3	611·4	2·2	17·1

Source: Compiled by NRI from *Management Analysis of World Companies*, Ministry of International Trade and Industry, 1975

TABLE 18 *Rate of earnings on total capital in major countries*

Country and no. of companies analysed	(Average, %)					
	1968	1969	1970	1971	1972	1973
Japan (104)	4·11	4·69	3·96	2·63	3·17	3·96
USA (186)	7·51	6·91	5·74	6·15	6·62	7·90
Canada (12)	6·51	5·50	5·38	4·03	4·92	7·65
UK (33)	5·98	5·40	4·70	4·82	4·06	7·02
West Germany (25)	4·37	4·34	3·34	2·00	2·28	2·67
France (7)	0·91	2·42	3·30	1·45	2·01	2·37
Italy (3)	1·60	0·98	0·50	−0·01	−0·37	0·22
Netherlands (3)	4·52	4·89	3·47	2·61	3·91	4·76
Belgium (6)	(4) 3·09	(4) 4·58	3·72	2·83	2·97	3·55
Switzerland (3)	4·80	5·10	3·31	2·84	2·89	2·91
Sweden (8)	5·10	4·82	4·08	2·83	2·77	3·68

Source: As Table 17.
Note Figures in parentheses indicate number of companies analysed.

2.4.2 DIFFERENCE IN NET PROFIT RATE

From 1968 to 1973, the average sales of 104 Japanese companies doubled but their gross profit rate declined slightly from 4·12% to 4·01%. During the same period, average sales of 186 American companies increased by only 26% but their after-tax profits to sales ratio levelled off at 5·92% to 5·93%, about 50% higher than the Japanese rate. The same is true of Canadian and British companies (Table 19). Since the difference in the after-tax profits-to-sales rates has prevailed for a long period, it seems to derive from structural factors.

TABLE 19 *Ratio of profits to sales in major countries*

Country and no. of companies analysed	(Average, %)					
	1968	1969	1970	1971	1972	1973
Japan (104)	4·12	4·66	4·15	3·05	3·45	4·01
USA (186)	5·92	5·58	4·87	5·16	5·36	5·93
Canada (12)	7·34	6·25	5·93	4·64	5·44	7·28
UK (33)	5·27	5·06	4·37	4·39	3·98	6·21
West Germany (27)	3·47	3·25	2·44	1·51	1·77	1·95
France (6)	0·90	2·20	4·49	1·86	2·32	2·59
Italy (3)	4·03	2·50	1·11	−0·01	−0·61	0·33
Netherlands (3)	5·32	5·30	3·90	2·88	4·24	4·80
Belgium (6)	3·56	4·91	3·97	3·08	3·21	3·58
Switzerland (3)	4·42	4·42	3·94	3·96	3·95	3·71
Sweden (8)	4·86	5·20	4·57	3·15	3·37	4·40

Source: As Table 17.

One factor is the difference in capital composition. The average equity capital to loan capital ratio or net worth of 104 Japanese companies in 1973 was only 22·5%, which was higher than the 17·6% of six Italian companies but lower than that of 186 American companies, 12 Canadian companies, 23 British companies, 27 West German companies and 10 French companies (*see* Table 20). Heavy borrowing from banks to finance continued equipment investment resulted in Japan's low equity capital ratio. As a result, Japanese companies use 3–6% of their sales revenue in interest charges, three times higher than that of American companies.

Another factor is that Japanese depreciation charges amount to 4–8% of sales revenue as the result of their continued investment in new equipment between 1956 and 1973. This is 1–3% higher than the American figure, reflecting the Japanese efforts to increase sales by expanding equipment with borrowings rather than to improve the earnings rate and financial position. Heavy dependence upon borrowed capital is a post-war phenomenon: in 1934–36 the equity rate of Japanese companies stood at about 61%.

2.4.3 ATTITUDE TOWARD COMPETITION

Japanese companies started from scratch after the Second World War and since 1956 they have aimed to surpass their competitors. In the process, competition to expand market share even at the cost of profit margins has become very sharp. When export markets appeared to be promising, there

TABLE 20 *Financial ratios in major countries (1973)*

Country and no. of companies analysed	(Average, %)			
	Net worth ratio	Quick ratio	Current ratio	Fixed assets ratio
Japan (104)	22·5	79·8	120·0	182·3
USA (188)	53·9	101·6	185·6	94·0
Canada (12)	49·3	103·1	207·2	110·2
UK (33)	49·5	111·8	176·6	98·8
West Germany (27)	32·0	97·4	192·1	144·5
France (10)	35·0	83·0	137·0	162·8
Italy (6)	17·6	85·0	110·0	322·7
Netherlands (3)	41·3	112·6	200·3	97·9
Belgium (6)	39·3	55·5	121·0	151·5
Switzerland (4)	54·5	103·1	152·5	90·6
Sweden (8)	27·5	101·0	195·2	118·9

Source: As Table 17.

was a "localized downpour" on them, which has caused international friction. The same is true of overseas operations; there has often been a rush to specific, promising, countries at certain times. This causes a bandwagon effect and in this sense decisions made by Japanese companies often depend on decisions made by competitors. This is also seen in Western companies but, since they are more profit-oriented, they are more inclined to avoid excessive competition.

2.4.4 IMPACT OF GROUP-ORIENTED MANAGEMENT

As mentioned earlier, Japanese companies make decisions through the *ringi* system. In such group-oriented management, a proper decision causes few problems because it benefits all of the people involved. However, when a poor decision is made, it is not clear where responsibility lies.

By contrast, in Western companies, specific individuals are responsible for decisions. Decisions involving large amounts of money are made after certain targets such as recovery of invested capital have been set. If the decision proves disastrous, the responsible individual is often discharged. This is quite rare in Japan.

2.4.5 DIFFERENCES DUE TO THE LIFETIME EMPLOYMENT SYSTEM

Under the lifetime employment system, it is difficult to lay off blue-collar workers, even in a recession. Surplus workers in Japanese companies are estimated at about 2 million, while 1 million workers do not have jobs. Western, particularly American, companies can adjust their workforce by laying off surplus workers in a recession. Therefore labour cost is a variable expense in the United States, whereas it is a fixed cost in Japan.

2.4.6 DIFFERENCES DUE TO THE SENIORITY SYSTEM

The seniority system, unique to Japan, is closely related to the lifetime employment system. Promotion of a talented few to high positions far ahead of others under the lifetime employment system would create bitterness and adversely affect the morale of others.

In the larger Japanese companies, employees are usually promoted to their first management position, *i.e.*, to section chief, fifteen to twenty years after they enter a company, and a select few are promoted to department managers at the age of 50–55. Only a few of them become president or executive vice-president, when they reach 60. Although Japanese executives are about ten years older than their Western counterparts, their decisions are not always excessively conservative or meticulous.

More often than not, Japanese top management do not present ideas with which to lead others, but encourage middle management and subordinates to work out better plans. Top management's role is to skilfully coordinate opposing interests among different departments. The initial stages of decision-making are proposed by subordinates, while management makes decisions based on these plans, using its judgement and experience.

Capable Western managers are usually younger than their Japanese counterparts. They take leadership roles themselves, and when they make decisions, they have the power and the responsibility for the decision.

2.4.7 CHANGES AFTER THE OIL CRISIS

In the wake of the oil crisis of October 1973, Japanese corporate growth has slowed considerably. During high economic growth, priority placed on increasing sales, expansionary policies based on borrowing and even excessive competition were tolerated. Group consciousness, the lifetime employment system and the seniority system proved useful. However, all this has become disadvantageous in the present slow economy. Not all of these features of Japanese management are outdated. The lifetime employment system is its best feature, in that it enhances employees' loyalty to the company. Although Japan does not have a management participation system, the organization of Japanese labour unions within the enterprise has the same effect.

However, to cope with the slow economic growth that is expected to continue, Japanese management will have to take on a Western merit system and rejuvenate management. This trend is beginning with recent personnel changes at the top management level in some big companies.

2.5 Joint Ventures

Japanese companies invest in two types of joint ventures, those with foreign companies operating in Japan and those set up abroad by Japanese companies.

2.5.1 JOINT VENTURES WITH FOREIGN COMPANIES OPERATING IN JAPAN

There are about 2,000 foreign-capital firms operating in Japan, including 1,300 in joint ventures with Japanese companies. Most Japanese companies participating in manufacturing joint ventures do so because their management participation was a collateral condition for the introduction of foreign technology. Other joint ventures are motivated by the introduction of marketing and management expertise and of well-known foreign brands. Foreign companies are motivated by the growth potential and earnings opportunities.

Of these joint ventures, 60% are in the manufacturing industry, using advanced technology for general machinery, chemicals, electrical machinery, and pharmaceuticals. The Japanese have set up joint ventures in fields which assure advantages through technical introduction. Foreign companies have set up joint ventures in the fields where they have superior technology.

These foreign-capital joint ventures account for only 2% of all Japanese industry and 3·8% of the manufacturing industry. Even in advanced-technology industries, joint ventures only account for 6·5% of general machinery, 3·7% of chemicals, 8·4% of pharmaceuticals and 3·7% of electrical machinery. Exceptional fields are oil and tyres, which have a long pre-war history of joint ventures. Joint ventures account for 50% of the oil and 22% of the tyre industry.

To evaluate the performance of these joint ventures, 477 foreign-capital companies with more than ¥100 million capital and annual sales of more

TABLE 21 *Performance ratios of foreign-capital and domestic firms in Japan*

	Earnings on total capital (%)		Profits on sales (%)		Turnover of total capital as a multiple	
	1972	1973	1972	1973	1972	1973
Foreign-capital firms						
All industries	2·5	5·1	2·5	4·6	1·0	1·1
Manufacturing industry	2·5	5·3	2·8	5·6	0·9	1·0
Domestic firms						
All industries	3·1	3·7	3·1	3·4	1·0	1·1
Manufacturing industry	3·6	5·4	4·5	6·0	0·8	0·9

Note % Earnings on total capital $= \dfrac{\text{Net profits after tax}}{\text{Total capital (total liabilities and net worth)}} \times 100$

% Profits on sales $= \dfrac{\text{Net profits after tax}}{\text{Net sales}} \times 100$

Turnover of total capital $= \dfrac{\text{Net sales}}{\text{Total capital (total liabilities and net worth)}}$ times

Source: *Movement of Foreign Capital Firms*, Ministry of International Trade and Industry.

than ¥1 billion are compared in Table 21 with 1,768 major domestic companies. In 1973, the after-tax earnings rate on the total capital of foreign-capital companies stood at 5·1%, while that of domestic companies was 3·7%. However, in the manufacturing industry, the foreign-capital rate is 5·3%, which is almost the same as 5·4% for domestic-capital companies. The after-tax profits to sales ratio of foreign-capital companies was 3·6% and that of domestic companies 3·4%. In the manufacturing industry, the rate of the former is 5·6% and slightly lower than 6% for the latter group.

These companies can be further compared by the ratio of the main costs to sales (*see* Table 22). The ratio of product cost to sales in 1973 was 77·4% for foreign-capital companies and 87·4% for domestic companies, indicating that foreign-capital companies are operating in higher value-added areas than Japanese companies. The ratio of selling and general administrative expenses to sales of foreign-capital companies in 1973 was 12·4%, 5·2% higher than that for domestic companies. The fact that the cost to sales rate was 10 percentage points lower for foreign-capital companies suggests that their gross profit to sales rate is 10 percentage points higher. This, as well as the 5% higher ratio of selling and general administrative expenses to sales, could indicate that these foreign-capital companies spend 5% more on marketing activities.

TABLE 22 *Ratios of main costs to sales in foreign-capital and domestic firms in Japan (1973)*

	(%)				
	Cost of sales	Selling and general administrative expenses	Personnel expenses	Depreciation expenses	Real financial expenses
Foreign-capital firms					
All industries	77·4	12·4	8·6	4·5	1·7
Manufacturing industry	75·3	12·8	10·2	5·3	2·0
Domestic firms					
All industries	87·4	7·2	7·4	2·3	2·8
Manufacturing industry	79·6	11·6	12·2	3·7	3·6

Source: As Table 21.

The ratio of personnel expenses to sales of foreign-capital companies was 8·6%, compared with 7·4% for domestic companies in all industries. In the manufacturing industry, however, the rate of the former group was 10·2%, or 2 percentage points lower than that of the latter group (*see* Table 22).

Since foreign-capital firms hire Japanese workers at the same wage level as Japanese companies, it is believed that in the manufacturing industry foreign-capital firms are operating in less labour-intensive areas. Foreign-capital firms register markedly higher depreciation in all industries, indicating that their equipment and facilities are relatively new and much remains to be depreciated.

The ratio of net financial expenses (interest paid minus interest earned) to sales of foreign-capital firms in 1973 was 1·7% in all industries, or 1·1% below that of domestic firms. The foreign-capital ratio in the manufacturing industry was 2%, or 1·6% lower than the domestic capitalized industries (*see* Table 22).

The equity capital ratio of foreign-capital firms in 1973 was 21·7% and 22·9%, for all industries and for the manufacturing industry, respectively, compared with 15·8% and 19·3%, respectively, for domestic firms. The ratio of real financial expenses to sales of foreign-capital firms is low because they are less dependent on borrowing and are in a better financial position (*see* Table 23).

TABLE 23 *Financial safety ratios of foreign-capital and domestic firms in Japan (1973)*

	(%)		
	Current ratio	Fixed assets ratio	Net worth ratio
Foreign-capital firms			
All industries	110·3	182·2	21·7
Manufacturing industry	103·7	160·9	22·9
Domestic firms			
All industries	107·9	253·6	15·8
Manufacturing industry	110·7	211·0	19·3

Source: As Table 21.

Many joint ventures operating in Japan are performing well, but some are operating in the red even after several years of operation. When 50–50 joint ventures show a poor performance over a long period, serious conflict of opinions arise and in some cases the joint venture breaks down. Mutual trust is essential for successful operation.

2.5.2 JOINT VENTURES SET UP OVERSEAS BY JAPANESE COMPANIES
Joint ventures set up by Japanese companies by direct investment abroad totalled about 3,600 in March 1975. They were mostly textile, electrical machinery and commercial firms and were concentrated in the developing countries of Asia and Latin America. In many cases when Japanese companies operate overseas, they set up joint ventures instead of wholly owned subsidiaries. Although they do not prefer this form, the national policy of the

host country usually requires joint ventures. As an exception to this rule, there are the wholly owned Japanese investments in Singapore, Europe and North America, where foreign ownership is not limited.

Generally, Japanese joint ventures in the developing countries face the following problems:

(a) The number of partner candidates in host countries is limited. There are some good commercial managers but few qualified industrial managers in those countries.

(b) Local partners have very limited financial resources. In almost all cases, regardless of the proportion of participation, Japanese companies have to guarantee long-term borrowings.

(c) The limited financial resources of local partners inevitably holds down the equity, and Japanese partners often must provide loans for local partners to finance their share of equity. On average, capital accounts for only one-third of the necessary funds and the rest have to come from loans raised by Japanese partners.

(d) Even if Japanese participation is limited by the policy of the host countries, local partners often lack management experience and Japanese partners take on the real leadership.

(e) In many cases, Japanese partners who plan reinvestment from the long-range viewpoint and local partners who demand short-term return on investment have differences of opinion.

According to a survey by the Ministry of International Trade and Industry, only 30% of Japanese joint ventures operating in South-East Asia pay dividends and the average dividend rate is only 4·4%, indicating that the number of successfully operating joint ventures is quite small.

Successful Japanese joint ventures abroad have the following factors in common:

(a) Their partners have a good understanding of modern business management.

(b) They obtain a high market share and are price leaders in local markets.

(c) They rely on reinvestment of earnings and on increased capital for funds and their equity capital rate is quite high.

(d) Their parent companies are leaders in respective Japanese industries and have a high level of management and marketing competence.

(e) They systematically train local employees and promote capable local employees to important positions.

3 JAPANESE INDUSTRY

3.1 The Outlook for Major Japanese Industries in 1980

The following is a forecast for the five-year period from 1976 to 1980 of the development of 50 major Japanese industries. It is derived from a review of the basic economic indicators for the past ten years. In this forecast, different methods are used to take account of the peculiarity of each industry or its major products. In addition, basic indicators vary from leading indicators (such as production, shipments, orders received or investments) to lagging ones, and from value indicators to quantitative ones. Since the purpose is not to produce a thesis on the industrial structure of Japan but to give an overview of each industry, a lack of consistency is inevitable. This is intended as a rough sketch of the possible course which each industry will follow until 1980.

3.1.1 EMERGENCE FROM STAGNATION

The growth rates (rates of increase in basic indicators) of 50 industries during three five-year periods, 1966–70, 1971–75 and 1976–80, are computed and classified in six groups according to their size, as shown in Table 24.

This table shows the terrible blow experienced by the Japanese economy during the 1975 recession. Ten industries registered a minus growth rate and 14 industries attained a sluggish growth rate of less than 5% during the five-year period from 1971 to 1975. This is in striking contrast to the showings in the previous five-year period.

The simple arithmetical average of growth rates of the 50 industries for the 1971–75 period remained low at 5.1% as a result of a sharp decline in 1975 which cancelled out the remarkable increase registered until 1974. The movement of the industrial production index for the same period also indicates the strong impact of a sharp decline in a short time on a five-year period growth rate. With 1970 as a base year of 100, the index rose from 102.6 in 1971 to 110.1 in 1972, to 127.3 in 1973, but it fell to 123.3 in 1974 and to 109·7 in 1975. As a result, the average year-to-year rate of increase in the index for the five years was 1·9%.

TABLE 24 *Average annual growth rates of 50 industries*

(%)			
Growth rate	1965–70 (Average 17·9)	1971–75 (Average 5·1)	1976–80 (Average 7·3)
Below zero	Natural fibres (−1·5)	Housing (−1·8) Sugar (−0·8) Firebrick (−8·9) Shipbuilding (−50·2) Fine chemicals (−0·4) Sanitary ware (−0·2) Synthetic resin (−0·1) Machine tools (−8·4) Land transportation (−0·9) Natural fibres (−2·7)	Marine products (−3·0) Firebrick (−3·3) Confectioneries (−0·2) Shipbuilding (−5·2)
Less than 5%	Flour milling (2·7) Private railways (4·6)	Marine products (2·4) Vegetable oils (2·6) Ethylene (1·9) Cement (3·9) Special steel (2·0) Paper (2·3) Heavy electrical machinery (4·7) Flour milling (3·3) Confectioneries (0·2) Petroleum (2·6) Ordinary steel (1·9) Copper (0·2) Electric wire (4·7) Private railways (2·2)	Housing (4·3) Sugar (1·6) Vegetable oils (4·0) Paper (4·4) Warehouses (2·7) Private railways (2·1) Sanitary ware (3·8) Flour milling (2·0) Synthetic fibres (0·8) Petroleum (4·2) Natural fibres (1·7) Brewing (3·3)
Less than 10%	Marine products (6·2) Vegetable oils (8·8) Warehouses (9·2) Sugar (7·7) Confectioneries (5·5) Brewing (8·6)	Meat products (6·3) Aluminium (9·6) Bearings (9·1) Electronic parts (5·0) Warehouses (6·9) Brewing (5·2) Synthetic fibres (5·7) Construction machines (8·5) Communications equipment (8·2) Automobiles (5·5) Shipping (7·4)	Meat products (6·8) Synthetic fibres (7·0) Ordinary steel (5·8) Copper (8·1) Electric wire (5·5) Communication equipment (9·8) Trading houses (9·5) Land transportation (5·2) Fine chemicals (6·5) Ethylene (7·0) Cement (5·1)

Growth rate	1965–70 (Average 17·9)	1971–75 (Average 5·1)	1976–80 (Average 7·3)
(Less than 10%)		Electric power (5·7)	Special steel (8·1) Aluminium (8·8) Bearings (8·4) Automobiles (5·2) Shipping (6·4) Electric power (6·7) Construction machines (6·0)
Less than 15%	Housing (12·0) Meat products (11·1) Cement (11·8) Copper (14·9) Apparel (11·1) Land transportation (14·9) Fine chemicals (12·7) Sanitary ware (12·1) Paper (10·9) Firebrick (12·8) Electric wire (12·0) Shipping (12·7) Electric power (12·6)	Construction (11·9) Computers (11·8) Acoustic instruments (13·0) Timepieces (12·7) Road paving (12·2) Household appliances (11·5) Trading houses (14·0)	Construction (12·3) Pharmaceuticals (12·3) Heavy electrical machinery (10·0) Electronic parts (12·0) Printing (11·5) Apparel (11·7) Timepieces (10·7) Road paving (12·8) Machine tools (11·4) Household appliances (11·3) Cameras (11·8) Department stores (12·4) Automobile parts (13·3)
Less than 20%	Construction (19·3) Timepieces (16·2) Pharmaceuticals (17·5) Ordinary steel (17·5) Household appliances (18·2) Cameras (15·8) Department stores (16·2) Road paving (18·0) Synthetic fibres (18·0) Petroleum (19·0) Communications equipment (17·5) Shipping (19·8) Printing (16·9) Tourism and amusement (18·5)	Pharmaceuticals (15·0) Printing (15·6) Apparel (17·3) Automobile parts (16·8) Cameras (15·0) Department stores (17·4) Tourism and amusement (15·6)	Computers (17·7) Tourism and amusement (15·6) Acoustic instruments (15·0)

Growth rate	1965–70 (Average 17·9)	1971–75 (Average 5·1)	1976–80 (Average 7·3)
20% and over	Ethylene (31·9) Special steel (24·9) Machine tools (34·4) Bearings (23·4) Automobiles (23·0) Trading houses (20·0) Acoustic instruments (33·0) Synthetic fibres (26·2) Aluminium (23·0) Construction machines (32·0) Heavy electrical machinery (20·6) Automobile parts (26·0) Computers (53·5) Electronic parts (30·0)		

3.1.2 FURTHER RAPID GROWTH NOT EXPECTED

The simple arithmetical average of the estimated growth rates of the 50 industries for 1976–80 can reasonably be expected to reach 7·3%. Compared with the previous five-year period, 25 industries will register an increase in growth rate, while 17 industries will see a decline. The growth rate is levelling off for the remaining eight industries (*see* Table 25).

The industries for which the growth rate is expected to be below zero for the 1976–80 period number only four (*see* beginning of Table 24). Although growth rates are expected to pick up for the 1976–80 period, they will remain at a relatively low level. The growth rate for 18 industries stands at less than 10% and that for 13 industries at less than 15%. Only three industries (computers, acoustic instruments and tourism and amusement) are expected to grow at a rate of more than 15% and none is expected to grow at a rate of 20% or over.

This is in striking contrast to the 1966–70 period, during which 14 industries grew at a rate of more than 15% and another 14 industries expanded at a rate of 20% or more. The average growth rate for the 50 industries stood at the high level of 17·9%. This indicates that Japan has definitely entered into a period of slower growth and can no longer expect rapid expansion. The slowdown of economic growth may exert greater influence on Japan than is currently imagined, and it is likely that many phenomena at present unforeseen will appear in the future. There is a possibility that this forecast of Japan's industrial growth for the five-year period ending 1980 will prove to be wide of the mark. The forecast is based on the assumption that 1980

TABLE 25 *Changes in annual growth rates of 50 industries*

Industries	1971–75	1976–80
Growth rate is increasing in the following industries:	%	%
Housing	−1·8	4·3
Sanitary ware	−0·2	3·8
Sugar	−0·8	1·6
Vegetable oils	2·6	4·0
Natural fibres	−2·7	1·7
Paper	2·3	4·4
Ethylene	1·9	7·0
Synthetic resin	−0·1	7·0
Fine chemicals	−0·4	6·5
Petroleum	2·6	4·2
Cement	3·9	5·1
Firebrick	−8·9	3·3
Ordinary steel	1·9	6·6
Special steel	2·0	8·1
Copper	0·2	8·1
Electric wire	1·3	5·5
Machine tools	−8·4	11·4
Heavy electrical machinery	4·7	10·0
Communications equipment	8·2	9·8
Computers	11·8	17·7
Acoustic instruments	13·0	15·0
Electronic parts	5·0	12·0
Shipbuilding	−50·2	−5·2
Land transportation	−0·9	5·2
Electric power	5·7	6·7
Growth rate is decreasing in the following industries:		
Marine products	2·4	−3·0
Flour milling	3·3	2·0
Brewing	5·2	3·3
Synthetic fibres	5·7	0·8
Pharmaceuticals	15·0	12·3
Aluminium	9·6	8·8
Construction machines	8·5	6·0
Bearings	9·1	8·4
Automobile parts	16·8	13·3
Cameras	15·0	11·8
Timepieces	12·7	10·7
Printing	15·6	11·5
Trading houses	14·0	9·5
Department stores	17·4	12·4
Apparel	17·3	11·7
Shipping	7·4	6·4
Warehouses	6·9	2·7

Industries	1971–75	1976–80
Growth rate is levelling off in the following industries:		
Construction	11·9	12·3
Road paving	12·2	12·8
Confectioneries	0·2	− 0·2
Meat products	6·3	6·8
Household appliances	11·5	11·3
Automobiles	5·5	5·2
Private railways	2·2	2·1
Tourism and amusement	15·6	15·6

will be neither prosperous nor depressed. Since the future course of the economy will probably be characterized not only by slower growth but also by clear cyclical change, it is probable that a cyclical peak or trough will fall in these years. It is necessary to add, therefore, that this forecast of growth rates is susceptible to changes in market conditions. Growth rates of industries vulnerable to cyclical changes and those requiring large-scale plant and equipment may diverge from the predictions for 1980, depending on business conditions.

3.1.3 NEW BUSINESS AND NEW MARKETS INDISPENSABLE FOR STABLE GROWTH

Of the 50 industries under review, 16 are expected to grow at a rate of more than 10% for the 1976–80 period, as shown in Table 24. They have the following characteristics in common:

(a) They are non-manufacturing industries such as construction, department stores and tourism and amusement, or they are processing or assembling industries. None of the material or intermediate goods manufacturing industries are included among them.

(b) Most of them are industries relating to personal consumption which grew at a rate of more than 10% for the 1971–75 period and still have a potential for growth. However, machine tools, heavy electrical machinery and electronic parts are exceptions. They are industries vulnerable to the cyclical change of business conditions. The present low level of growth rates is due to a large decline during the 1971–75 period and thus contributes to their higher prospective growth rates for the 1976–80 period.

Of these 16 industries, except the seven which, by their very nature, are entirely dependent on the domestic market, the following nine industries are active in expanding overseas markets: construction, machine tools, heavy electrical machinery, household electrical appliances, electronic parts, acoustic equipment, automobile parts, cameras and timepieces. It would thus seem imperative for Japanese manufacturing industries to expand their markets abroad, despite the increasing pressure to limit their products sold in foreign markets. In addition, almost all of the 16 industries have so far succeeded in launching new lines of business, compared with those growing at a slower pace. In the future, no industry can attain a high rate of growth unless it aggressively expands markets, creates demand or launches new lines of business. As it happens, industries in processing or assembling, as well as those manufacturing consumer goods, can make such efforts more easily than others.

On the other hand, Table 24 indicates that 16 industries expect a negative or less than 5% growth rate for 1976–80. The following common characteristics are found in these industries:

(a) Their growth rates are chiefly determined by such quantitative indicators as output, orders received in terms of quantity, the volume of transport and so on. Taking into account price upswing, their growth rates will be a little higher than those indicated in Table 24, but a large increase in growth rate cannot be expected without a sizable quantitative expansion. Exceptions are such industries as petroleum, private railways and housing, because in each case their largest cost factors (i.e., prices of crude oil for petroleum refineries, wages for private railways and land prices for housing) are beyond their control.

(b) They cannot expect a further expansion of the overseas market. For example, the ratio of exports to the total output in the shipbuilding industry has reached its limit; also, natural and synthetic fibres and paper have completely lost their competitiveness in the international market. By nature, firebrick, sanitary ware and houses are difficult to place on the world market. Therefore, these industries have no alternative other than concentrating on the domestic market.

(c) Many of them are material or intermediate goods manufacturing industries and largely depend on imports for their raw materials.

(d) It is difficult to improve the quality of their products simply because of their nature. In addition, there is internecine competition with similar products in each of these industries.

Table 26 shows the numerical distribution of the 50 industries under review by factors affecting their growth.

3.1.4 BASIC INDUSTRIES WILL MAINTAIN THEIR INFLUENCE

The economic growth of Japan was centred on synthetic fibres, synthetic resin, household electrical appliances and automobiles during the 1960s, joined by steel and heavy machinery in the early 1970s. This section is a forecast of expectations for these key industries. It is a foregone conclusion that industries such as steel, automobiles and construction will have greater influence than before in cyclical business fluctuations, although they have lost some steam as the driving forces of Japan's economic growth.

For instance, in 1974, the steel industry was the largest in Japan, accounting

TABLE 26 *Factors affecting growth in 50 industries*

| Growth rate | Factors affecting industrial growth | | | | | | Number of industries at each growth rate |
| | Volume and price | | Market expansion | | Products or lines of business | | |
	Increase in volume	Price upswing	Domestic market	Overseas market	Existing products	New lines of business	
15% and over	1	2	2	1	1	2	3
10% to 14%	8	5	5	8	3	10	13
5% to 9%	7	11	10	8	14	4	18
0 to 4%	3	9	12	0	8	4	12
below zero	1	3	3	1	1	3	4
Total	20	30	32	18	27	23	50

for 10·8% of the aggregated output of all industries in terms of value. It is expected that crude steel output will increase at a rate of 6·6% on a year-to-year basis for the 1976–80 period, and that the rate of increase in value will be greater than this. That is to say, the industry's output in terms of value will probably continue to account for 10%-plus of the nation's total production even in 1980. The steel industry has a great effect on private plant and equipment investment. It was to the fore in the wage rises of the 1977 "spring labour offensive", as it was in 1976. It also affects almost all commodity prices, through the pricing of steel products. This heavy influence of the steel industry is likely to continue until 1980.

The automobile industry is expected to increase its influence on the Japanese economy. According to the 1974 industrial statistics, its value output reached $32,850 million, next only to $42,140 million for steel and $40,000 million for electrical machinery. It employs 600,000 workers in the manufacturing sector and 900,000 in the sales and service sector. If the 1,800,000 employees engaged in road transport are added, the automobile manufacturing and auto-related industries employ 4,400,000, or one-tenth of Japan's working population. Vehicle output for the 1976–80 period is likely to increase at a low rate of 5·2% in terms of volume, but in value it will maintain a 12%–13% level. Also, as the number of vehicles in use increases, the auto-related sector of the economy is expected to increase. Thus, the automobile sector, including related industries, will approach 15% of the total economic output, the level of the American automobile industry.

The construction industry employs more workers than the motor industry; its labour force totals 4,700,000. Realignment within the industry seems to be inevitable, since it contains 400,000 enterprises. However, the total of construction works completed is expected to increase at a rate of 12% for the

1976–80 period. The construction industry will continue to be vital to employment in Japan.

The electrical machinery industry, which includes household electric appliances, electronic parts and computers, is expected to grow. This sector of the Japanese economy, as the latest and most active leader of technological innovation in Japan, will increase. The development of electronics and information systems indirectly affects other industries, in addition to the industry's direct influence on production, export and employment.

These four basic industries account for 30–50% of the total production, exports and employment of Japan. It is likely that their further growth will be limited, but that they will continue to influence the nation's economy heavily. Control over these pivotal industries, to minimize the adverse effects of business fluctuation on the nation's economy, is a difficult problem for government and business leaders.

3.1.5 THE THREE MAJOR EXPORT INDUSTRIES WILL KEEP THEIR PLACE
Japan must continue to live by international trade in the future. The three largest export items, steel, cars and electrical machinery, earned $10 billion, $8 billion and $6 billion respectively in 1975, accounting for some 45% of Japan's exports. The ratio of their contributions will probably be maintained.

The volume of steel exports is expected to expand at a rate of 6·7% on a year-to-year basis during 1976–80, falling short of 9·3% for the preceding five-year period. Mounting criticism against the flood of Japanese-made steel in various parts of the world will limit exports. Japanese steel received a large share (26%) of the world's steel trade in 1974, and although it is still cost-competitive and has an excess supply capacity, other factors limit its export possibilities. Sustainable expansion of exports to less developed countries and to petroleum-producing countries where there are no local steel producers cannot be expected, due to their limited foreign exchange reserves and to insufficient infrastructure, such as port facilities. However, there is strong pressure for an increase in export prices due to the upswing of material costs and the necessity of making up deteriorating earnings in the domestic market, where mark-up is more difficult. The value of Japan's steel exports, therefore, is expected to increase at a rather rapid pace and to reach $15 billion in 1980.

Vehicle exports also increased rapidly for the 1971–75 period at the high rate of 17·6%, but this is likely to slow to 8% for the 1976–80 period. This will still be higher than the prospective rate of increase in the domestic demand. Thus, the ratio of export volume to the total output will rise, to 46% in 1980 from 42% in 1975. A rise in unit prices of vehicles for export seems to be inevitable and automobile exports in 1980 are expected to reach the $15 billion level, more than 1.5 times that of 1976, continuing to rank above all other exports in value.

Exports of electrical machinery are also expected to increase at a rate of

10% to 15% and to approach the $15 billion level. Exports will expand, led by electronic parts, information-related equipment such as computers and their peripheral equipment, and plant involving various kinds of heavy electrical machinery. However, the increase in exports of household appliances will slow down.

Thus, total exports of steel, automobiles and electrical machinery will rise to $45 billion in 1980 from the present level of $25 billion (*see* Table 27). These items will continue to be the mainstay of Japan's exports.

TABLE 27 *Export levels of the main exporting industries*

	1970	1975	1980 (projections)
		($ million)	
Steel	2,843	10,716	15,000
Automobiles	1,874	8,105	15,500
Electrical machinery	2,866	6,133	14,500
Ships	1,409	5,998	4,500
Total exports	19,317	55,753	110,000

However, such a forecast cannot be accepted blindly, as rising Japanese exports will inevitably add fuel to overseas criticism. Unfortunately, nothing is likely to replace any of the above three items in the nation's main exports.

3.1.6 THE GAP BETWEEN REALITY AND THE IDEAL

Many people believe that Japan's industrial structure should be remodelled in accordance with changes in circumstances. Even the Industrial Structure Council, an advisory body to the Ministry of International Trade and Industry, takes this line.

It cannot be denied that the Japanese economy should give less emphasis to heavy industries and realign structurally defective industries such as textiles and aluminium which have completely lost their competitiveness. At the same time, technology-intensive and resources-saving industries should be fostered. The Japanese economy may be reoriented along these lines in the next ten years, but drastic innovations cannot be expected for the five-year period under review. The trend dominant in the past is likely to survive for some years. Existing circumstances cannot be changed at a stroke.

From a wider viewpoint, the industrial expansion in Japan that centred on resources and energy-hungry heavy industries is coming to an end, but the heat caused by this frantic expansion will remain until 1980. It should be noted that the present industrial structure, relying on heavy industries and export-led expansion, is directly attributable to government policy. Needless to say, the government should decide how to remodel Japan's industrial structure and frame a firm, long-range policy to encourage new industries. From this point of view, attention must be paid to the form which the government's various industrial policies take. Investment promotion (*e.g.*, asset revaluation, exemption of investment tax), industrial conversion (*e.g.*, employment adjustment fund, redevelopment of workers' abilities) and fostering of new industries (*e.g.*, development of new technology, financing of corporate expansion) will indicate the direction of government policy. These questions cannot be discussed in the limited space available here, but one must take account of the effects produced by these policies.

3.2 Iron and Steel

3.2.1 CHARACTERISTICS
Japan's steel industry is composed of:

(*a*) Eight integrated steel manufacturers who use blast furnaces to produce pig iron and crude steel from iron ore and process this into various steel products.

(*b*) Around 70 steel manufacturers who use open-hearth or electric furnaces to produce crude steel and some steel products from iron and steel scrap.

(*c*) Around 30 steel manufacturers who specialize in rolling and produce rolled steel from steel ingots or half-finished steel products (chiefly billets and hot coils) supplied by steel mills equipped with blast, open-hearth or electric furnaces.

(*d*) About 170 manufacturers who specialize in rolling and produce small bar steel and other steel products from steel scrap.

(*e*) About 130 manufacturers who produce mainly cast and forging steel, as well as iron castings, and approximately 1,500 foundries which produce iron castings.

(*f*) A large number of manufacturers of secondary steel products.

The manufacturers cited in (*a*), (*b*), (*c*) and (*d*) above produce rolled ordinary steel; the 1975 output of this is broken down by type of manufacturers as follows:

Integrated manufacturers	84%
Open-hearth and electric furnace operators	14%
Others	2%

The structure of Japan's steel industry is characterized first by the distinctly different production systems of the major integrated manufacturers and the minor ones. The former profits by economies of scale using mass production systems with large-scale production facilities; the prices of iron ores and coking coal are relatively stable, owing to their long-term purchase contracts. On the other hand, the minor manufacturers adopt a flexible small production system suitable for supplying local needs. Output and price of iron and steel scrap vary with the locality, and production fluctuates according to business conditions.

Major integrated steel manufacturers turn out plates and sheets, pipes and tubes, large shapes and wire rods. The production of these items requires large-scale facilities, and therefore a large amount of capital, as well as advanced technology. These products are supplied to such relatively stable consumers as car manufacturers, shipbuilders, machinery manufacturers, large construction companies and manufacturers of secondary steel products. Minor steel producers put out small bars, medium- or small-sized shapes, according to demand, which is vulnerable to the fluctuation of business trends and regional disparities. Demand from construction firms accounts for 80% of the total for these products.

Major manufacturers sell at a stable price under a detailed and conditional contract with specific consumers, which accounts for 80% of their total sales. The small producers sell almost all products through wholesalers at a market price which reflects the contemporary supply–demand situation.

The second trait of the Japanese steel industry is its oligopolistic structure, which is dominated by the Nippon Steel Corporation. Nippon Steel, the largest steel manufacturer in the world, was created by the merger of Japan's two largest steel producers, Yawata and Fuji Steels, in March 1970. Its annual crude steel output in 1970 came to 33·6 million tons, accounting for 36% of the total production in Japan. The previously fierce competition among leading blast furnace operators for plant and equipment investment and expansion of market share ("competitive oligopoly") subsided. It has been replaced by a "cooperative oligopoly", led by Nippon Steel, giving them more leeway for production cutbacks and price rises during recessions.

Another characteristic of Japan's steel industry is the wild fluctuation in steel demand and prices. The fluctuations are so wild that the steel industry finds itself either "on the throne, or in beggary". Private and public capital investments in Japan, which account for a large percentage of the GNP, lead the sizable increases in steel demand. The large stock cycle in Japan's steel-producing and steel-processing industries also affects the fluctuations. Japan's ordinary steel consumption in fiscal year 1974, broken down by industry, is as follows: construction 45%, automobiles 12%, shipbuilding 14%, industrial machinery 9%, electrical machinery 4%, secondary steel products 9%, and others 7%. The following is a breakdown by the final demand sector: personal consumption expenditure 6%, private housing construction 10%, private plant and equipment investment 40%, gross domestic fixed capital formation by the government 19% and indirect exports 24%. The wild price fluctuation is a result of the steel producers requiring large-scale facilities and the difficulty of cutting production. They generally depend on external funds for expanding production facilities.

TABLE 28 *Steel production and supply in Japan*

Fiscal year	Crude steel output (000 tons)	Ordinary steel products			Unit export price (dollars)
		Shipments (1,000 tons)			
		Total	Domestic market	Exports	
1970	92,406	64,051	48,412	15,638	142
1971	88,441	65,231	45,028	20,202	136
1972	102,972	77,816	58,199	19,617	157
1973	120,017	91,558	68,735	22,824	210
1974	114,035	84,976	55,139	29,837	328
1975	101,596	76,186	49,532	26,654	288
1976	108,309	82,059	49,719	32,340	268

The Japanese steel industry depends on imports for nearly all of its basic materials, 99% of the iron ores and 88% of the coking coal, while it exports 30% of its products. About 48% of the iron ores come from Australia, 26% from South America, 13% from India and 5% from Africa. Recently, imports from Australia and South America have been increasing. In coking coal, 38% of the imports come from Australia, 35% from the United States and 19% from Canada. Imports from Australia and Canada have been increasing, and imports from Canada are expected to rise sharply. In 1974, Japan's steel exports accounted for 26% of the world's total steel exports. The breakdown of Japan's steel exports by destination is: Asia 32% (China only 13%), North America 20% (United States 19%), Europe 18%, Middle East 17%, Central and South America 8%, Africa 3% and Oceania 2%. Japanese steel products account for more than half of the steel imports of developing nations.

The post-war recovery of the Japanese steel industry was striking. Output in terms of crude steel rapidly expanded from 560,000 tons in 1946 to 7,660,000 tons in 1953, exceeding the past peak attained in 1943. In 1964, Japan outpaced West Germany in steel output and became the world's third largest steel producer next to the Soviet Union and the United States. Steel output of the four largest steel producing nations in 1976 is (in thousand tons); USSR 145,000, USA 116,310, Japan 107,380, West Germany 42,410.

3.2.2 OUTLOOK

Eleven blast furnaces are expected to be put into operation between 1976 and 1980. Five new furnaces will be constructed and six are replacements. As a result, Japan's crude steel production capacity will increase by 34 million tons and its real operating capacity will reach at least 150 million tons in 1980. A capital outlay of $18 billion will be required for this expansion.

Domestic demand for steel has been growing at an annual rate of 10%, but its growth rate is likely to slow down to 5–6% and will be subject to greater fluctuations. The elasticity of steel consumption in relation to the GNP will probably fall below 1·0, due to a decrease in public and private capital outlays, which usually boost steel consumption. Increases in personal consumption expenditure and a shorter business fluctuation cycle with enlarged amplitudes will directly affect steel demand. Demand from ship-builders is likely to stagnate, while that from automobile and machinery industries is expected to rise 5–8%, but this will be too small to boost demand for steel as a whole. It is expected that public investment in such projects as land and ocean development and urban renewal will boost demand for steel, but it will be some time before these projects get under way. However, demand for steel for private housing and consumer goods is expected to increase gradually.

In July 1976, the Industrial Structure Council, an advisory body to the Ministry of International Trade and Industry, estimated the domestic demand for steel in 1980 at 110 million tons, with a prospective average annual increase of 10·7% between 1976 and 1980. However, in the steel industry, some believe that the estimate is too high. Probably a more reasonable estimate would be 85–90 million tons. The world demand for steel is expected to rise from 680 million tons in 1976 to 830 million tons in 1980.

TABLE 29 *Steel production capacities of the world*

	(million metric tons)				
	1974			1980	
	Crude steel output	Operating capacity	Operation rate (%)	Operating capacity	Increase rate (%) 1980/1975
Japan	117·1	121·0	96·8	150·0	3·6
Western Europe	181·0	191·3	94·6	231·0	3·2
Central and South America	17·8	19·5	91·3	39·6	12·5
North America	148·8	152·8	97·4	174·0	2·2
Others	27·8	33·3	83·5	60·8	10·6
Sub-total	492·5	517·9	95·1	655·4	4·0
Communist bloc	212·2	221·7	95·7	281·4	4·1
Total	704·7	739·6	95·3	936·8	4·0

The steel supply capacity of the United States is not expected to increase by more than 18 million tons between 1976 and 1980 because of a shortage of funds, despite American steel producers' ambitious investment plans. European Common Market nations' steel supply capacity is expected to increase by 25 million tons during the same period. In addition, a considerable delay in programmes for self-sufficiency of steel in developing countries seems inevitable because of soaring construction costs and insufficient monetary reserves in these countries in the wake of the oil crisis. Also, steel producers in advanced nations are reluctant to invest overseas due to the recent recession.

As a result, the operational capacity of all steel mills in the world is expected to reach 940 million tons at an operating rate of 88%. However, supply and demand for steel products will become tighter after 1980, because advanced nations are unlikely to further increase the operating capacity of their steel mills, while demand will expand, especially that of the developing countries.

In fiscal year 1976, Japan exported 42·8 million tons of steel (in terms of crude steel). It is possible that its exports will exceed 50 million tons after fiscal year 1980, but it will remain at 45 million tons if import curbs on Japanese steel are tightened. Consequently, the operational rate of Japanese steel mills is likely to increase to nearly 90%, even if the output of crude steel in fiscal year 1980 is estimated at 135 million tons.

There is some concern in business circles about the weakening of Japanese steel's competitiveness in the international market, due to rising material costs and soaring wages. However, the difference in production costs between the United States and Japan at the end of 1975 was still estimated at $40–50 per ton. It is true that the CIF price of imported Japanese steel is at a disadvantage relative to American steel, but Japan has an advantage over the United States in various Third World markets.

The competitive power of Japanese steel will be maintained for some time. Japanese steel producers have constructed efficient production facilities at low cost. The average construction cost per ton of crude steel stands at $170. On the other hand, the United States and Europe have old and inefficient facilities, and sizable investments would be required for their replacement ($500 per ton) or construction of new steel mills ($1,000 per ton). The smaller interest payments and depreciation for Japanese steel manufacturers will help sustain the competitiveness of their products on the world market.

The sharp rise in salaries and wages of Japanese steel workers has begun to subside, contributing to Japan's continued competitiveness. After the recent round of price increases, material costs are levelling off, reflecting slack demand. Japanese steel producers have achieved better results in production rationalization than their American and European counterparts. For example, a rise in yield rate and a decrease in the basic unit of energy consumption have supported Japan's position. The ratio of investments in anti-pollution devices relative to the total investments for the United States and European steel industries rose to 15%, approaching Japan's 20%. For these reasons, Japan's steel producers will retain their competitive edge over those of the United States and Europe.

3.3 Shipbuilding

3.3.1 CHARACTERISTICS

Ever since exceeding Britain's gross annual tonnage of ship construction in 1956 and thus ranking first among shipbuilding countries in the world, the Japanese shipbuilding industry has had an unbroken command of the world market for 20 years. Since 1973, it has held a share of 50% or more of the global market (*see* Table 30).

TABLE 30 *Major shipbuilding nations' shares of the world market*

	(%)			
	Japan	Britain	Sweden	West Germany
1950	7	43	11	2
1955	11	27	10	19
1960	22	15	8	13
1965	42	11	11	9
1970	48	6	7	6
1971	48	5	7	7
1972	48	5	7	6
1973	50	3	8	6
1974	51	4	6	6
1975	50	4	7	7

Note Shares are calculated on a launching basis
Source: Lloyd's statistics

The remarkable growth of the Japanese shipbuilding industry may be attributed to the following factors:

(a) Technological innovation in the construction process – control of costs and time required for shipbuilding by means of block systems, block welding sequence, outfit in advance, etc.

(b) Success in coping with different types of ships, especially in meeting the growing demand for larger vessels. The Japanese shipbuilding industry now ranks foremost in the construction of supertankers and specialized carriers.

(c) The special financing system of the Export–Import Bank of Japan. Financing plays an important role in ship construction because of its enormous costs and the increasing loans of the Export-Import Bank have made a significant contribution to the industry's growth.

The Japanese shipbuilding industry is now confronted with two major problems: a worldwide sluggish demand for ships, resulting in a decrease in orders, and mounting criticism in Europe of the sharp increase in the export of Japanese ships. In the medium term, the world demand for ships is likely to remain sluggish, because an over-supply of bottoms makes new ships less attractive to shipowners. Idle tankers totalling 40 million dead-weight tons were laid up at the end of August 1976, and a 25–30% slowdown of navigation speed is now being put into practice. Surplus tankers total just under 100 million dead-weight tons, approximately one-third of the world's total tonnage, which reaches 305 million dead-weight tons. Taking account of the projected increase in tankers, the supply and demand will not balance until 1980, presuming that marine transport of crude oil and petroleum products will increase at a rate of 8% per year. At the end of August 1976, laid-up bulk carriers and cargo ships totalled 1·5 million dead-weight tons. Supply pressure will increase due to orders for tankers which have been switched to those for bulk carriers and cargo ships.

In June 1976, the Shipping and Shipbuilding Rationalization Council, an advisory body to the Ministry of Transport, made a forecast of the demand for bottoms in 1980, as a preparation for the government's anti-recession programme which hopes to avoid possible future confusion in the industry. According to the forecast, the total tonnage of ships to be built in Japan in 1980 is estimated at 6·5 million gross tons, or 33% of the all-time high attained in 1974, assuming that Japan's 50% share of the global market will be maintained. Utilization rate of the shipyards' capacity in 1980 is expected to remain at 65% of the all-time high, due to the increase in the number of ships to be built which have resulted from a shift in demand from huge tankers to small bulk carriers. However, many in the industry believe it will be difficult to secure as many orders as expected, and the demand for bottoms will fall far short of 6·5 million gross tons in and after 1978.

To cope with a decrease of work in process, the Japanese shipbuilders have attempted to expand their overseas business network and stressed canvassing by executives. They have succeeded in obtaining orders accounting for more than 90% of the total tonnage of orders received by OECD member countries during the third quarter (July to September) of 1976. European shipbuilders are concerned at such aggressive canvassing, though they have a larger backlog of orders than Japan at present. Japan holds an exorbitantly large share of the global shipbuilding market and Japanese shipbuilders offer far lower prices than their European counterparts, which caused the Association of Western European Shipbuilders (AWES) to blame Japanese shipbuilders for snatching orders at prices 40% lower than theirs. In fact, shipbuilders in Europe are now in great difficulty.

Under such circumstances, Japan could not ignore a demand for import restrictions. Therefore, Japanese shipbuilders have decided to refrain from accepting orders from German shipowners for two years. The Ministry of Transport has decided to watch contract prices more carefully and to permit only contracts with a 5% price increase over that of 1976. The Ministry will press shipbuilders to refrain from a "torrential" export of ships to a single country, and curb each shipbuilder's capacity utilization. These steps may appease European criticism, but it is unlikely that Japan's "voluntary restriction" on ship exports will contribute to a gain in orders by European shipbuilders. It is more likely to result in an increasing market share for newly-rising powers, such as the Republic of Korea, Taiwan, Singapore and Brazil.

3.3.2 OUTLOOK

The most serious problem is to control the huge construction capacity of the Japanese shipbuilding industry, which doubled from 10 million gross tons in 1970 to 20 million gross tons in 1974. The six major shipbuilding firms are Mitsubishi Heavy Industries Ltd, Ishikawajima-Harima Heavy Industries Co Ltd, Kawasaki Heavy Industries Ltd, Mitsui Engineering & Shipbuilding Co Ltd, Hitachi Shipbuilding & Engineering Co Ltd and Sumitomo Heavy Industries Ltd. They have vied to expand their yards, emphasizing huge docks to meet the growing demand for mammoth tankers.

TABLE 31 *Trend and projection of orders received by the shipbuilding industry*

(000 gross tons)							
	1965	1973	1975	1976	1980 (fore- cast)	Average rate of increase (%)		
						1965–73	1973–75	1975–80
For all ships	7,976	33,790	8,504	8,422	6,500	19·8	−50·2	−5·2
Tankers	3,185	27,630	606	456	500	31·0	−85·2	−3·6
Non-tankers	4,791	6,160	7,898	7,966	6,000	3·4	13·2	−5·3
Ships for export	5,520	27,706	6,899	6,825	5,000	22·3	−50·1	−6·2
Ships for Japanese owners	2,456	6,084	1,605	1,598	1,000	12·0	−48·6	−1·3

Source: Ministry of Transport Ship Bureau

Docks for building 1 million-ton ships have been brought into operation since 1972, for instance the Koyaki Dock of Mitsubishi, the Chita Dock of IHI, the Sakaide Dock of Kawasaki, the Ariake Dock of Hitachi and the Oppama Dock of Sumitomo. These large docks have now become unnecessary, because Japanese shipbuilders are no longer awarded new orders for supertankers and their backlog is decreasing. As long as excess of supply capacity exists, cut-throat competition will continue.

The only countermeasure would be a slash of supply capacity. In response to a report by the Shipping and Shipbuilding Rationalization Council, which estimated the demand for bottoms in 1980 at 6·5 million gross tons, the Ministry of Transport drew up a rough plan for cutting the shipyards' capacity usage rate. It would reduce the rate to 63% for major shipbuilders, to 70% for medium-sized ones and to 75% for minor ones during fiscal year 1978, as measured against the 1974 base level. The purpose of this plan is to limit ship construction at all shipyards, helping all shipbuilders survive.

The operational rate cut threatens the existence of many shipbuilders, unless it can be carried out along with the lowering of their fixed cost level. Then personnel cutbacks and partial scrapping of shipbuilding facilities will become the problems to solve. Depreciation expenses relating to equipment are modest, in addition to the difficulty of selling docks and other facilities. Personnel cutbacks seem more viable, since personnel costs account for 20% of gross sales. It seems necessary to reduce the workforce by approximately 100,000 workers to cut operations back to 65%. Most shipyards employ a large number of temporary workers other than their regular personnel (in 1975, 29% of their employees). It would seem possible to discharge these temporary workers, but there are constraints on such a lay-off, for the following reasons:

(a) At a dockyard, many jobs (e.g., painting, work at dizzy heights) cannot be carried out without these workers.

(b) Opposition by the local community. Lay-off of these workers would seriously affect the local economy, especially in towns where the shipyard is the main industry.

Consequently, lay-offs or redeployment of regular employees would also be required.

In previous recessions, Japanese shipbuilders made every effort to expand their machinery departments. They achieved good results between 1960 and 1965, in which time demand for heavy machinery sharply increased. "The Second Rationalization Programme" of the steel industry, intended to integrate production, required the construction of a number of blast furnaces, and large-scale capital outlays by the electric power and petroleum industries created a demand the shipbuilders could fill. However, domestic demand for materials and intermediate goods, which encourages corporate capital spending, has dwindled, and there is little prospect of its recovery in the foreseeable future.

There has been a steady increase in plant exports to oil-producing countries. Japanese shipbuilders can afford to supply various kinds of plant such as steel mills, hydropower or atomic power stations, cement plants, fertilizer plants, desalination plants and material stockpiling centres. For example, in 1975 Mitsubishi Heavy Industries received an order for a fertilizer plant worth $670 million from Iraq. Many other firms have also been awarded orders for various plants, each in the $100 million range. Japan's plant exports on a licence basis in fiscal year 1975 reached $5·2 billion, ranking next to exports of steel, automobiles and ships. Shipbuilding firms expect to make up the decrease in their earnings from ship construction with plant exports. The export of plant is expected to play a more important role for shipbuilding firms.

3.4 Construction

3.4.1 CHARACTERISTICS

The construction industry in Japan is composed of approximately 428,000 companies and employs 4,700,000 workers. It plays an important role in the nation's economy as well as in people's daily lives. The construction industry is used by almost all sectors of the economy, from government agencies to business corporations and individuals. Since construction investments reflect economic trends, orders received for construction are regarded as an effective leading indicator of business prospects. In Japan, private sector construction orders, which account for 55–60% of the industry, are susceptible to monetary policies, such as an increase or decrease of the official discount rate. The effects are noticeable after a lag of two or three quarters, especially on orders from the manufacturing industry.

On the other hand, construction orders in the public sector, accounting for 40–45% of the industry, are affected by fiscal policies such as early placement of public works orders, compilation of a supplementary budget or additional treasury investments and loans. The government often utilizes public works as a means of business adjustment, because its fiscal policy produces the desired effect in a short period, and because these works have a large inducement factor, promoting business activity. Consequently, in Japan, construction investments follow a cycle in which the private sector orders increase in a boom, while those of the public sector increase during a recession.

The construction industry is specifically characterized by its integration into the economy, as examined below. Construction is carried out to order and, accordingly, constructors are compelled to assume a passive attitude towards their clients. They are in a completely different position from manufacturers who produce and stock products in anticipation of demand. Constructors give top priority to the obtaining of orders and attach importance to the turnover of their own assets and capital. Also, construction works are executed in many different places. Accordingly, construction companies have difficulty in keeping a regular labour force and fixed equipment. They inevitably have to emphasize "site management". In addition, their profits are often influenced by weather, and production management and cost control are difficult.

Construction firms largely depend on subcontractors, who procure most of the necessary materials and appliances, and need the cooperation of many specialists and advisers. In general, the expenditure on subcontracted work and services accounts for 55–70% of the total construction costs. In most cases, subcontracting exists in tiers: subcontractors of a construction firm usually sublet a portion of their work to their own subcontractors, and so forth. A construction company takes charge of design, procurement of materials and supervision of the work. In some cases, they also raise the funds necessary for the work. Thus, they occasionally take on the characteristics of a *sogoshosha* (general trading company).

Tenders are made in the following ways: open bidding, restricted bidding and bidding by negotiation. There are few examples of open bidding in Japan's construction industry. Bidding by negotiation is made only for construction works in the private sector. The restricted bidding system, inviting plurally designated contractors, is most widely adopted. When a government agency invites a tender, it designates a number of contractors who have achieved a certain level of rating, in accordance with the scale of the projected construction works. Construction firms wishing to be invited for tenders offered by government agencies must apply yearly to the government for designation. In rating, the greatest importance is usually attached to construction revenue. This is why construction firms are apt to emphasize an increase in revenue rather than the quality of the work.

The construction industry is composed of civil engineering and building businesses. They are entirely different in organization, technology, appliances needed, subcontracting system, etc. This further complicates the management of construction companies. Of the Japanese construction companies, Kajima, Taisei, Shimizu, Ohbayashi-Gumi and Takenaka are the most important. They are followed by Kumagaigumi, Hazama-Gumi, Fujita and Toda Construction.

3.4.2 OUTLOOK

The government's "Medium-term Economic Programme" serves as an indicator for a medium-term projection of the future trend of construction investment. The government programme estimates an average annual economic growth rate from 1976 to 1980 at 13%-plus in nominal and 6% in real terms. Investments for improving the quality of dwellings are expected to increase private residential construction. Improvements requiring special overhead capital, especially sewerage, carry a high priority, and investments in public utilities are also expected to increase. The increase in the government's investment is likely to continue. Strong inflationary pressures such as energy costs and public utilities charges are expected to persist. holding down ambitious development.

Private construction investments will pick up with an improvement of corporate earnings and a need to increase supply as demand picks up. However, this tempo is expected to slow down with the advent of sustained economic growth. In addition, finding appropriate sites for constructing plant and other facilities whilst avoiding environmental pollution will be difficult, because of citizens' movements to protect the environment. These conditions will restrict construction investment in both public and private sectors. However, the housing-related industry, environmental improvement, urban renewal and modernization of distribution structure are the areas in which increases are expected. Construction investments are expected to rise in parallel with the GNP, following business fluctuations, without the previous rapid growth.

TABLE 32 *Orders received and revenue of the construction industry*

($ million)							
						Rate of increase (%)		
Fiscal year	1965	1970	1975	1976	1980 (esti- mates)	1965–70	1970–75	1975–80
Total orders received	517	1,286	2,123	2,172	3,821	20·0	10·6	12·5
Private sector	238	741	1,031	1,086	1,821	25·0	6·8	12·1
Public sector	244	460	910	929	1,714	13·5	14·8	13·5
Construction revenue	482	1,168	2,046	2,057	3,660	19·3	11·9	12·3

As expansion of domestic construction investments is expected to ebb with a slowdown of the nation's economic growth, Japan's construction industry must cope with decreasing demand. As a result, many construction firms have stressed overseas construction. Overseas construction work on a commercial basis has been increasing since 1965, taking the place of that made as war reparation to South-East Asian countries. However, until 1973, Japanese construction firms had been occupied with rapidly increasing domestic orders and, feeling uneasy about the profitability of overseas construction works, they hesitated to move into this field. 43 major construction firms received orders from abroad amounting to $94 million in fiscal year 1972, but this accounted for only 0·5% of the total orders.

Since 1973, construction investment in developing countries has increased for national development and for improvement of industrial foundation, including construction of roads, power plants and port facilities. Japanese construction firms began to actively solicit orders from these countries because of decreasing domestic orders. Those received from abroad increased to $1,130 million, accounting for 5·5% of the orders accepted, including large-scale construction works such as repair and expansion of the Suez Canal, subway construction in Hong Kong, etc. At present, Japanese construction firms have inquiries for large-scale construction works, mainly from Middle

East and South-East Asian countries, including a petrochemical complex in Iran.

The volume of overseas construction will continue to increase but it will remain below 10% even in 1980. Improvement of financial and tax systems to insure the various risks involved in overseas construction works has been delayed, along with low-interest loans earmarked for tender money and for carrying out construction works. Experience is required in managing local workers or understanding particular contract methods due to differences in religion, ways of thought and life, and habits. Training of experts with a long-range outlook is vital as there is a possibility that a shortage of expertise will be a great disadvantage. Time will be required to solve these problems.

Domestically, Japanese construction firms should strive for:

(a) increased activity in the residential construction sector, which has bright prospects;
(b) creating new demand through research and technological development;
(c) increased participation in planning and design;
(d) expanding their spheres of business activity by establishing a closer contact with local constructors, as well as with the local community.

In residential construction, leading construction firms have generally engaged in building high-rise apartment houses for the Japan Housing Corporation and local semi-governmental organizations. They have little experience of building single family houses or small apartment houses because of the localized demand for this type of house and the small scale of construction involved. However, more than one-third of the construction investments are now of this latter type, and a further increase can be expected. Therefore, leading construction firms will increase their activity in this field.

Construction companies may find a new demand in energy-related fields, such as construction of LNG or crude oil storage facilities and of pumping power plants, or in improving the living environment, in projects like prevention of pollution, urban renewal and ocean development. Obtaining orders from local government, which account for two-thirds of the public works orders, is another challenge for major construction firms.

3.5 Automobiles

3.5.1 CHARACTERISTICS

Japan's automobile industry has been fully developed since the mid-1960s. Japan's vehicle production increased 3·7 times between 1965 and 1975, by far outpacing the corresponding figures of 0·75 for Great Britain, 0·81 for the United States, 1·07 for West Germany and 2·01 for France. In 1975, it reached 6,940,000 units, 60% of which were passenger cars, second only to the US output of 8,990,000 units, 75% of which were passenger cars. The number of vehicles in use increased sharply from 6,300,000 units in 1965 to

28,090,000 units in 1975, and Japan now ranks second in car population after the United States. In 1966, sales of small and low-priced cars, suited for the use of the general public, seemed to trigger Japan's motorization. At present, one out of four Japanese owns a car. The vehicle dissemination rate in Japan is coming close to the international level.

TABLE 33 *World automobile industries in 1975*

		(000 units)		
Ranking	Produc- tion	Domestic demand	Exports	Imports
1 USA	8,990	10,660	910	2,200
2 Japan	6,940	4,310	2,680	50
3 France	3,300	1,690	1,940	440
4 West Germany	3,190	2,220	1,650	790
5 United Kingdom	1,650	1,420	700	470
6 Italy	1,460	1,130	710	410

Source: Japan Automobile Manufacturers Association

Japan's automobile exports have increased remarkably, due to the strength of their mass production system, established in the 1960s. Since 1974, Japan has been the largest automobile exporting country in the world, exporting 2,680,000 vehicles in 1975. At present, Toyota and Nissan are numbered among the world's "big four", together with General Motors and Ford, indicating that Japan's automobile industry is international in scope.

Nearly 30,000 components and parts are required to construct an automobile. The automobile industry, supported by many related industries, has grown into a key industry, ranking with the steel and electric power industries.

The output of Japan's automobile industry in 1974 was $32,850 million, accounting for 8.4% of the manufacturing industry's output as a whole. This compares with $42,140 million for the steel industry and $40,000 million for the electric power industry. The automobile industry is playing an increasingly important role in Japan's exports, on a par with steel and ship construction. In 1975, exports of automobiles, excluding two-wheelers, reached $6,830 million, or 12.2% of Japan's total exports. In 1972, automobile exports exceeded ship construction and ranked second in exports, and they have been gaining on steel, the most important export item. Automobiles have expanded from one-fifth of the steel exports in 1965 to two-thirds in 1975. If rapid increases continue, they will soon gain the lead in exports.

In the field of employment, the automobile industry can be called "a comprehensive industry", as it has far-reaching effects on employment in various related industries. The industry, including the manufacture of chassis and various parts, employs around 600,000 workers and the sales and service sector employs 900,000. In addition, approximately 1,800,000 persons are employed to drive the resultant vehicles, and 300,000 work in various supporting industries. The total number of workers in the automobile and auto-related industries approaches 3,600,000. If the labour force in the basic material manufacturing sector is added, it reaches 4,500,000, more than one-tenth of Japan's working population (44,000,000).

The automobile industry accounts for approximately 10% of the nation's production, exports and labour force, greatly influencing the nation's economy. Incidentally, employment, output and sales of the US auto industry account for 15%, 11% and 26% respectively of the industrial economy.

3.5.2 OUTLOOK

The expansion of domestic demand has already begun to slow down. Domestic demand increased 6% per year during the 1970–73 period, but it declined below the preceding year for the first time, in the wake of the oil crisis in the autumn of 1973. This was due to a slackness in demand for transport, a sluggish growth of personal income, and the fact that Japan's consumption of vehicle production has reached the maturity stage. The number of vehicles used in Japan has already topped the 30 million mark, and automobile are widely considered a modern convenience. At present, one out of four Japanese, or every household in Japan, has a car, and there is little room for an increase in new owners. However, as the function of vehicles gradually expands, saturation will be delayed. As the role of the car expands from one for family use to the second car and then to a personal car, there is a positive longer-term outlook. However, this depends on a continued increase of spending on social projects like roads.

TABLE 34 *Growth of the automobile industry*

					1980 (estimates)	Rate of increase (%)		
(000 units)								
	1965	1970	1975	1976		1965–70	1970–75	1975–80
Number of vehicles in use	7,240	18,160	28,370	30,000	35,000	22·0	9·8	4·3
Domestic demand	1,710	4,090	4,200	4,100	5,050	18·7	0·5	3·5
Exports	200	1,220	2,990	3,710	4,150	44·0	17·6	7·0
Production	1,940	5,450	7,130	7,840	9,200	23·0	5·5	5·2

Source: Japan Automobile Manufacturers Association

In 1980, domestic demand for automobiles will reach 5,050,000, exceeding the all-time high of 4,910,000 attained in 1973. An active demand for passenger cars will probably contribute to such an increase in domestic demand for vehicles, since the present dissemination rate is relatively low compared with the international level. In 1980, domestic demand for passenger cars in Japan will certainly reach 3,150,000, exceeding the past peaks.

In the medium term, a sluggish increase in demand will probably be an issue. It will drive car manufacturers to more intensive competition for a larger market share, widening the gap between large and small producers with their differing merchandizing ability and price competitiveness. With a shift from new demand to replacement demand, the automobile industry will become more vulnerable to cyclical business fluctuation. Productivity will slow down, and manufacturers must increase the value added to their products, by reviewing the total cost through rationalization of their production set-up and improvement of their financial position. Previously they have been reducing costs through economies of scale.

Generally, competitiveness in the world market is achieved through the following stages: moderate price; good quality and performance; innovation in both technology and styling; and prestige. Rolls Royce is a representative of the last stage. Japanese cars' competitiveness is passing from the first stage (price competitiveness) into the second one where performance carries the most weight. Since 1973, Japan's "big two", Toyota and Nissan, have emphasized "performance" more than "moderate price" as their main selling point. Fortunately, demand has also emphasized function or performance. Japanese models enjoy a high reputation in the world small car market. This is further enhanced by an increasing concern for fuel economy since the 1973 oil crisis.

The Japanese have little fear about competitiveness, even in the medium term. In the US market, their real prices, including cost of options, are nearly 10% less than those of their competitors. The Big Three's (Toyota, Nissan and Honda) strategy for developing smaller cars has shifted emphasis from minicars to town-size cars. Small cars priced at $3,000 form a small portion of each of the Big Three's earnings, which are dependent on those with an average price of $5,000. Consequently, there has been no direct impact on sales of Japanese cars in the United States. The biggest obstacle facing the export of Japanese cars lies in the non-economic realm and includes such things as import restrictions.

If there are no great changes, the export of Japanese cars will increase through the expansion of their share of the American and European markets and through the diversification of their markets. In 1980, Japan's automobile exports are expected to reach 4,150,000 units, boosting the ratio of exports to the total output to 45%.

In 1980, domestic demand and exports will probably reach 5,050,000 and 4,150,000 units respectively. Assembly production of Japanese cars in developing countries will progress further, but production in advanced countries on a full scale will not be realized by 1980. Total domestic production is estimated at 9,200,000 units, and the average annual rate of increase from 1976 to 1980 is expected to be over 5%. This is almost the same as that for the previous five-year period, from 1971 to 1975.

The weight of the Japanese automobile industry in the international arena will further increase. Japanese automobile producers will be strengthened by an increase in size, expansion of their earning capacity and an improvement of their financial position. Japan's automobile industry can take advantage of a stable labour–management relationship and active union cooperation in improving productivity. The political and economic stability in Japan, along with an abundant, highly-educated labour force, will contribute to make Japan one of the world's vehicle production centres. It should be noted that General Motors and Chrysler are strengthening their ties with Japanese automobile producers, a change in their strategy for development as multi-national corporations, recognizing the increasing demand for smaller cars in the world market.

The world vehicle output is expected to reach 39 million units in 1980. Japan's share in the world's production will rise to 25% in 1980 from 21% in 1975, and it is not unrealistic to predict that Japan will become one of the largest sources of automobiles in the world, ranking with the United States, which accounted for 27% of the world production in 1975. At present, there are 11 vehicle manufacturers in Japan. The combined share of the "big two", Toyota and Nissan, in the domestic market has been expanding rapidly from 40·4% in 1965, 49·7% in 1970, to 60·8% in 1975. Their share of the passenger car market reached 70·4% in 1975. This was a result of their domination in the production of small and low-priced cars suitable for the use of the general public, as well as their excellent fund-raising capacity.

It seems essential for the smaller manufacturers to use market segmentation appropriate to their marketing capacity. Even now, some motor manufacturers are making stable profits on such products as light-duty or heavy-duty trucks. With regard to cars, Honda's single-car strategy has succeeded in breaking through the big two's full-line array, demonstrating an alternative route. However, an oligopolistic tendency in the Japanese automobile industry will inevitably develop, as the gap between the stronger and weaker widens.

3.6 Consumer Electronic and Electrical Products

3.6.1 CHARACTERISTICS

Consumer electronic and electrical products can be generally defined as electrical machinery for household and personal use. From a technical point of view, they are classified into

(a) consumer electronic appliances and
(b) consumer electrical appliances.

Consumer electronic appliances include such products as radios, television sets, tape recorders and stereo systems, which make use of the physical characteristics of conductivity in vacuum tubes and semi-conductors; consumer electrical appliances include refrigerators, washing machines and electric irons, which utilize electrical or thermal energy. The production systems of these two kinds of appliance differ because of their technical characteristics.

The technology of consumer electronic products is closely related to that of the electronics industry. In other words, it advances in step with progress in the electronics industry. The production of these electronic products centres on the assembly of a large number of electronic components, which is a labour-intensive process. Even small manufacturers, therefore, can enter this market, if they become experienced in electronics technology; in fact, there are a large number of small manufacturers in the field of relatively simple electronic products, including radios and tape recorders. In addition, this field is very competitive, as is illustrated by the fact that developing nations, where labour costs are low, have recently started production (this also includes local production by Japanese manufacturers). However, products with a large number of parts and components and a complicated production process, such as colour television sets, require large amounts of capital funds and an extensive sales network. Inevitably there is only a small number of manufacturers of these products. Since the oil crisis, the manufacturers have been switching to a more automated production process. Even in the field of simple electronic appliances, the large manufacturers have expanded their market share.

Consumer electrical appliances, on the other hand, are the applied products of electrical motor and heating equipment. Production is somewhat capital-intensive because the ratio of skilled labour to technological development is low and mechanical facilities are required. Therefore, the production of consumer electrical appliances is limited to a small number of large manufacturers. The major Japanese companies whose manufacture is limited to consumer electronic and electrical products are Matsushita Electric Industrial, Sanyo Electric and Sharp. The major companies which manufacture heavy electric machinery in addition to these products are Tokyo Shibaura Electric (Toshiba), Hitachi and Mitsubishi Electric Corporation.

The consumer electronic and electrical industry manufactures consumer durables and accordingly, demand depends largely on

(a) the development of promising products which will stimulate demand,
(b) consumers' disposable income, which fluctuates according to economic conditions, and
(c) the degree of market penetration of the products.

The industry occupied a secure position only after 1955. After succeeding in the development of such glamour products as television sets, refrigerators and washing machines, it has grown to become a major industry which has led the high growth Japanese economy.

Japan's high economic growth since 1955 resulted in an improved standard of living. As national income as a whole increased sharply, domestic demand for consumer electronic and electrical products expanded substantially. The successive development of leading products continued to stimulate domestic demand. In addition, manufacturers realized the efficiency of producing in volume in the light of growing demands. Technological advancement in the electronics industry contributed to a drastic cost reduction in consumer electronic appliances and a lowering of retail prices. These factors were responsible for the high growth of the industry.

In the export market, consumer electrical appliances, for which technological development has been less relevant, are at a disadvantage because of high transportation costs. Consumer electronic appliances account for a greater volume of exports. Japan is currently the world's major supplier of consumer electronic appliances with the highest level of production in the world. This industry has strengthened its price competitiveness according to the following cycle: from an increase in demand to a realization of the efficiency of volume production, to a cut in prices. The United States, which is the most advanced nation in electronics technology, has so far concentrated its production in industrial, space development and defence fields, depending largely on imports for household products, which are very labour-intensive. These factors have contributed to Japan's strong international competitiveness.

The industry has enjoyed high growth. However, the degree of growth has varied according to the life cycle of its major products. The life cycle of a product is composed of

(a) the exploitation period in the market (market penetration of not more than 10%);
(b) the growth period (market penetration of not more than 60%);
(c) the maturity period (market penetration of more than 60%);
(d) the declining period.

After the declining period, the replacement demand for the product accounts for its marketability and the overall demand for this industry begins to grow again only after the development of new products. Such products as black-and-white or colour TV sets, which are highly attractive to consumers, have an extremely short growth period and their market expands very rapidly. Meanwhile, such products as stereo systems and tape recorders, which depend more on personal taste, experience a slow rate of market penetration. Their penetration ratio generally increases only to 60–70%. Consumer electrical appliances are usually considered necessities and are used most often by housewives. It takes a considerable period of time for these products to penetrate from the high-income consumers into the low-income group.

TABLE 35 *Changes in exports of consumer electronic and electrical products*

(¥ billion)				
	1965	1970	1975	1976
Consumer electrical appliances	10·3	47·7	113·6	139·0
Consumer electronic appliances	143·4	577·9	883·0	1,427·0
Both	150·7	625·6	996·6	1,566·0
Ratio to total shipments	26%	31%	39%	47%

Source: *Japan Exports and Imports*, Ministry of Finance

When the growth process of the consumer electronic and electrical industry since 1955 is reviewed (*see* Table 36), a higher growth rate is seen for the periods 1956–60 and 1966–70. This is because the industry placed powerful leading products on the market during these periods.

The differences among the manufacturers of this industry are rarely evident in their technology or prices. They are, instead, seen in marketing power, advertising or product design. Although the market share of large retailers increased recently, the sales by small retailers as a whole still account for 70% of total sales in Japan of consumer electronic and electrical products. Most small retailers are contracted to one of the major manufacturers (the "contracted store" system). Accordingly, the domestic market share of the respective manufacturers depends on the number of their contracted stores. Most small and medium-sized manufacturers concentrate their efforts on exports, since they have difficulty in establishing nationwide sales networks. Some manufacturers producing consumer electronic appliances of a highly personalized nature attain a unique status by means of advertising, design or technology.

TABLE 36 *Growth pattern of consumer electronic and electrical products*

Period	Average annual growth rate	Major products	Market penetration
1956–60	56%	Black and white TV	from 5% to 63%
1961–65	10%	Refrigerator	from 17% to 57%
		Stereo system	from 4% to 10%
1966–70	29%	Colour TV	from 0·6% to 33%
1971–75	6%	Air-conditioner	from 10% to 24%
		Stereo system	from 26% to 47%

3.6.2 OUTLOOK

The products currently experiencing a growth period are room air conditioners and deep freezers. The demand for room air conditioners and freezers is expected to grow substantially with the increased installation of air-conditioning facilities in office buildings and trains. A growing number of house-

TABLE 37 Changes in production of consumer electronic and electrical products

(¥ billion)

	1965	1970	1975	1976 (esti-mated)	1980 (esti-mated)	Annual increase rate (%)		
						1965–70	1970–75	1975–80
Consumer electrical appliances	246·7	575·0	990·0	1,188·0	1,600·0	18·2	11·5	10·0
Refrigerator	94·6	111·8	212·6	262·6	460·0	3·4	13·7	16·7
Room air conditioner	10·2	64·3	227·2	276·9	360·0	43·0	29·0	9·6
Consumer electronic appliances	344·7	1,465·8	1,560·4	2,139·0	3,130·0	34·0	1·3	14·9
Colour TV	13·1	681·3	564·8	747·0	1,140·0	120·0	-3·7	15·0
Tape recorder	44·7	196·5	346·1	505·0	560·0	34·0	12·0	10·1
Total	591·4	2,040·8	2,550·4	3,327·0	4,730·0	28·0	4·5	13·1

Source: *Year Book of Machinery Statistics*, Ministry of International Trade and Industry.

holds will probably regard freezers as one of their daily necessities, due to the increased marketing of frozen foods.

After the colour TV set experiences saturation in the market, it is generally considered that the videotape recorder (VTR) will be the most promising product, combining the high profit potential of a quality product with the wide market of domestic usage. Also, the price is dropping to the level at which average households can afford to purchase one. However, the VTR will not be a market leader in the near future because it is still in the exploitation period and is not as attractive as the colour TV set. Meanwhile, the replacement of colour TV sets purchased between 1968, when the demand went into full swing, and 1971, when the new demand reached its peak, is expected to begin soon.

In addition, changes have been seen in other products; for example, refrigerators have changed from the conventional to the two-door type or to larger models, electric ovens have given way to microwave ovens, the conventional type of washing machine has changed to the automatic twin-tub type or the fully automatic type. Also, a large number of new products is to be placed on the market, although demand for them is small compared with that for major products.

Because of the above factors, the domestic demand for consumer electronic and electrical products is expected to grow at an annual rate of nearly 10% until around 1980. The international competitiveness of Japanese-made consumer electronic and electrical products is now the highest in the world. The world market is likely to expand further in the future, due to the increasing use of these products. However, the concept of free trade, based on a theory of the international division of labour in which exports are permitted to expand without restraint in line with their competitiveness on the world market, has faded quickly since 1970. This is due to the fact that industrial nations have placed a higher priority on the protection of domestic industries than on free trade. Because of increasingly serious problems, such as the slowdown of economic growth, uniform industrial structures and higher unemployment, the United States has, for example, introduced import restrictions on colour television sets. Japan's colour TV exports to the United States increased sharply from 1,220,000 sets in 1975 to 2,960,000 sets in 1976 because of the business recovery in the United States, coupled with Japanese manufacturers' efforts to cut their production cost. As a result, the percentage of Japanese-made colour TV sets on the US market rose drastically from 16% in 1975 to 33% in 1976. In particular, the share of small sets (screens smaller than 20-inch), which Japan is highly experienced in producing, expanded to 47%. In an attempt to cope with this situation, marginal manufacturers of colour TV sets in the United States, together with trade unions, urged the US government to impose import restrictions. Under these circumstances, Japan agreed to restrict voluntarily its colour TV exports to the United States (including semi-manufactured products) to the 1,750,000-set level per annum for three years from July 1977. The outlook for Japanese exports of consumer electronic and electrical products depends largely on the degree of such import restrictions.

3.7 Audio Equipment

3.7.1 CHARACTERISTICS

Broadly speaking, audio equipment includes all devices which produce sound, from radios to tape recorders and stereo systems. This section is limited to equipment capable of high quality sound reproduction, which consists mainly of stereo systems. Audio equipment is more of a luxury item than is a television set or a radio. Accordingly, the market has the following characteristics:

(a) Users or consumers range from beginners to hi-fi enthusiasts, depending on their taste and purchasing ability. Consequently, the product needs in this market are multidimensional, calling for sound quality-oriented, design-oriented and price-oriented items.

(b) The needs also vary with time and product appeal is sensitive to changes in fashion.

Therefore, audio equipment manufacturers have to produce a wide range of products varying in capability, price and design, in order to cope with these diverse needs. As a result, they have adopted a system of manufacturing relatively small numbers of diverse products. Large-scale manufacturers do not enjoy a superiority in production costs relative to smaller producers, since the production of audio equipment generally is unable to benefit from the economies of scale as in, for example, television manufacturing. In addition, since audio equipment is basically a personal luxury item, the user's evaluation is subjective, depending on personal taste and brand name image. Therefore, each manufacturer's basic production technology is not necessarily related directly to the competitive power of its products. Lower-priced products will not necessarily enjoy higher sales.

Large as well as small manufacturers of audio equipment have established a unique status by producing specialized, high-quality products. Some of the small producers are not yet publicly listed companies. In high-quality products, such specialist makers enjoy higher prestige with purchasers than general manufacturers of consumer electronic and electrical products, since the former maintain a lead in the ability to develop new products. There are also a large number of specialist stores which handle only audio equipment. Because of the growth of audio specialist shops, this unique distribution channel allows the relatively small specialist producers to compete with large general manufacturers which have a nationwide sales network of contracted stores.

The production of stereo systems in 1975 in terms of value totalled $1,230 million, which was 60% of the production value of colour television sets. Considering that the ratio was a modest 40% in 1970, stereo systems have obviously had a higher growth potential than colour televisions. In addition, the export ratio of stereo systems (the ratio of exports to total shipments) has reached as high as 45%, while that of colour TV sets is 30%. In particular, the export ratio of high-quality audio components (including tuners, speakers, amplifiers and decks) is an outstanding 50%. The components are chiefly exported to industrial nations: 45% of the exports are to the United States and 38% to Europe. The Japanese audio industry is highly competitive internationally, leading the world market in design and ability to develop new products, while producing high quality at a low cost. This international competitiveness is due to the following:

(a) Japan's advanced television and transistor industry makes domestic buying-in of good-quality electronic parts simple. Major audio parts, such as power transistors and ICs (internal circuits), can be developed jointly with highly experienced and technologically advanced parts manufacturers.

(b) In addition to the highly competitive electronic parts, audio equipment manufacturers' technologies for circuit design and volume production based on the technology of Japan's household electronics industry are more advanced than those of foreign manufacturers.

(c) Japanese manufacturers have become very sensitive to the quality and design of audio equipment because of sharp domestic sales competition. As a result, their products lead the international market.

(d) Pioneer, Sony and other small audio manufacturers have established unique sales networks in the international market and have popularized their own brand names. US audio manufacturers have focused their attention on hi-fi enthusiasts and, consequently, have not introduced volume production systems. On the other hand, Japanese manufacturers, led by Pioneer, have adopted a marketing strategy and distribution policy aimed at popularizing high-quality products and have thus succeeded in exploiting new overseas markets.

(e) While foreign manufacturers specializing in audio equipment are small-scale and usually produce only one audio component, there are some general manufacturers in Japan which produce many of these components. This provides Japanese manufacturers with superior capital strength.

Under these circumstances, in the field of low-priced products or "compact stereo systems", local manufacturers in the United States and Europe generally have higher market shares. In the field of high-quality audio components, Japanese manufacturers have an overwhelmingly high share of the world market.

3.7.2 OUTLOOK

In Japan, market penetration of stereo systems has reached 54%. This is lower than the 94% of colour television sets but can still be considered a high rate for personal luxury items. The stereo system has become almost one of the necessities of life for the young generation. Accordingly, penetration is expected to shift from the conventional "one set per household" to a "one set per person" pattern. Currently, replacement demands for higher-class models and demands for additional purchase, indicating that a household possesses more than one stereo system, already account for 40% of the total sales. Since trends in purchasing stereo systems are more sensitive to fashion than colour television sets, there is a strong tendency to replace them with higher-class models. Replacement of colour television sets is generally made at a seven- to eight-year interval, but stereo systems are replaced every five to six years. In particular, consumers can purchase replacement audio components separately as their income increases. Within the sales of audio equipment, audio components are occupying an increasingly large share of the market compared with stereo systems. Replacement demand is therefore expected to grow in the future.

Meanwhile, manufacturers will make efforts to stimulate demand by frequently changing the specifications of products, including design and mechanical performance, thus speeding up changes in fashion. Consequently, the domestic demand for audio equipment, with stereo systems as the leading product, is likely to see a steady rise in keeping with an increase in personal income. The export demand will probably expand more rapidly than domestic demand, which is expected to grow at a stable rate (*see* Table 38).

This prediction is based on the following points:

(*a*) Market penetration of audio equipment is lower in the United States and Europe than in Japan. It is estimated to be 30% in the United States, slightly less than 20% in West Germany and Britain, 25–30% in the Netherlands and Sweden, and 8% in Australia and France. Therefore, there is still room for market expansion in those countries.

(*b*) US and European consumers have increasingly recognized the high quality and comparatively low price of Japanese products. Pioneer, in particular, has made a great contribution to this end. Japanese products are becoming highly regarded not only in the fields of amplifiers and tuners, traditionally competitive Japanese fields, but also in decks and speakers, traditionally European fields. Therefore, the market share of Japanese products, including decks and speakers, has been expanding steadily.

(*c*) In the United States, popularization of audio equipment progressed as a result of the abolition of the Fair Trade Act. As in Japan, audio components have been penetrating rapidly into the young people's market. Therefore, the US market is expected to experience a high

TABLE 38 *Production and exports of audio equipment*

(¥ billion)

	FY 1965	FY 1970	FY 1975	FY 1976 (esti-mated)	FY 1980 (esti-mated)	Average annual growth rate (%)		
						1965–70	1970–75	1975–80
Stereo system								
Production	37·5	117·3	178·2	120·0	130·0	26	–	38
Exports	n/a	21·8	43·1	60·0	90·0	n/a	14	16
Audio components								
Production	7·6	71·5	236·3	350·0	570·0	58	27	19
Exports	n/a	n/a	124·1	190·0	350·0	n/a	n/a	23
Total								
Production	45·1	190·8	344·5	470·0	700·0	33	13	15
Exports	n/a	n/a	167·2	260·0	440·0	n/a	n/a	21

Sources: *Year Book of Machinery Statistics*, Ministry of International Trade and Industry; *Japan Exports and Imports*, Ministry of Finance; NRI forecast

Notes (i) "Audio components" does not include tape decks.
(ii) n/a – figures not available.

growth in the medium term, depending on the economic trend in that country.

Japanese manufacturers specializing in audio equipment have emphasized exports and have already established their overseas sales networks, popularizing their brand names internationally. So far, these manufacturers have usually supplied their products to a relatively limited number of users, the so-called hi-fi enthusiasts, through stores specializing in audio equipment. Their future marketing strategy will centre on the establishment of an effective network for mass sales, in line with the increasing popularity of audio equipment in overseas markets. Such Japanese manufacturers as Matsushita Electric Industrial, Hitachi and Sanyo, Electric have been trying to establish sales networks of specialist audio stores in addition to their existing overseas sales networks for consumer electronic and electrical products. For instance, Sanyo took over a local manufacturer of audio equipment in the United States and has been energetically attempting to expand its market share of audio components drastically, using its existing sales network and the popularity of its brand name.

The overseas markets will probably experience severe competition among the internationally competitive Japanese manufacturers. In this process, the exploitation of overseas markets is expected to accelerate and Japanese manufacturers are likely to expand their market share as a whole. Meanwhile, American and European manufacturers specializing in audio equipment will probably be forced to concentrate on the production of specific high-quality components.

Unlike in the colour television industry, there are no major foreign manufacturers of audio equipment. Speakers are usually produced by small and medium-sized local manufacturers and are sold in combination with Japanese-made components. This makes it very unlikely that foreign manufacturers will call for import restrictions on Japanese products to protect local manufacturers or to ensure employment opportunities for local workers. In the medium-term perspective, Japanese manufacturers expect their export-led growth to continue. Major Japanese manufacturers specializing in audio equipment include Pioneer Electronic Corporation, Victor Company of Japan, Nippon Columbia, Trio Kenwood, Sansui Electric, Akai Electric, TEAC and AIWA.

3.8 Synthetic Fibres

3.8.1 CHARACTERISTICS

Since the commercial production of vinylon by Kuraray Co Ltd in 1950 and nylon by Toray Industries Inc in 1951, Japan's synthetic fibre production has increased rapidly at an annual rate of more than 20%. It now accounts for about 15% of the total world production, making Japan the world's second largest producer after the United States. Initially, nylon was produced solely by Toray and polyester was produced by both Teijin and Toray under a government policy of industrial promotion and protection by the basic patent. As a result, supply and demand were balanced and the price stabilized. However, when the term of the patent expired in the mid-1960s, synthetic fibres became a more market-sensitive industry, with an increasing number of producers.

At present there are six nylon, eight polyester and seven acryl producers, and the top three producers of each of these synthetic fibres account for about 60% of the respective total productions. The market is characterized by sharp competition and varying technological advances made by different manufacturers. For instance, Toray leads the nylon market but is a latecomer in acryl, while the top acryl producer, Asahi Chemical Industry, is a latecomer in polyester.

Keen competition with market-sensitive natural fibres makes synthetic fibres, in turn, more sensitive to the market. The synthetic fibre industry depends entirely on the petrochemical industry for raw materials. Cost reduction due to an increase in production facilities, together with a reduction in the raw materials price resulting from the growth of the petrochemical industry, have expanded the synthetic fibre market. In the late 1960s, synthetic fibre producers stepped up integrated production in an effort to cut further the cost of raw materials.

TABLE 39 *Composition of domestic demand for fibres, by type of fibre*

	(%)		
	Natural	Regenerated	Synthetic
1960	59·1	24·1	16·8
1965	49·2	25·1	25·6
1970	44·1	20·1	35·8
1975	47·5	11·0	41·5

Of the total demand for synthetic fibres in terms of yarns, clothing accounts for 43%, industrial use 15% and exports 42%. Of the total demand for fibres, synthetics account for 32%, 84% and 75%, respectively, of these items. The reasons for the heavy industrial use of synthetic fibres lie in their strength and water resistance. The proportion of synthetic fibres used for clothing has also been rising since polyester fibres, which are excellent for spinning with other fibres and for wash-and-wear, were put on the market.

The percentage of synthetic fibres exported has been rising rapidly since the late 1960s and is now 50%. The primary reasons are the rapid increase in production capacity with the latecomers' entry into the market in the early 1960s, as well as renewed efforts for increased exports to cope with the 1965 recession and sluggish domestic demand. This trend coincided with the worldwide expansion of demand for synthetic fibres.

About 40% of synthetic fibres for export are shipped to South-East Asia, 15% to the Communist bloc, 10% to the Middle East, 10% to North America and 7% to Western Europe. The export environment has changed rapidly in the 1970s owing to:

(a) Japan's export restraint under the Japan–United States textile agreement of 1971;
(b) sharp revaluation of the yen in 1971;
(c) rapid expansion of synthetic fibre production capacities by South-East Asian countries.

As a consequence, exports increased at an annual rate of 24% in the late 1960s but, after reaching a peak of 510,000 tons in 1972, declined to 430,000 tons in 1973 and have not yet returned to that peak level.

Growth of demand for synthetic fibres in the 1950s and the 1960s was the result of expanding production, cost reduction through technological innovation and the development of new products, and the replacement of natural and regenerated fibres. The percentage of domestic demand accounted for by synthetic fibres has risen rapidly (see Table 39). In the 1970s, however, domestic demand has undergone major changes, including:

(a) a slowdown of domestic demand as a whole;
(b) a rise in the relative volume of demand for natural fibres due to renewed recognition of their qualities;
(c) a sudden decline in the relative demand volume for regenerated fibres.

This change is a result of a shift in the consumption pattern from quantity to quality. Since hitting the bottom in 1970, the relative volume of demand for natural fibres has been rising and the price spread between natural and synthetic fibres has been expanding. With 1970 as the base year of 100, the 1975 wholesale price index was 133 for cotton, 140 for wool, 69 for synthetic filament and 107 for synthetic spun yarn. Nevertheless, the demand for natural fibres has been increasing. For example, cotton has won renewed recognition, as evidenced by its use in jeans in recent years. This is a major departure from the past pattern in which a purely economic factor – price – caused a shift from one type of material to another.

3.8.2 OUTLOOK

There will be no significant increase in demand for synthetic fibres in the future because the growth rate of domestic demand will slow down and exports will decrease.

Domestic Demand is Expected to Grow at About 4% a Year.
Domestic demand for all textiles is expected to increase from about 1,600,000 tons of yarn in 1975 to 1,850,000 tons in 1980 at an annual rate of 2·8%. This is a sharp decline from the annual growth rate of 6·9% in the 1960s. Actual

domestic demand for synthetic fibres is expected to rise from 670,000 tons in 1975 at an annual rate of 4·4% (*see* Note (i), Table 40).

TABLE 40 *Demand for synthetic fibres*

(000 tons)							
	1965	1970	1975	1976	1980 (esti- mated)	Average annual growth rate (%)		
						1965–70	1970–75	1975–80
Domestic demand	269	517	508	688	830	14·0	−0·4	10·3
Exports	113	356	481	469	370	25·8	6·2	−5·1
Total demand	382	873	989	1,157	1,200	18·0	2·5	3·9
Imports	1	10	34	53	100	58·5	27·7	11·9
Production	388	898	942	1,095	1,100	18·3	1·0	3·1
(Production capacity)	(1,150)	(3,110)	(3,894)	(3,930)	(3,900)	(22·0)	(4·6)	(0)

Source: Ministry of International Trade and Industry, *Annual Textile Statistics.*
Notes (i) NRI estimate actual domestic demand for 1975 at 670,000 tons. MITI's figure of 508,000 tons is set lower than on an actual consumption basis because it does not take into account fluctuations in final product inventories between 1973 and 1975.
(ii) All figures are for the calendar year and are given in terms of yarn.

Among synthetic fibres, the demand for polyester will grow at an annual rate of 6–7%. The reasons are probable cost reduction due to substitution of raw materials, rising relative weight of demand for outer garments due to advanced yarn processing technology and increasing demand from industrial users.

Exports to Decrease

Keener competition with South-East Asian countries will be the most important problem in the future. As shown in Table 41, the total production capacity of South-East Asian countries amounted to 65% of that of Japan at the end of 1975. Their production capacity in the three major types of synthetic fibre is approximately 70% of Japan's, and in polyester it is almost equal. The higher figures of South Korea and Taiwan are a result of their emphasis on synthetic fibres in order to earn foreign currency.

It should be noted that Japanese companies have invested in about 35% of these South-East Asian synthetic fibre companies. Japanese participation in these ventures began in 1970 in an attempt to set up export bases and, since then, they have become strong competitors. Except in Indonesia and Malaysia, most of these Japanese companies do not control the majority capital. The expanding production capacity in South-East Asia not only affects Japan's exports to this area, which takes up 40% of her total synthetic fibre exports, but also contributes to competition elsewhere – competition

TABLE 41 *Synthetic fibre production capacities in South-East Asia* (*end of 1975*)

	Nylon	Polyester	Acryl	3 major fibres	Synthetic fibre total
			(tons/day)		
South Korea	165	321	224	710	766
Taiwan	333	769	140	1,242	1,242
Thailand	42	127	–	169	169
Philippines	25	60	–	85	85
Indonesia	18	42	–	60	60
Singapore	8	15	–	23	23
Malaysia	–	72	–	72	72
Total	591	1,406	364	2,361	2,417
Japan	955	1,411	930	3,296	3,894

in the Middle East and other areas is intensified by the fact that the United States and European countries set quotas on imports from South-East Asia.

The advantages of South-East Asia over Japan lie, first of all, in cost competitiveness, including labour costs. As these amount to only 25% of Japan's labour costs, South-East Asian competitiveness is especially strong in highly processed products such as spun and woven fabrics. Another advantage is the availability of lower-priced raw materials, due to easier international supply and demand of synthetic fibre materials.

Although prediction is difficult due to many uncertain factors, Japan's exports of synthetic fibres will probably decrease by 5% a year. What is more, it may be difficult to maintain the price level that ensures certain profits. Since little increase is expected in fibre demand, including exports, production will at best level off in the future.

To cope with this situation, the Japanese synthetic fibre industry will have to:

(*a*) retain only those factories with sufficiently competitive products,

(*b*) raise the relative weight of the products that do not compete with South-East Asian output and

(*c*) strengthen overall international competitiveness by competing in processing and distribution.

However, no immediate effect is expected from these efforts. Since the industry has lost much of its vitality, the current slow process of industrial reorganization is causing concern.

3.9 Trading Companies

3.9.1 CHARACTERISTICS

Japan's major trading companies play a unique and important role in the

Japanese economy. Although their business is essentially sales and distribution of merchandise, it is different from that of retailers and small traders because it covers an extremely wide range of commercial activities.

These major trading firms handle diversified products from cheap popular foodstuffs to missiles; invisible services are also covered in their business activities. Therefore, they have relationships with a wide range of industries.

They conduct active overseas business. At present, more than 800 Japanese corporations have set up over 3,200 overseas offices. As many as 30% of these offices are operated by Japan's nine major trading companies: Mitsubishi Corporation, Mitsui & Co, Marubeni, C. Itoh & Co, Sumitomo Shoji Kaisha, Nissho-Iwai, Toyo Menka, Nichimen and Kanematsu-Gosho. A quarter of all their employees are stationed at overseas offices, totalling about 17,000 people. These employees account for 46% of the personnel sent overseas by Japanese corporations. In addition, 28% of the local staff recruited by Japanese corporations abroad are working at the overseas offices of these nine companies.

Their international networks effectively back up these major trading companies by collecting information. For example, the telex network linking the 150 overseas offices of Mitsui & Co covers 400,000 kilometres, and the number of messages between these offices totals 1,500,000 per month. The company spends $53 million a year in collecting and exchanging information.

The wide variety of business activities of major trading companies is indicated by the size of their sales. The collective sales of the nine major trading companies totalled $164,280 million in fiscal year 1975. Their business activities were concerned, in some form or another, with 56% of Japan's exports and imports and 18% of the domestic distribution of goods. In addition, taking into consideration the trade between their overseas branches and local subsidiaries, which is not conducted through Japan, these major trading companies were involved in about 10% of the world's total trade volume of $880 billion in 1975.

A unique function of Japan's major trading companies is "financing", which strengthens their trading activities and covers not only domestic financing but also the financing of exports and imports. In fact these trading companies play an important role in the Japanese financial system. Short-term credits (sales credit, advance and short-term loans) extended by Japan's six largest trading companies totalled $38 billion at the end of March 1976. In a broad sense, inventories can also be regarded as credit by trading companies; therefore with the inventories added, the short-term credits amounted to $41·42 billion, almost equivalent to the combined loans of the two major city banks in Japan.

Financing by trading companies came into existence because the post-war financial market in Japan was underdeveloped. Trading companies financed smaller enterprises, which found difficulty in borrowing from city banks, and newly established enterprises with weak financial bases. This system currently occupies a strong position in Japan's financial market, involving large corporations such as steel producers.

Under these circumstances, major trading companies play the role of buffers between banks and manufacturers. Through them, banks can avoid taking risks, improve their operational efficiency and ensure constant borrowers of large funds. Manufacturers can concentrate on production or plant and equipment expenditure by entrusting the sales financing to trading companies. This pattern was clearly evident in heavy industry, including steel and chemical production, a main contributor to the growth of the major trading companies. Service through credits between enterprises has been a key factor in their expansion of business.

Since 1970, trading firms have experienced a dramatic change in their economic situation. The change began with the international currency realignment triggered by President Nixon's announcement in 1971 that in future the dollar would not be exchanged for gold. This was followed by excessive liquidity, excessive easing of monetary control and sharp increases in the international commodities markets. Furthermore, as a result of the oil crisis in late 1973, the Japanese economy experienced rising inflation, excessively high interest rates, and a tight long-term monetary policy; in short, it experienced the most serious recession since the end of the Second World War.

Under these circumstances, the nine major trading companies' business performance fluctuated wildly: profits climbed 63% in fiscal year 1972, rose again 51% for fiscal year 1973, but dropped 45% in fiscal year 1974 and 52% in fiscal year 1975. Between fiscal years 1964 and 1971, their profits increased at an average annual rate of 18% and the highest annual increase was 39% in 1971.

Major trading companies are influenced by international as well as domestic economies because of the wide variety of their business activities. At the same time, they are generally stable, because negative factors are offset by positive factors. But even these powerful trading companies could not cope with the wild changes in the economic environment after President Nixon's announcement in 1971. Ataka & Co Ltd, one of the then ten major trading companies, failed to survive these changes and merged with C. Itoh on 1 October 1977.

Since 1965, major trading companies have begun to emphasize advance investments in order to secure stable business blocs. These investments include the strengthening of domestic distribution networks by establishing distribution centres, constructing food complexes, etc. The trading companies have also entered new business areas, such as housing, ocean development, the leisure industry, and overseas loans and investments aimed chiefly at the development and import of natural resources. The four largest trading companies, Mitsubishi, Mitsui, Marubeni and C. Itoh, have increased the ratio of their overseas loans and investments to their total assets from 8% in 1965 to 15% in the 1970s.

This is in line with Japan's increasing overseas investments which rose dramatically after 1971: they totalled $1·0 billion between 1951 and 1965, $3·5 billion between 1966 and 1971, $2·3 billion in 1972 and $3·5 billion in 1973. The sharp increases since 1972 are attributable to:

(a) the large upward revaluation of the yen;
(b) the growing need for the development of natural resources;
(c) the necessity for corporations to secure lower-cost labour forces in developing countries;
(d) the growing environmental pressure to restrict the construction of factories causing pollution.

As a result, Japan's major trading companies have played leading roles as "business organizers" because of their extensive overseas information networks, fund-raising abilities and experience in overseas activities. According to a Ministry of International Trade and Industry survey conducted in August 1974, the outstanding overseas loans and investments of the six largest trading companies totalled about $2·5 billion, accounting for 40% of Japan's overseas investments.

3.9.2 OUTLOOK

Major trading companies are expected to actively seek new business opportunities, such as plant exports. As overseas investment projects increase in scale, arrangements for multilateral fund-raising and measures to lessen investment risk will be an important consideration in increasing orders. Accordingly, the large trading companies' ability to collect information, raise funds, reduce risks and organize investment projects is expected to be very effective.

TABLE 42 *Changes in trade volume of nine major trading companies*

						Average annual growth rate (%)		
	FY 1965	FY 1970	FY 1975	FY 1976 (estimated)	FY 1980	1965–70	1970–75	1975–80
Exports	1,610	3,510	9,600	10,960	17,110	16·9	22·3	12·3
Imports	1,890	4,870	9,670	11,160	16,760	18·3	17·2	11·6
Domestic trade	4,620	11,160	22,550	26,310	35,580	20·4	14·0	9·6

(¥ billion)

Source: Financial statements of the trading firms.

Exploitation of markets in developing countries and the Communist bloc will increase. These nations have more diversified needs than advanced nations, including barter trade, construction of infrastructure and co-operation for economic development. Major trading companies are capable of coping with these diversified needs and are expected to take advantage of such business opportunities.

The trading companies can promote an international division of labour and economic development in less advanced nations, as in Mitsui's large-scale pioneering projects. This company has invested in Alumax and started construction of a petrochemical complex in Iran. In the former case, it plans to use a United States refinery for bauxite produced in Australia and the refined mineral will be imported into Japan.

From the mid-1950s to the early 1960s, Japan's major trading companies began to handle a wider range of merchandise. From the late 1960s they developed more comprehensive economic functions and enhanced their status as business organizations within the Japanese economy. This change has been supported by Japan's high economic growth.

The future strategy of the major trading companies will be to seek business opportunities abroad on the basis of overseas assets and business experience rather than develop other industries. In line with this strategy, they are currently promoting trade expansion between overseas subsidiaries and not with their headquarters in Japan. They are notably among the most flexible of Japanese industries capable of coping with changing business environments. It is difficult to forecast the direction of their medium-term development, because their functions change and multiply with changes in the business environment. However, assuming a substantial development of their overseas business activities, the following is a fair prediction.

Major trading companies are expected to absorb various risks. Their ability to absorb risks in foreign exchange, the commodities markets and interest rates is evident. They are also capable to some extent of recovering invest-ments prior to the completion of a particular project by exporting plant and equipment or through barter trade. By cooperating in overseas operations by Japanese corporations, they will be likened to insurance companies, playing a growing role in reducing overall risks. They will also act as holding com-panies, shifting the primary responsibility for regional business activities to their overseas subsidiaries. For example, Mitsui's North, Central and Latin American regions are supervised by Mitsui & Co (USA) Inc, Europe by Mitsui & Co Europe GmbH, and Australia by Mitsui & Co (Australia) Ltd. The parent company supervises the other regions, centred in South-East Asia. Mitsui intends to introduce a system of establishing four headquarters to cover the world. The parent company is transferring the management of overseas investment projects which are already in operation to its overseas subsidiaries. In the long run, a subsidiary controlling South-East Asia may be established and Mitsui of Tokyo may become purely a holding company for its overseas subsidiaries.

For the medium-term outlook, the sales of the major trading companies are projected to grow at an average annual rate of 11–12%. During this period some of the loans and investments are also expected to produce profits. In the short term, the quality of their business activities and their funding policies will vary. In future, their business performances will differ more widely and will be affected by their ability to develop new opportunities.

3.10 Department Stores and Chain Stores

3.10.1 CHARACTERISTICS

Department stores and chain stores are the large-scale retailers in Japan and are under the control of the Large-Scale Retailer Law, effective from 1 March 1974. Although department stores and chain stores have different business patterns, both have contributed to the modernization of Japan's retailing industry. The retailing business is a typically regional industry, so even very small "corner shops" can survive, since it is difficult for the industry to utilize economies of scale. Accordingly, it has been slow to modernize.

Department stores played a pioneering role in the modernization of Japan's retail industry. They succeeded in increasing the scope of operations through a management style in which each business division operates separately and can realize economies of scale. However, the passing of the Department Store Law in 1966 imposed various restrictions on department stores, the only modern enterprises in the retailing industry, thus easing competition among department stores. Since the late 1960s, the ratio of department store sales to total sales in the retailing industry has been almost unchanged at the 9% level.

Chain stores, meanwhile, which appeared in Japan in the 1950s, grew rapidly during the 1960s and 1970s. The ratio of their sales to total sales in the retailing industry increased to the 9% level by 1975. Chain stores introduced a modern management style which department stores could not adopt and which includes self-service merchandising and discount sales. They have also had an impact on the modernization of the retailing industry, by increasing the scope of their individual business and realizing economies of scale.

The market share of department and chain stores rose from 14% in 1970 to 18% in 1975. Small retail stores, with less than ten employees, account for 55% of the total sales volume. Under these circumstances, there is still room for further rationalization.

Department store sales in Japan rose at an average annual rate of 17·5% between 1971 and 1976, while consumer spending also increased at an annual rate of 17·8%. However, the selling floor space of department stores only expanded at an annual rate of 5·8%, showing a declining growth trend.

The 1975 sales breakdown by commodity was: 42% for clothing, 7·5% for personal effects, 12·6% for sundry goods, 14·2% for household goods, 18·5%

TABLE 43 *Japan's top 20 retailers*

Ranking FY 1976	FY 1975	Company	Chain or department store	Head office	FY 1976 Sales (¥ million)	Increase rate (%)	No. of stores	FY 1977 Sales (Target) (¥ million)
1	1	Dai'ei	C	Osaka	788,496	11.7	137	880,000
2	2	Mitsukoshi	D	Tokyo	429,851	5.5	14	466,000
3	3	Seiyu Stores	C	Tokyo	392,294	11.5	125	470,000
4	4	Daimaru	D	Osaka	356,433	6.5	6	382,000
5	6	Ito-Yokado	C	Tokyo	316,454	24.7	66	n/a
6	5	Takashimaya	D	Osaka	310,374	9.4	5	338,000
7	8	Jusco	C	Osaka	301,539	25.1	108	400,000
8	10	Nichii	C	Osaka	283,067	23.6	126	330,000
9	7	Seibu	D	Tokyo	276,000	9.8	10	304,000
10	9	*Tetsudo Kosaikai		Tokyo	262,032	9.4	4,134	276,829
11	12	Uny	C	Nagoya	253,026	17.5	85	290,000
12	11	Matsuzakaya	D	Nagoya	244,103	8.3	8	265,000
13	14	Hankyu	D	Osaka	202,188	13.5	7	222,400
14	13	Nagasakiya	C	Tokyo	200,009	10.0	86	220,000
15	15	Isetan	D	Tokyo	180,027	5.6	5	190,000
16	16	Tokyu	D	Tokyo	173,304	10.6	4	188,000
17	17	Marui	D	Tokyo	169,036	13.5	34	189,000
18	19	Izumiya	C	Osaka	143,509	14.9	50	167,000
19	18	Sogo	D	Osaka	142,962	9.5	3	160,000
20	20	Tokyu Store	C	Tokyo	126,953	12.9	75	150,000

*Tetsudo Kosaikai is a subsidiary of the Japanese National Railways.

for foodstuffs, 2·5% for the restaurant business and 2·7% for others. The average annual rate of sales increase by commodity from 1971 to 1976 was 18·7% for foodstuffs, 18·7% for the restaurant business, 17·7% for clothing, 14·8% for household goods and 15·9% for sundry goods. This indicates that market penetration of consumer durables, including consumer electrical products, has reached a peak. Also, consumers hoarded or refrained from buying unnecessary goods from late 1973 to 1974 when retail prices rose sharply because of the oil crisis. During the consequent recession, consumers have been cautious in their spending and this has had a large impact on department store sales.

According to a nationwide survey of consumer spending conducted in 1974 by the Prime Minister's Office, 9·3% of householders' consumer expenditure was absorbed by department stores. The latter maintained sales superiority in certain goods, absorbing 31·1% of household clothing expenditure, 12·4% of furniture and utensil expenditure and 2·5% of foodstuff expenditure. The top 20 items which consumers purchased at department stores included 14 items of clothing, 3 items of personal effects and 2 items of sundry goods.

The sales pattern at department stores is basically on a face-to-face basis. The sales growth of these stores has depended chiefly on their ability to attract customers and on the sale of higher-priced merchandise, together with urban development. Location and merchandising ability account for the differences in sales growth among stores and companies. The "out-of-store sales", especially to business corporations, also affected the growth rate of sales of department stores.

Chain store sales rose at an annual rate of 27% during 1971–76, according to statistics issued by the Japan Chain Store Association. The number of their stores increased sharply from 1,569 in 1970 to 2,411 in 1975. Moreover, energetic efforts were made to expand the scale of their individual stores and the expansion of selling floor-space has apparently contributed to sales growth. Rapid progress in the operation of chain stores was due to the following:

(a) Funds invested per store were small and could be recovered in a short period.
(b) Excess operating funds brought about by cash sales and credit purchases were used for investment.
(c) Large chain stores increased their fund-raising abilities through the public offering of stock.
(d) No legal restrictions existed concerning the opening of new stores.
(e) Efficiency of funds and personnel was improved through merger and reorganization.

The sales breakdown by commodity in 1974 was 37·4% for foodstuffs, 34·4% for clothing, 10·9% for sundry goods, 2·3% for medicine and cosmetics, 3·4% for furniture and interior goods, 4·2% for consumer electrical products, 3·4% for other merchandise, 1·9% for the restaurant business and 2·1% for services. The sales of foodstuffs and clothing were outstandingly high. There is a growing trend for chain stores to sell all kinds of merchandise as they expand the size of each store. Accordingly, the relative sales percentages of foodstuffs and clothing have been declining. The chain stores maintained a high sales growth even during the recession, since they concentrated on daily necessities and middle-priced fashionable goods. Therefore, their market share in the retailing industry continued to expand.

The 1974 nationwide survey of consumer spending showed that 19·2% of householders' consumer expenditure was absorbed by chain stores. This was a sharp increase on 7·8% in 1964 and 12·1% in 1969. The survey also indicated that chain stores were superior in the following areas: they absorbed 26·6% of the household foodstuff expenditure, 11·8% of the furniture and utensil expenditure and 14·6% of the clothing expenditure. However, there is still room for expansion of foodstuff sales. Chain stores are used in both big cities and in small municipalities, indicating that they are located over a wide geographic area and that their customers come from various groups.

At the early stage, chain stores differed clearly from each other, depending on the merchandise they handled. Those specializing in foodstuffs differed from those specializing in clothing. However, as selling floor-space per store expanded and merchandise was diversified, the differences gradually disappeared. The stores which rely on the self-service and discount sales system are divided into the following categories:

(a) the original supermarket, handling mainly foodstuffs and sundry goods;

(b) the superstore, handling mainly clothing;

(c) the discount store, handling hard goods such as consumer electrical products, glasses and watches;

(d) the general merchandise store, covering a full range of products.

3.10.2 OUTLOOK

As the growth rate of consumer spending is slow, expenditure on food, housing and clothing is expected to continue to decline as a percentage of total consumer expenditure. The percentage was 55% in 1965, 51% in 1970 and 48% in 1975. The sales increase in the retail industry is likely to be lower than the rise in consumer spending.

Furthermore, with the growing diversification of consumption and personal tastes, sales of popular consumer products will probably fluctuate wildly. In this connection, selling and merchandising strategies to cope with consumer needs will become more important. The differences between chain stores as a result of the different strategies, or overall management abilities, will widen. In the process, a reorganization of the chain store industry is expected to occur.

An increasing number of local department stores have entered into business arrangements with major department stores since the late 1960s. The chain store industry has also experienced several mergers since the latter half of the 1960s, as demonstrated by the establishment of Nichii and Jusco. The first round of reorganization has been completed in both the department store and the chain store industry. Future reorganization is expected to take the form of the strong companies taking over the weaker ones. The increasing distinctions among companies caused by differing management abilities in a low-growth economy, the restrictions on opening of new stores under the Large-Scale Retailer Law, and the growing similarity of department stores and chain stores, will encourage this trend. Local department stores and chain stores suffering from the business slump, together with nationwide major chain stores, will probably be involved in the second round of reorganization.

Department stores are expected to strengthen their basic management structure and to increase the number of stores. They will take on the characteristics of high-class speciality stores by promoting the sales of fashionable and high-quality products. Their flexible buying and marketing systems are likely to remain effective. However, local department stores are expected to suffer, in the continuing business slump, from severe competition with chain stores. Consequently, the ratio of department store sales to total sales in the retailing industry is expected to continue unchanged. Department store sales are estimated to grow at an annual rate of 12% until 1980.

Meanwhile, more new chain stores will be opened, and their market share is expected to continue growing. In particular, major chain stores will increase their competitive power, since their ability to raise funds will be strengthened further by the issue of stock. The expansion as well as strengthening of their chain store operations will lead to a substantial profit gain. Local chain stores will probably reorganize their management under the control of major chain stores. Some original supermarket or discount stores are expected to experience conspicuous growth. Although the restrictions on the opening of new stores may be increased, there is still room for this kind of expansion over the next five years from an economic point of view. The competition is expected to further modernization. Consequently, chain stores will expand their market share and the ratio of chain store sales to total sales is expected to exceed 12% in 1980. The sales of member companies of the Japan Chain Store Association are expected to rise at an annual rate of slightly more than 18%.

TABLE 44 *Sales volume of department and chain stores*

(¥ billion)

| | 1965 | 1970 | 1975 | 1976 (esti-mated) | 1980 (esti-mated) | Average annual increase rate (%) | | |
						1965–70	1970–75	1975–80
Department stores	860·3	1,824·2	4,065·1	4,440·0	7,300·0	16·2	17·4	12·4
Chain stores	–	1,206·8	3,966·8	4,640·0	9,200·0	–	26·8	18·3

Sources: Japan Department Store Association; Japan Chain Store Association.

4 THE JAPANESE FINANCIAL SYSTEM

4.1 The Structure of the Financial Market

Fig. 4 shows the structure of the Japanese financial market, classified in terms of types of financial institutions.

4.1.1 ORDINARY BANKS (COMMERCIAL BANKS)

In Japan, ordinary banks perform commercial banking functions. In 1901, when the number of ordinary banks reached its peak, it stood at 1867. Following the financial crisis of the late 1920s, and more particularly, through the government's one-bank-in-each-prefecture policy enforced during the Second World War, the ranks of small- and medium-sized banks were thinned on a nationwide scale, to 61 banks (eight city banks and 53 local banks) at the end of 1945. Following the end of the war, some of the special banks (such as Nihon Kangyo Bank, Hokkaido Development Bank and Yokohama Specie Bank) changed from their statutory status into ordinary banks, and in recent years, certain mutual banks have followed suit, with the result that the number of ordinary banks has increased to 76 as of 31 March 1977 (13 city banks, including one foreign exchange bank, and 63 local banks).

City Banks

City banks form the base of Japan's banking system. Although their relative weight in the nation's banking system in terms of their share of business financing and of assets has declined as a group, they still account for 30% (25·6% of the deposits and 29·0% of the outstanding loans) of the business, the largest of all groups (*see* Tables 47 and 48).

The operation of city banks is characterized, first and foremost, by a chronic state of over-borrowing.

As shown in Table 45, the ratio of "borrowings, etc." to total assets stood at 9%. This suggests that, owing to excessive loans made to customers, fund shortages of city banks depend upon external liabilities such as Bank of Japan credit and call money. At the end of 1976 the Bank of Japan's outstanding

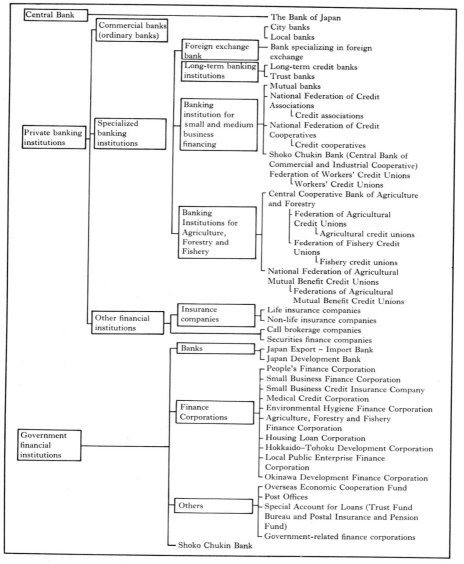

Fig. 4 Structure of the financial market

lendings stood at ¥1,955·8 billion, of which ¥1,625·3 billion, or 83%, were to city banks. The considerable external liabilities constantly force city banks to improve their fund positions. One way is to sell some of their bonds. In Japan's secondary bond markets, city banks are always net sellers. Therefore, city banks' fund positions, as well as the Bank of Japan's guidelines, are important factors in the bond markets.

Local Banks

While city banks maintain a nationwide network of branches based in big

TABLE 45 *Balance sheet of city banks (31 March 1977)*

Assets (¥ billion)		%	Liabilities and capital (¥ billion)		%
Cash and deposits	7,915	(8·6)	Deposits	60,714	(66·0)
Loans outstanding	53,778	(58·5)	Borrowings, etc.	8,574	(9·3)
Securities	11,232	(12·2)	Net worth	2,672	(2·9)
Total assets	91,969		Total liabilities and capital	91,969	

Note "Borrowings, etc." refers to the sum of borrowings, call money and bills negotiated.

cities, local banks operate within a limited geographical area and cater closely to the banking needs of their areas.

Local banks are also distinguished from city banks by the size of their assets. On 31 March 1977, local banks held deposits amounting to ¥39,220 billion against ¥60,710 billion for city banks. However, there are exceptional local banks whose assets are larger than those of some of the city banks. Local banks differ from city banks in that a larger percentage of business is accounted for by dealings with their local public bodies. In fact, local banks' subscription to local government bonds has swollen to such an extent that these holdings have come to strain their financial positions.

4.1.2 LONG-TERM FINANCIAL INSTITUTIONS

Long-term Credit Banks

Long-term credit banks were founded in 1952 under the Long-term Credit Bank Law. To help businesses finance their capital spending and long-term operation funds, they make long-term loans out of the funds raised through offering bank debentures. These banks are authorized to issue debentures up to 20 times their capital and reserves, and to receive deposits only from local public bodies and their loan clients. The reasoning behind such a restriction is that it is not proper to finance long-term credits with short-term deposits. By their very nature, these banks should avoid competing with commercial banks for deposits. At present, the long-term credit banks issue two kinds of debentures: interest-bearing debentures (with a maturity of five years) and discount debentures (with a maturity of one year). About one-half of their coupon issues are subscribed to by financial institutions, while most of their discount debentures are sold to individual investors through securities companies.

In the decade that followed 1955, when the economy of Japan grew at a rapid pace, the long-term credit banks played an important role in financing capital spending projects, increasing the amount loaned by 20–30% each year. Utilities, steel mills and chemical plants were the major beneficiaries from such loans. In the decade following 1965, however, loan demand for capacity expansion and working capital flattened, and the fall-off in such demand became particularly pronounced after the oil crisis of 1973.

The long-term credit banks are also authorized to engage in securities business, including:

(a) acting as a trustee for trusts involving government bonds, local bonds, corporate bonds and other securities;
(b) running trusts involving secured corporate bonds;
(c) acting as an agent for the registration of corporate bonds under the Corporate Bond Registration Law.

Through these activities, the long-term credit banks carry considerable weight in the nation's bond markets.

Trust Banks

At present, there are seven banks exclusively engaged in the trust business, and one city bank so engaged whilst concurrently providing a regular banking service. Services provided by these trust banks include loan trusts, trust cash funds, securities investment trusts, annuity trusts, movable property trusts, real estate trusts, securities trusts and secured corporate bond trusts. Of these services, the first three are the most important ones. The loan trusts, in particular, account for approximately 50% of the funds of the trust banks and thus play a central role in raising their funds. In recent years, the annuity trusts have grown dramatically, and the operation of these funds has an important impact on the bond market.

4.1.3 FINANCIAL INSTITUTIONS FOR SMALL BUSINESSES

Because of the larger risks and small amounts involved in loans to small businesses, the credit costs tend to be larger than those to big corporations. To meet this loan demand at a lower cost, specialized financial institutions were established. At the private-sector level, they include mutual banks, credit associations and credit cooperative unions. City banks also make loans to small businesses but these cater for those having a relatively large scale of operation, while the financial institutions specifically intended to serve small businesses provide for those which operate on a small scale.

Mutual Banks

In addition to monthly instalment deposits, unique to mutual banking, these banks are authorized to provide the whole range of ordinary banking services, such as acceptance of deposits, extension of loans, discounting of notes and foreign exchange transactions. However, in keeping with their status as a financial institution for small business, in principle mutual banks restrict their loan service to businesses which employ less than 300 persons and are capitalized at less than ¥400 million. However, they may lend their funds to

TABLE 46 *Current state of financial institutions (30 September 1976)*

Type of institution	No. of operators	Total no. of branches	Assets		Loans outstanding	
			Amount (¥ billion)	Proportion (%)	Amount (¥ billion)	Proportion (%)
Commercial banks	86	7,950	140,347·4	61·4	111,517·4	63·2
City banks	12	2,557	62,348·5	27·3	52,037·8	29·5
Local banks	63	4,973	36,596·2	16·0	28,582·4	16·2
Foreign exchange banks	1	71	4,623·6	2·0	2,689·2	1·5
Long-term credit banks	3	51	16,041·6	7·0	12,203·0	6·9
Trust banks	7	298	20,737·5	9·1	16,005·0	9·1
Small business financial institutions	1,034	10,486	47,631·2	20·8	38,763·4	22·0
Mutual banks	72	3,386	17,357·4	7·6	13,679·5	7·8
Credit associations	470	4,705	21,028·7	9·1	16,963·7	9·6
Credit cooperatives	488	2,311	5,470·4	2·4	4,455·1	2·5
Central Bank of Commercial and Industrial Cooperative	1	84	3,774·7	1·7	3,665·1	2·1
Workers' credit unions	47	428	1,498·0	0·7	1,146·2	0·6

Type of institution	No. of operators	Total no. of branches	Assets Amount (¥ billion)	Assets Proportion (%)	Loans outstanding Amount (¥ billion)	Loans outstanding Proportion (%)
Agriculture- and forestry-related financial institutions	6,500	12,881	21,960·7	9·6	14,466·1	8·2
Central Cooperative Bank of Agriculture and Forestry	1	33	4,139·2	1·8	3,021·2	1·7
Agricultural cooperative unions	4,764	12,273	16,996·4	7·4	10,822·3	6·1
Fishery cooperative unions	1,735	575	825·1	0·4	622·6	0·4
Insurance companies	43	1,994	17,315·8	7·5	10,596·0	6·0
Life insurance companies	21	1,510	13,793·5	6·0	9,355·2	5·3
Non-life insurance companies	22	484	3,522·3	1·5	1,240·8	0·7

Notes (i) Agricultural cooperative unions include the Federation of Agricultural Credit Cooperation Unions, and fishery cooperative unions include fishery processing cooperative unions and fishery credit cooperative unions.

(ii) The total assets of the agriculture- and forestry-related financial institutions are net of inter-institutional accounts maintained among themselves.

(iii) The assets of the insurance companies represent their total operating assets.

other customers for amounts up to 20% of the outstanding balance of their loan. Lately, the balance of instalment deposits has decreased, so that the regular deposits have become their main source of funds. As of 31 March 1977 there was a total of 71 mutual banks in the country.

Credit Associations

A credit association is a non-profit organization affiliated with small and medium-sized businesses and workers residing in a certain area. It accepts deposits from members and non-members alike, makes loans to and discounts notes of members, lends money to non-members against the collateral of their deposits and handles domestic exchange. It is not authorized to handle foreign exchange. The object is to facilitate the financing of small and medium-sized businesses and to serve the general public in its area through these services. The number of credit associations has decreased through mergers and there were 469 on 31 March 1977. To facilitate and coordinate the flow of funds of the credit associations, they founded a national organization called the National Federation of Credit Associations.

Credit Cooperative Unions

Credit cooperative unions accept deposits from, and make loans to, their members. A union is also authorized to accept deposits from public agencies and non-profit-making corporations. It can accept deposits from private individuals who are not members only up to a level of 20% of its deposits. The credit cooperative union is more cooperatively organized than the credit association, in that it is restrained from wholesale acceptance of deposits from the general public. As of 31 March 1977, there were 488 such unions, with an aggregate balance of deposits of approximately ¥5,800 billion. Its national organization is called the National Federation of Credit Cooperative Unions.

4.1.4 AGRICULTURE-, FORESTRY- AND FISHERY-RELATED FINANCIAL INSTITUTIONS

Financial institutions catering to agriculture and fishery form two lines of three-tiered structures: one line is composed of the Central Cooperative Bank of Agriculture and Forestry, the Federation of Agricultural Credit Cooperative Unions and agricultural cooperative associations; and the other, the Central Cooperative Bank, the Federation of Fishery Cooperative Associations and fishery cooperative associations. Agricultural cooperative associations also provide an insurance service called the "agricultural mutual aid programme". Those within the same prefecture are organized into a Federation of Agricultural Mutual Aid Cooperative Associations, and these, in turn, are organized into a national organization called the "National Federation of Agricultural Mutual Aid Cooperative Associations".

Agricultural Cooperative Associations

The main business of an agricultural cooperative association consists of accepting deposits from, and making business and personal loans to, its members, who are predominantly farmers. As such, it constitutes the base of the pyramid of the agriculture- and forestry-related financial machinery.

Federation of Agricultural Credit Cooperative Unions

A Federation of Agricultural Credit Cooperative Unions is established in each prefecture and acts as an upper-level organization to the local agricultural cooperative associations. Among the agriculture- and forestry-related financial institutions, the Federations of Agricultural Credit Cooperative Unions rank in the middle. Agricultural cooperative associations deposit their surplus funds with the Federation of Agricultural Credit Cooperative Unions of their prefecture, which, in turn, deposits its surplus fund with the Central Cooperative Bank of Agriculture and Forestry. If there is a shortage of lendable funds on the agricultural cooperative association level, the funds flow in reverse. This is not to say that all surplus funds of agricultural cooperative associations are deposited with superior institutions. They are free to – and in fact, they do – invest their surplus funds in the short-term money or bond markets. Similarly, the institutions do lend their funds to outside institutions.

Central Cooperative Bank of Agriculture and Forestry

The Central Cooperative Bank is the supreme institution of the nation's agriculture- and forestry-related financial machinery. Its capital was drawn from contributions by the government and various organizations related to agriculture, forestry and fishery. In addition to deposits accepted from organizations lower in the financial hierarchy, public agencies and non-profit corporations, the Central Cooperative Bank is authorized to issue debentures (agricultural and forestry debentures). Being a superior institution to the nation's agriculture- and forestry-related financial institutions, the Central Cooperative Bank receives lump sum payments from the government for the rice to be purchased from farm operators and acts as an agent for transferring funds to lower-level financial institutions.

4.1.5 OTHER FINANCIAL INSTITUTIONS

Workers' Credit Unions

The workers' credit union is the financial arm of the workers' cooperative structure and is charged with the promotion of mutual aid activities of labour unions, livelihood cooperative associations and other workers' organizations. Its business consists of accepting deposits and making loans, to and from its members. On 31 March 1977, there were 47 workers' credit unions with an aggregate balance of deposits of ¥1,700 billion.

Insurance Companies

Insurance companies are divided into two categories: life insurance and non-life insurance companies. At present, there are 21 life insurance companies and their aggregate operating assets were approximately ¥14,150 billion at the end of 1976. Approximately 60% of their operating assets are

TABLE 47 *Balance of deposits, by banking groups*

(%)

Fiscal year ended 31 March	1965	1966	1967	1968	1969	1970	1971	1972	1973	1974	1975
Private banking institutions (total)	87·2	86·7	85·9	85·2	84·8	84·2	84·5	84·5	83·5	82·1	81·4
Banks	49·0	47·8	46·1	45·9	44·8	44·0	44·8	45·0	43·7	41·4	40·8
City banks	27·0	25·6	23·9	23·9	24·0	23·3	24·5	24·4	22·8	21·2	20·8
Local banks	14·7	14·8	14·9	14·9	13·8	13·6	13·1	13·2	13·6	13·2	13·0
Trust banks	1·8	1·8	1·8	1·7	1·7	1·8	1·9	1·9	1·8	1·7	1·6
Long-term credit banks	5·5	5·6	5·6	5·5	5·3	5·3	5·4	5·5	5·5	5·3	5·3
Other banks	38·3	38·9	39·8	39·3	40·0	40·3	39·7	39·5	39·7	40·7	40·6
All banks (trust accounts)	5·2	5·3	5·4	5·5	5·5	5·5	5·6	5·6	5·8	5·9	5·8
Small- and medium-sized banking institutions	17·0	17·2	17·6	16·9	17·1	17·3	17·1	16·9	17·2	18·2	18·2
Mutual banks	6·7	6·7	6·8	5·9	6·0	5·9	5·6	5·6	6·2	6·2	6·1
Credit associations	6·5	6·6	6·8	6·9	7·1	7·3	7·0	7·1	7·6	7·5	7·4
Credit unions, etc.	3·8	3·9	4·0	4·1	4·0	4·0	4·5	4·2	3·5	4·5	4·7
Agriculture-, forestry- and fishery-related institutions	10·7	10·7	11·0	10·8	11·2	11·0	10·8	11·1	10·6	10·4	10·6
Insurance companies	5·4	5·6	5·9	6·1	6·2	6·5	6·2	5·9	6·1	6·2	6·0
Government-related funds (total)	12·8	13·3	14·1	14·8	15·2	15·8	15·5	15·5	16·5	17·9	18·6
Trust Fund Bureau	10·2	10·9	11·7	12·4	12·9	13·4	13·3	13·3	14·3	15·4	16·1
Postal insurance and postal pension funds	2·5	2·5	2·4	2·4	2·3	2·3	2·2	2·1	2·3	2·4	2·5
Total	100·0	100·0	100·0	100·0	100·0	100·0	100·0	100·0	100·0	100·0	100·0

Note "Credit unions, etc." refers to the Central Bank of Commercial and Industrial Cooperative, the National Federation of Credit Cooperative Unions, credit unions, the National Federation of Credit Unions, worker's credit unions and the Federation of Workers' Credit Unions.

Source: Keizai Tokei Geppo (Monthly Statistical Report, Bank of Japan).

TABLE 48 *Balance of outstanding loans, by banking groups*

(%)

Fiscal year ended 31 March	1965	1966	1967	1968	1969	1970	1971	1972	1973	1974	1975
Private banking institutions (total)	79.1	78.5	78.3	77.8	78.0	78.1	78.3	78.6	78.1	76.2	74.2
Banks	47.6	47.4	45.9	45.4	44.3	43.3	44.7	45.1	43.2	41.7	40.0
City banks	26.9	26.1	24.9	24.6	24.6	24.1	24.5	24.7	23.4	22.5	21.5
Local banks	13.6	13.9	13.9	13.8	12.9	12.8	12.8	13.0	12.7	12.4	12.0
Trust banks	1.5	1.6	1.6	1.5	1.4	1.5	1.8	1.8	1.7	1.5	1.4
Long-term credit banks	5.6	5.7	5.6	5.5	5.4	5.3	5.6	5.6	5.3	5.2	5.0
Other banks	31.5	31.2	32.4	32.4	33.7	34.3	33.7	33.5	34.9	34.5	34.1
All banks (trust accounts)	5.5	5.4	5.6	5.7	5.7	5.7	5.9	5.9	5.7	5.6	5.5
Small and medium-sized banking institutions	16.3	16.6	17.1	16.4	17.0	16.9	16.4	16.9	17.2	16.9	17.0
Mutual banks	6.6	6.6	6.5	5.7	5.7	5.7	5.6	5.8	5.7	5.6	5.7
Credit associations	6.0	6.2	6.6	6.7	7.1	7.2	6.6	7.0	7.2	6.9	7.0
Credit unions, etc.	3.7	3.8	4.0	4.0	4.2	4.1	4.1	4.0	4.3	4.3	4.4
Agriculture-, forestry- and fishery-related institutions	6.1	5.8	6.2	6.4	6.9	7.1	6.8	6.3	7.6	7.5	7.2
Insurance companies	3.5	3.3	3.5	3.8	4.1	4.6	4.7	4.4	4.4	4.4	4.4
Government-related funds	20.9	21.5	21.7	22.2	22.0	21.9	21.7	21.4	21.9	23.8	25.8
Government-run financial institutions	8.5	8.7	8.8	8.9	8.8	8.7	8.5	7.9	8.0	8.5	8.9
Trust Fund Bureau	10.4	10.9	11.2	11.6	11.6	11.7	11.7	12.1	12.6	13.8	15.5
Postal insurance and postal pension funds	2.0	1.8	1.7	1.6	1.6	1.5	1.5	1.3	1.3	1.4	1.5
Total	100.0	100.0	100.0	100.0	100.0	100.0	100.0	100.0	100.0	100.0	100.0

Note As for Table 47.

accounted for by loans and 23% by securities holdings. Most of the loans were directed to financing capital expenditure but with the lack of demand for long-term loans, the percentage of loans in their operating assets has declined in recent years. There were 22 non-life insurance companies as of 31 March 1977 and their aggregate balance of operating assets was approximately ¥3,700 billion at the end of 1976, of which 37% was accounted for by securities holdings, 35% by loans outstanding and 22% by cash, deposits and call loans. The functioning of non-life insurance companies is characterized by a high ratio of liquid assets, which must be maintained to provide against contingencies inherent in their business.

Call Brokers

Call brokerage companies act as intermediaries on the call and bill discount markets, and at present, there are six companies so licensed by the Minister of Finance. Call brokers are subject to regulations as moneylenders but unlike general moneylenders (subject to the control of the prefectural governor), call brokers are under the direct supervision of the Minister of Finance. In addition to coordinating short-term funds on the call money market, call brokers also act in accordance with the Bank of Japan's monetary policy, under its guidance.

4.1.6 GOVERNMENT-RELATED FINANCIAL INSTITUTIONS

Government-related financial institutions include the Japan Development Bank, the Japan Export–Import Bank, ten financial corporations (such as the Small Business Finance Corporation and the Housing Loan Corporation), the Overseas Economic Cooperation Fund, and various other loan associations. These financial institutions make loans in line with government policy in their respective areas. Their loans carry low interest and are designed to achieve policy goals of industrial development, promotion of trade and overseas economic cooperation, development of small business, agriculture, forestry and fishery operations and public housing projects. Their lending activities are carried out within the framework of the government's Treasury Investment and Loan Plans.

Treasury Investment and Loan Plans

These plans are financed by funds drawn from the government's industrial investment special account, loans from the Trust Fund Bureau and from postal insurance and by funds raised by government-related financial institutions under government guarantees. The investments made thereunder are directed to areas essential for the implementation of government policies.

In fiscal year 1976, Treasury investment and loans amounted to ¥12,538·2 billion, which represented more than 40% of the ¥28,514·3 billion appropriated initially to the general budget account. More than 90% of the funds appropriated to Treasury investment loans came from the government's financial funds, the largest part of which were drawn from the Trust Fund Bureau. (The financial funds accounted for 93% of the funds of the original

Treasury investment and loan program, of which 83% were drawn from the funds of the Trust Fund Bureau.) The funds of the Trust Fund Bureau are derived from postal savings, welfare annuity premiums and the surpluses of the various special accounts. The operating funds of the Trust Fund Bureau as of 31 March 1977 were ¥51,900 billion, equal to about 85% of the aggregate deposits held by the nation's city banks.

Principal Government-related Financial Institutions

Japan Development Bank The object of this Bank is to finance industrial development projects. Its scale of operation is the largest among the government-related financial institutions. The main business of the Bank consists of long-term loans for industrial development projects, guarantees for the repayment of loans and subscription to corporate bonds. Its loans are primarily made to basic industries, such as utilities and shipping. In recent years, loans to urban renewal and technological development projects have risen.

Japan Export–Import Bank This Bank supplements private banking institutions by supporting and assisting the financing of export, import and overseas investment. The largest part of its activities is devoted to financing plant exports. Lately, the Bank has been increasingly involved in overseas investment loans and loans to foreign governments.

Small Business Finance Corporation This Corporation is primarily interested in loans for small businesses' capital expenditures and long-term operating funds that general banking institutions find difficult to finance. It also makes special loans for the modernization of small business, structural improvement and pollution control facilities. About one-half of its loans are made through city banks, local banks, mutual banks, credit associations and credit co-operative unions. It raises its working capital from loans by the Trust Fund Bureau, bonds sold to the government and government-guaranteed bonds.

People's Finance Corporation This Corporation specializes in smaller loans than those made by the Small Business Finance Corporation. In addition to general business loans, it also makes loans against the collateral of pension rights.

Shoko Chukin Bank (Central Bank of Industrial and Commercial Cooperatives) This Bank caters for the fund requirements of cooperative associations of small businesses. More than 60% of its working capital is contributed by the government, and the rest is drawn from private financial institutions. Part of its lending funds is derived from deposits received from its affiliated organizations and members, but the largest is derived from the sale of its debentures. As a rule, loans are restricted to its affiliated organizations and members.

Housing Loan Public Corporation This Corporation makes low-interest, long-term loans to individuals to help finance the construction or purchase of homes. Its funds are drawn mainly from loans of the Trust Fund Bureau and from funds transferred from the general account in the national budget.

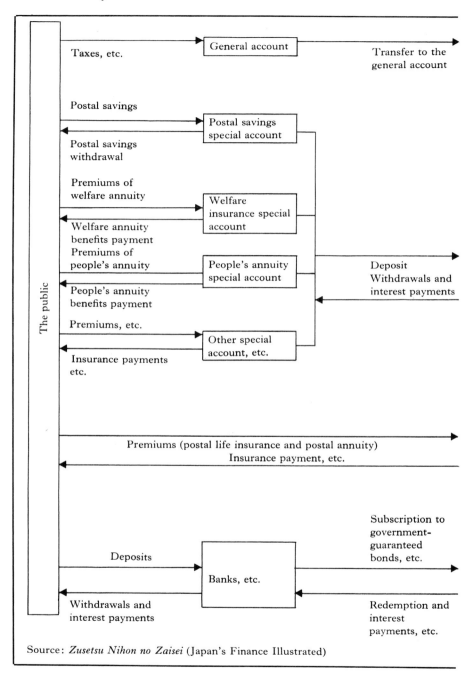

Source: *Zusetsu Nihon no Zaisei* (Japan's Finance Illustrated)

Fig. 5   Mechanism of Treasury investment and loans

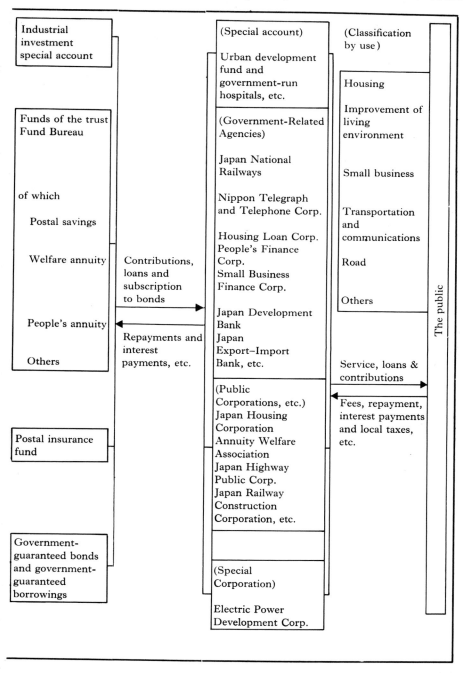

4.2 Monetary Policy and its Instruments

4.2.1 POLICY INSTRUMENTS

The Japanese monetary authorities employ four major instruments for the implementation of policy:

- (*a*) control of the official discount rate;
- (*b*) control of the call and bill discount markets;
- (*c*) adjustment of the reserve ratio;
- (*d*) "window" operation.

The last instrument is the most effective, especially in tightening the flow of credit by virtue of its direct control over banks' lendable funds. In addition, the buying operation of government bonds affects the movement of long-term interest rates, and with the government debt management policy, it is an important factor of the operation of monetary policies.

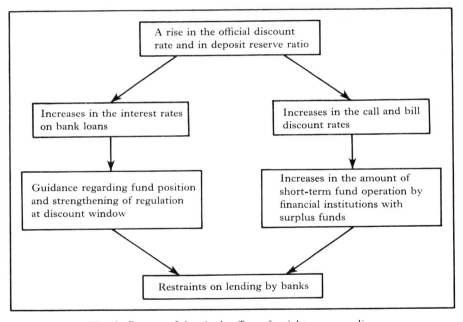

Fig. 6   Process of the ripple effect of a tight money policy

The control instruments may be divided into those affecting the flow of funds and those directly affecting the interest rates. Adjustments of the reserve ratio, window operation and the government bond-buying operation belong to the former group, while control of the official discount rate belongs to the latter. Control of the call and bill discount markets affects both the flow of funds and the interest rates. The Bank of Japan lines of credit are granted mainly to city banks, and this constitutes a powerful tool for achieving the goals of monetary policies. Given the peculiarity of the Japanese interest structure, where the official discount rate is lower than call rates, this system strengthens the Bank of Japan's control. The central bank directly controls bank lending through regulation at the discount window. However, its effect is little more than moral persuasion. The sense of private bank's indebtedness to the Bank of Japan created by the extension of a line of credit reinforces this moral persuasion, enabling the central bank to control the activities of private banks.

Official Discount Rate

At its simplest, the official discount rate represents an interest rate on loans made to banks by the Bank of Japan. Any change in such official discount rate has a cost effect as well as a psychological effect. In Japan, the interest structure is such that a change in the official discount rate directly affects the bank rates.

It has been customary among the city banks of Japan to set their prime rate at a level 0·25% higher than the official discount rate, meaning that their prime rate moves with the official discount rate.

The more highly a bank is geared, the higher the cost effect becomes. As call and discount rates also move in step with the official discount rate, a change in the latter affects not only the interest costs on loans from the Bank of Japan but also those from other outside sources. A change in the call and discount rates also prompts the agriculture- and forestry-related financial institutions and small business-oriented financial institutions (mutual banks and credit associations, in particular) to change their lending policy.

Adjustment of the Reserve Ratio

In 1959, the Bank of Japan established a reserve ratio, but because the ratio was so small, it proved to be ineffective as an instrument of monetary policy. The reserve ratio was not set at a higher level because city banks were heavily dependent on loans from the Bank of Japan. Even if the reserve ratio had been established at a higher level, it would merely have increased the banks' borrowings from the Bank of Japan, as the banks suffered from chronic shortages of loanable funds. In the meantime, local banks, mutual banks and credit associations had surplus funds which they operated in the call money market, and a higher reserve ratio could have siphoned off these surplus funds. However, because their scale of operation is so small, tying their funds to a non-interest bearing reserve would cause more problems than it solved.

In a drastic departure from previous policy, control of credit in 1973 began with a rise in the reserve ratio. Since then, the ratio has been changed more frequently and the adjustment of the reserve ratio came to be more important as an instrument of monetary policy.

Window Operation

Regulation of credits at the discount window has played the most important role in the execution of monetary policies. Since the 1960s, this method has been employed time after time whenever the monetary authorities decided

TABLE 49 *Changes in the reserve ratio of all Japanese banks*

(%)			
Date of change	Time deposits	Demand deposits	Applied to banking institutions with deposit balance of more than
Sept 1959	0·50	1·50	¥20 billion
Oct 1961	1·00	3·00	¥100 billion
Nov 1962	0·50	1·50	
Dec 1963	0·50	3·00	
Dec 1964	0·50	1·50	
July 1965	0·50	1·00	
Sept 1969	0·50	1·50	
Jan 1973	1·00	2·00	¥1,000 billion
Mar 1973	1·50	3·00	
Jun 1973	1·75	3·25	
Sept 1973	2·00	3·75	
Jan 1974	2·25	4·25	
Nov 1975	2·00	3·75	¥1,500 billion
Feb 1976	1·75	3·00	

TABLE 50 *Changes in the flow of credits to city banks through regulation at the discount window (1973–)*

Year	Period	Increases in amounts authorized (in ¥ billion)	Increase/decrease over/below the same period of previous year (%)
1973	Jan–Mar	1,320	+12·7
	Apr–Jun	1,000	−16·0
	Jul–Sept	1,250	−34·0
	Oct–Dec	1,300	−41·0
1974	Jan–Mar	840	−37·0
	Apr–Jun	840	−15·7
	Jul–Sept	980	−21·9
	Oct–Dec	1,270	−2·6
1975	Jan–Mar	910	+5·3
	Apr–Jun	920	+12·7
	Jul–Sept	1,278	+30·4
	Oct–Dec	1,580	+22·0
1976	Jan–Mar	1,180	+26·3
	Apr–Jun	1,050	+19·7
	Jul–Sept	1,300	+1·7
	Oct–Dec	1,550	−4·3
1977	Jan–Mar	1,130	−1·4
	Apr–Jun	960	−7·9
	Jul–Sept	1,130	−13·1

to tighten the money market. In recent years, they have used these regulations even in times of easy money after bitter experience of the results of lifting the controls in 1971–72: in the absence of credit control at the discount window at that time, banks competed with one another in making loans and thereby created excessive liquidity. The central bank establishes a quarter-to-quarter ceiling on loan increments in light of the market's fund requirements. It has been following this practice even now that loan demand has dried up, resulting in some banks not using all of their loan authority.

The practice of regulation at the discount window also includes guidance of the banks' fund position. In deference to the central bank's guidance, banks carrying large external liabilities attempt to reduce such liabilities by cutting down on loan commitments or by selling securities holdings.

4.2.2 MONEY SUPPLY

Cash supply by the Bank of Japan to the banking system follows one or more of three routes:

   (*a*) loans;
   (*b*) purchase of notes;
   (*c*) bond operations.

Of these, the outright operation of bonds is usually conducted to match the expected shortage of funds. During fiscal year 1976, the government bond-buying operation amounted to ¥900 billion. However, the amount of outright operation of bonds will probably increase in order to lighten the burden on city banks, whose government bond holdings have been increasing rapidly. Loans of the Bank of Japan are available at the official discount rate against the collateral of fine eligible bills or eligible bonds. Since the adoption of a new credit regulation policy in 1962, the outstanding balance of the central bank's loans has remained almost unchanged. In July 1977, the ceiling on credits extendable to city banks was raised from ¥875 billion to ¥1,200 billion. The practice of purchasing bills is designed to control the supply and demand of funds through the intermediary of the bill discount market, a cashing of trade credits by the Bank of Japan. The funds thus supplied by the Bank of Japan through purchases of bills reached its peak at ¥4,961·8 billion in August 1974.

4.3 The Money Market

The short-term money market of Japan consists of

   (*a*) the call market,
   (*b*) the discount market and
   (*c*) the repurchase market.

Transactions in the first two markets are intermediated exclusively by call brokers, while those in the third market are processed through securities companies, and this market constitutes the only short-term money market in which businesses can directly participate.

4.3.1 THE CALL AND DISCOUNT MARKETS

Membership in the call and discount markets is confined to financial institutions. Members are permanently divided into lenders and borrowers. Call brokerage houses are not authorized to act as dealers; their activities are restricted to the brokerage business. The call market is the market place where the shortest-term reserve assets are operated, while the discount market is one where funds which are free for two to three months can be operated. The present discount market was launched in May 1971. The related launching was due to the fact that as late as in 1970, 80% of the ¥2,000 billion balance of the call market was accounted for by funds that could be carried forward into the following month.

TABLE 51 *Changes in the volume of the short-term money market*

	(¥ billion)			
Year ended 31 Dec	Call market	Discount market	Repurchase market	Total
1967	1,001·8	–	152·1	1,163·9
1968	985·1	–	290·5	1,275·6
1969	1,546·4	–	407·7	1,954·1
1970	1,816·9	–	619·1	2,436·0
1971	1,472·3	368·7	881·5	2,722·5
1972	1,048·2	1,791·9	1,224·4	4,064·5
1973	1,226·7	4,088·8	1,737·5	7,053·0
1974	2,159·7	5,206·8	1,504·7	8,871·2
1975	2,331·6	4,403·3	1,679·0	8,413·9
1976	2,567·1	5,091·0	2,083·9	9,742·0
1977 (Mar)	2,938·5	4,775·7	2,543·6	10,257·8

One of the aims of establishing the discount market was to absorb funds of longer duration and let the call market operate in the shortest-term payment reserves. In those days, since the balance of outstanding government bonds was relatively low, there was a possibility of the central bank developing a shortage of buying vehicles. Therefore, to prepare the way for the introduction of a bills operation system, the discount market was launched.

4.3.2 MOVEMENTS OF THE CALL AND BILL DISCOUNT RATES

The call and bill discount rates, in theory at least, are supposed to move freely in response to the supply and demand situation of funds. In the case of Japan, however, these rates are set under the guidance of the Bank of Japan – so much so that they have become a captive tool of the central bank.

The interest rate structure is rooted in the peculiar banking structure of Japan. The relationships between the different interest rates may be represented by the following formula: official discount rate < call rates < discount

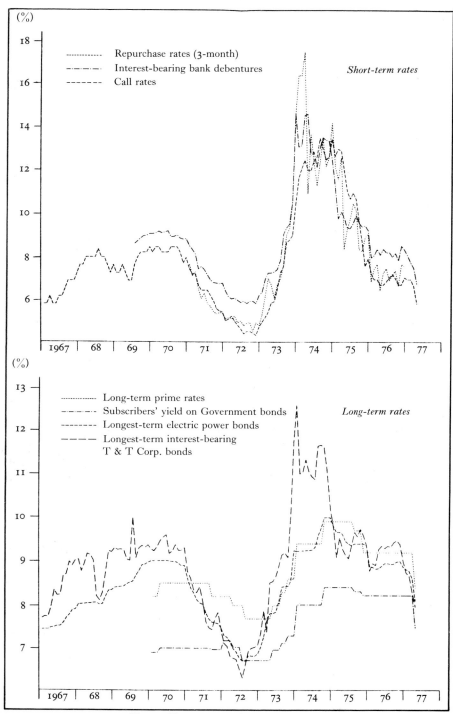

Fig. 7 Short-term and long-term rates

rates. The call rates do not go below the official discount rate because the city banks suffer from chronic shortages of loanable funds. The official discount rate does not act as a penal rate but as a guiding rate (usually below the market rates) supported by the system of allocating the Bank of Japan's funds. Even if the call rate goes below the official discount rate temporarily, it is bound to regain its previous rate because such a low rate will cause city banks to take in increased amounts of call money, pushing the call rate upward. The countervailing force on the upward movement of the bill discount rates is the subscribers' yield of government bonds. The increasing volume of government bonds held by city banks creates a growing pressure to reduce their outside debt service costs.

TABLE 52 *Recent highs and lows of the short-term money rate*

	(%)		
	Official discount rate	Call rate (unconditional, lender)	Discount rate (buyer)
Jun 1972 (recent low)	4·25	4·25	5·00
Dec 1974 (recent high)	9·00	13·50	13·75
May 1977 (latest low)	5·00	5·125	5·75

4.3.3 REPURCHASE MARKET

The repurchase market is the only money market in which businesses can participate directly for the operation of their short-term funds, for raising funds, and in which the interest rates are free from government control. On 31 March 1977, the outstanding balance of the market stood at ¥2,543·6 billion, compared with an average balance of ¥2,254·7 billion of the call market for the same month.

Initially, the repurchase market developed out of the inventory financing of the bonds held by securities companies. In other words, the repurchase market provided the market facility for financing short-term fund requirements by taking advantage of the long- and medium-term bonds held by the participants of the market. As such, it is utilized on an important scale by securities companies for the purpose of financing their own fund requirements. Financial institutions accounted for approximately 25% of the bonds supplied to the market, the largest part having come from the agriculture- and forestry-related institutions which raised short-term funds with their long-term bond holdings. Through the arbitration activities of these financial institutions on the call and discount markets, a linkage has developed between the call and discount rates and the repurchase rates.

On the supply side of the equation, funds supplied by business corporations account for approximately 70% of the total. In the absence of a market for Treasury bills, commercial papers and certificates of deposit, business

TABLE 53 *Structure of the repurchase market (31 March 1977)*

	Balance of funds raised (¥ billion)	(%)	Balance of funds operated (¥ billion)	(%)
Banking institutions	622·2	24·5	281·2	11·0
Life insurance companies, government agencies and mutual aid associations, etc.	71·4	2·8	464·4	18·3
Business corporations	476·2	18·7	1,787·8	70·3
Securities companies	1,373·8	54·0	10·2	0·4
Total	2,543·6	100·0	2,543·6	100·0

corporations take a keen interest in the repurchase market, because they are prohibited from participating in the discount market. In fact, many corporations come to the repurchase market with their idle three- to six-month fund, which they have accumulated for the payment of summer and winter bonuses or corporation taxes.

4.4 Changes in the Structure of the Financial Market

The environment surrounding the nation's money and capital markets has undergone profound changes in recent years as a result of the following factors:

(a) As the economy has shifted to slower growth, opportunities for lucrative investments have decreased, on the one hand, and there is plenty of cash to go around (increasing self-financing capability), on the other.

(b) Businesses have become increasingly liquid and their securities holdings have also increased.

(c) Deficits in the public sector are rising and government and local public bodies have been issuing bonds on a massive scale.

(d) The nation's capital market has become increasingly involved in international capital transactions.

(e) The financial resources of the nation's institutional investors, such as pension trusts, investment trusts, life insurance companies and mutual aid associations, have grown substantially.

These factors brought about a gradual change in the structure of Japan's money market, which had been characterized by:

(a) predominance of indirect financing,

(b) over-borrowing by businesses and

(c) over-lending by the banks (borrowing in excess of reserves).

Massive offerings of public bonds and the increase in their volume traded

TABLE 54 Changes in investment preferences

(¥ billion) (% of all investment)

	1965	1970	1971	1972	1973	1974	1975	1976
Cash and currency deposits	5,768	13,019	15,442	19,968	24,510	27,344	29,853	33,568
	18·7	*18·9*	*19·0*	*20·1*	*20·5*	*19·3*	*17·8*	*17·0*
Time deposits and savings accounts	13,035	31,835	37,597	46,978	58,142	69,799	84,894	100,378
	42·3	*46·1*	*46·2*	*47·2*	*48·4*	*49·4*	*50·6*	*50·8*
Trusts	1,436	3,925	4,713	5,793	6,823	8,170	9,944	12,031
	4·7	*5·7*	*5·8*	*5·8*	*5·7*	*5·8*	*5·9*	*6·1*
Insurance	3,616	9,049	10,850	12,932	15,249	18,036	21,375	25,243
	11·7	*13·1*	*13·3*	*13·0*	*12·7*	*12·8*	*12·7*	*12·8*
Securities (total)	5,558	9,742	11,501	12,742	14,196	16,077	19,478	23,770
	18·0	*14·1*	*14·1*	*12·8*	*11·8*	*11·4*	*11·6*	*12·0*
Stocks	3,303	4,427	4,604	4,328	4,393	4,785	5,206	5,514
	10·7	*6·4*	*5·6*	*4·3*	*3·7*	*3·4*	*3·1*	*2·8*
Bonds	1,186	4,095	5,428	6,704	7,868	9,072	11,779	15,386
	3·8	*5·9*	*6·7*	*6·8*	*6·5*	*6·4*	*7·0*	*7·8*
Investment trusts	1,069	1,219	1,469	1,710	1,935	2,220	2,492	2,869
	3·5	*1·8*	*1·8*	*1·7*	*1·6*	*1·6*	*1·5*	*1·5*
Others	1,404	1,446	1,302	1,177	1,097	1,985	2,302	2,725
	4·6	*2·1*	*1·6*	*1·1*	*0·9*	*1·3*	*1·4*	*1·4*
Total	30,816	69,016	81,406	99,590	120,019	141,410	167,846	197,714
	100·0	*100·0*	*100·0*	*100·0*	*100·0*	*100·0*	*100·0*	*100·0*

Source: *The Flow of Funds*, The Bank of Japan.

accelerated the development of the bond market, and the rising level of participation of institutional investors added to the depth of the capital market.
Meanwhile, corporations have come to rely more heavily on bond issues as a
means of raising funds, and this was further encouraged by raising the
statutory limits on the amount of bonds issuable. Thus the stage is being
set for the expansion of direct financing as opposed to indirect financing
(bank borrowings).

4.4.1 INCREASING WEIGHT OF LONG-TERM FINANCIAL ASSETS

As financial assets have accumulated, long-term financial assets, such as life
and non-life insurances, long-term bonds and money and loan trusts, have
gained influence. In the past, indirect financing has been the dominant form
of business financing, because bank deposits accounted for roughly one-half
of individuals' financial assets. However, individuals have become increasingly selective in their choice of investment vehicles, with a pronounced
tendency to choose long-term financial assets with higher yields.

4.4.2 INCREASING LEVEL OF BUSINESSES' SECURITIES INVESTMENT

The majority of corporate cash was traditionally deposited with banks, with
little invested in securities. However, as the profit margin declined, corporations drew down their bank deposits to repay debts owed to banks and began
to invest their surplus funds in bonds which brought larger yields. Toyota
Motors and Matsushita Electric are totally free of debts and are devoting
large percentages of their surplus funds to bond investments. In the meantime, the number of corporations, highly geared or otherwise, which operate
their short-term funds in the repurchase market is rising. Business corporations are now playing an increasingly important role as suppliers of funds.

4.4.3 INCREASING ROLE OF INSTITUTIONAL INVESTORS

As individuals invest their savings in long-term financial assets, institutional
investors have come to play an important role. Individuals' investment in
long-term assets translates into increased funds for life and non-life insurance
companies, pension funds and investment trusts. Due to the declining business loan demand following a slowdown in economic growth, a larger share
of these funds is being invested in securities.

At the end of 1976, life insurance companies had aggregate assets of
¥14,000 billion and non-life insurance companies ¥3,700 billion. In addition,
the total assets of agricultural cooperative mutual aid associations, the
insurance arm of the agriculture- and forestry-related financial institutions,
stood at ¥3,400 billion. Those of public employees' annuity mutual aid
associations stood at ¥6,000 billion, those of corporate pension funds at
approximately ¥3,000 billion, those of stock investment trusts at approximately ¥2,000 billion and those of bond investment trusts at approximately
¥1,500 billion. The total assets of the insurance, pension and investment
trusts comes to approximately ¥34,000 billion, roughly equal to 50% of the
funds of city banks.

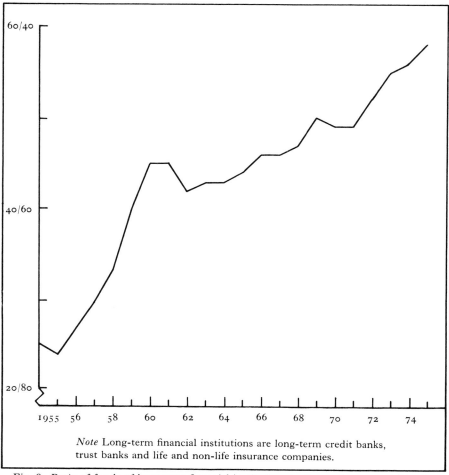

Note Long-term financial institutions are long-term credit banks,
trust banks and life and non-life insurance companies.

Fig. 8   Ratio of funds of long-term financial institutions to those of commercial banks

4·4·4 OUTLOOK

In Japan, the financial market has played a role as an allocator of funds and
controller of the market to fuel the rapid growth of the economy. It fixed
the interest rate at a low level to reinforce the competitive position of the
Japanese industry and gave priority to basic industries in its allocation of
funds. In the process, it helped establish the present order of the financial
market.

With the economy gearing to a slower rate of growth, the factors which
were used to prop up such a market structure have outlived their usefulness
and are being replaced by a market mechanism – the liberalization of interest
rates. As a matter of fact, changes in bonds' market yield have already
affected the long-term rates, narrowing the gap between the bond issuing
market and the secondary market rates.

The development of the bond markets and the increasing international involvement of the Japanese capital markets are making it difficult for the monetary authorities to control financial markets by regulating the interest rates. A complete liberalization of interest rates may not be realized soon, due to the difficulty of adjusting the interests of the various sectors involved, but obstacles are being removed one after another.

Expansion of direct financing and liberalization of interest rates go hand in hand and this will bring about an increasing diversification of the short-term money markets. Healthy development of the short-term money markets is indispensable for the growth of the capital market. However, the present short-term money markets are considerably distorted, because securities companies are restricted from raising funds in the call and discount markets, while city banks are barred from the repurchase market – *i.e.*, each is barred from one of the two important segments that constitute the overall short-term money market.

Any innovations in the short-term money market must start with the cultivation of the Treasury bills market. At present, the Treasury bill rates are pegged to a low level (call rates > official discount rates > Treasury bill rates) and the bulk of Treasury bill issues have been bought up by the Bank of Japan.

Future development in the structure of the nation's financial market will depend on the instruments (such as certificates of deposits and commercial paper) that the market introduces and on the rules of market participation that it adopts. It would be fair to say that the market is developing in the direction of a free market where diverse financial assets can freely find their optimum employment through the market mechanism.

5 THE JAPANESE SECURITIES MARKET

5.1 History and Development

5.1.1 BEFORE THE OUTBREAK OF THE SECOND WORLD WAR

Japan's emergence as a modern state commenced, as we saw in Chapter 1, with the advent of the Meiji era (1868–1912), and the history of its stock market likewise can be traced back to early Meiji period. The Tokyo Stock Exchange Co. Ltd, the predecessor of the Tokyo Stock Exchange, was established in 1878, following the enactment of the Stock Exchange Regulation in the same year. In the Meiji era, most industrial capital came from government funds and the *zaibatsu*. Its accumulation went on independently of the securities market. Consequently, in sharp contrast to the development achieved by banks, the stock market was unable to function as a source of long-term industrial funds. Speculative trading, centred around a few "specified stocks", became the order of the day.

This characteristic of the Japanese securities market remained unchanged throughout the Taisho era (1912–25). The establishment of the short-term futures trading system in 1922 only contributed to the speculative trends of the market. It was not until the Showa era (1926 to the present) that the securities market began its full-scale development through the increased use of spot trading. This increase in spot trading was brought about by the growing war industry, which stimulated the issue of stocks of the *zaibatsu* corporations. With the outbreak of the Sino-Japanese War in 1937, the situation changed drastically. The securities market, placed under war-time economic controls, was subject to a number of measures, including restrictions on dividend and capital increases. In 1943 the Tokyo Stock Exchange Co. Ltd was reorganized into the Japan Securities Exchange, a quasi-governmental organization. Thus, the securities market was under the direct and full control of the government during the war, and had virtually lost all its economic functions by the time the war terminated in August 1945.

5.1.2 POST-WAR PROGRESS

The Japan Securities Exchange closed on 9 August 1945, just before the end of the Second World War. In September, the General Headquarters of the Allied Occupation Forces postponed resumption of securities transactions indefinitely. As a result, securities were traded over the counter or on the private market for some time. In 1947, the Japan Securities Exchange was dissolved. In the same year, a huge number of stocks were released through the SCLC – Securities Coordinating Liquidation Committee – in the wake of the dissolution of the *zaibatsu* and reorganization of various business organizations executed by order of the Occupation Forces. With the release of these stocks, the number of individual stockholders increased rapidly, and the stock market in Japan underwent a complete transformation, which was called the "Securities Democratization Drive".

In May 1948, a new Securities and Exchange Law, introducing American legislation into Japan, was enacted. Since the basic law regulating the securities market in Japan was modelled on American legislation, the Japanese securities market resembles its American counterpart in many respects, even now. In 1949, securities exchanges, based on a membership system, were created under the new law. Before opening up securities transactions, the Occupation Forces' General Headquarters suggested the following three principles:

(*a*) Every transaction in a listed security by any member of a legal securities exchange shall be effected on the exchange.

(*b*) Every transaction on a legal securities exchange shall be recorded chronologically.

(*c*) No future trading shall be effected in the country.

The post-war Japanese securities market developed on the basis of these principles. Then, American-type margin transactions were introduced for the first time in Japan in June 1951. Differing from the futures transactions under a clearing contract in pre-war days, they are similar to spot transactions in their form. At the same time, the Law for Securities Investment Trusts was enacted, allowing securities companies to transact investment trusts concurrently.

The Japanese economy had been rehabilitated by 1955, and began to move toward expansion with the slogan "Now the post-war age is over". With the rapid growth of the Japanese economy, which experienced booms twice during the period between 1955 and 1961, stock prices made big gains. The bond market resumed its functions in April 1956 at the Tokyo and Osaka Exchanges after being closed for 11 years. In August 1955, provisions regarding securities finance companies were added to the Securities and Exchange Law, and in April 1956, three licensed securities finance companies started their operations. In February 1960, stock investment trust business, which had been carried on by securities companies, was transferred to newly-formed investment trust management companies, which, in January 1961, obtained permission also to operate bond investment trusts. In October 1961, the second section of the Tokyo, Osaka and Nagoya Exchanges came into existence.

Triggered by monetary restraints, the stock market crashed in July 1961 due to realization sales by institutional stockholders. However, corporate desire for expansion of production facilities was still so strong that many firms rushed to raise funds to finance growing capital, making stock prices plunge further. From the spring of 1963, repurchase of stock investment trusts from individual investors began to increase and pulled stocks down further, giving rise to a vicious circle. To stop a further decline of stock prices, the Japan Joint Securities Co. Ltd was set up in January 1964 with the cooperation of banks and securities companies. In January 1965, the Japan Securities Holding Association was formed by securities companies to take over surplus stocks accumulated by repurchase, together with stocks held by investment trusts. But the situation deteriorated, and the government had to take a series of remedies during the year: an all-out suspension of capital increases in February; the Bank of Japan's special loan to the ailing Yamaichi Securities Co. Ltd in May; and extension of the maturity term of unit-type investment trusts in June as their amount of redemption went down below par value. As a result of these supportive measures, stock prices ceased to fall, from July onwards.

The nation's economy turned upward in the autumn of 1965 and was back on the road to growth. Thus, the stock market gradually recovered from the hard blow dealt by the panic. An amendment of the Securities and Exchange Law introducing a licensing system in the securities business came into effect in October 1965, with a grace period of two and a half years. The Law for Securities Investment Trusts was also modified with a view to increasing the protection of investors, and this amendment came into force in October 1967. In order to improve securities transaction methods, amelioration of the margin transaction system and the prohibition of cross transactions successively came into effect in the same year. Stock exchanges were also restructured in April 1968 in order to give them more of a public character. In the meantime, regulations against window-dressing in the corporate settlement of accounts had been tightened since 1965, along with promotion of a disclosure system. The Certified Public Accountant Law was amended, with effect from June 1966. Stock prices continued a sustained rise from the spring of 1968 to that of 1970. As a result, the Japan Securities Holding Association was dissolved in January 1969 and the Japan Joint Securities Co. Ltd was wound up in January 1971, both having accomplished their mission.

The new US economic policy announced by President Nixon on 16 August 1971 drove stock prices down sharply but business turned upward after 1972 on the strength of the multinational currency realignment realized towards the end of 1971. In the meantime, monetary conditions experienced a drastic change as the money supply eased, with an abundant flow of foreign currencies into Japan. Consequently, chronic overlending by city banks came to an end. Against such a backdrop, the supply–demand relationship of funds on the capital market underwent a great change. The gap between issuer's cost and secondary market yield of bonds was closed with the fall of the latter. Stimulated by the active transactions on the market, the issuing market also began to show new developments. It had been customary for Japanese corporations to increase capital by allotting new shares to shareholders at par value, but since around 1972, capital has been financed on a large scaie by issuing new shares and convertible bonds at market price. Meanwhile, the number of bonds floated in each issue increased considerably, and issuing terms, including diversification of maturity period, became more acceptable to the public. Thus, an increasing number of individual and institutional investors began to buy bonds.

Liberalization of investment in securities, beginning in April 1970 with the government's approval of the acquisition of foreign securities by investment trust funds, increased during this period. In November 1972, a curb on the sale of foreign stock investment trusts in the domestic market was lifted, and investment in foreign securities by the Japanese was almost completely liberalized. Starting with the floatation of Asian Development Bank debentures in December 1970, floatation of yen-denominated foreign bonds increased in 1971 and 1972. Thus, internationalization of the Japanese securities market made remarkable progress.

In 1973, the economic and financial climate at home and abroad changed drastically. The government had to restrict aggregate demand in order to hold down rising commodity prices, as well as tighten monetary restraints by raising the official discount rate from 4·25% to 9·00%. In addition, a crude oil price boost by OPEC in the autumn of that year contributed to the commodity price upswing. With the continued restriction of aggregate demand, the economy in 1974 was stagnant and the GNP dipped below the 1973 level. Reflecting this situation, the stock market slackened and the total amount of corporate capital increase by stock issue at market price tapered off. In the meantime, bond issuing terms were revised in accordance with a rise of the secondary market yield of bonds caused by monetary tightening. In December 1973, several foreign issues were listed on the Tokyo Stock Exchange for the first time. At present, a total of 15 foreign issues are listed on the TSE.

Along with the change in the nation's economic growth pattern after the oil crisis, a change was also seen on the securities market. One aspect of this was the issue of a large number of government bonds and other public bonds, the purpose of which was to compensate for the shortfall in fiscal revenue caused by the slow growth of tax revenue due to the prolonged recession. The bond market will inevitably be affected to a greater extent in the future. With the deceleration of the nation's economic growth, corporations began to feel the necessity of increasing equity capital and securing long-term stable funds. Thus, they began to attach more importance to fund raising through the securities market. The role of the securities market, therefore, will probably become more important in the future.

5.2 Stocks and Bonds in Japan

5.2.1 STOCKS

In Japan, corporations can issue new shares by a decision of the board of directors within the limits of the authorized capital that are set by the general meeting of shareholders. From a legal point of view, no pre-emptive right is given to shareholders. But approval at the general meeting of shareholders is required if the right to pre-empt shares at a lucrative price is given to a third party. In addition to ordinary shares, corporations may issue stocks of a special character such as preferred and deferred stocks. However, there are few cases in which these stocks are issued by a company quoted on the Stock Exchange. The issue of preferred stock by Hitachi Shipbuilding & Engineering is the single exception in recent years.

Corporations also have a right to issue both par value and non-par stocks, but there are only a few cases where the latter were issued. The Commercial Law now in force stipulates that the face value of a share should be set at ¥500 and over. However, since this clause is not applied to corporations founded under the former Commercial Law, most listed stocks have par value of ¥50. In a few cases, such as the electric power companies' stock, the face value is set at ¥500. In addition, almost all stocks issued in Japan are registered, and there are few bearer shares.

5.2.2 BONDS

Bonds are usually classified by issuer, as follows:

(a) Government bonds
(b) Municipal bonds
(c) Special bonds
  (i) Government-related organization bonds (government-guaranteed bonds)
  (ii) Bank debentures
  (iii) Others
(d) Corporate bonds (industrial bonds)
(e) Foreign bonds

Government bonds are issued by the government under the Law Concerning Government Bonds after obtaining Diet approval. They are divided into short-term, medium-term and long-term bonds according to the terms of

TABLE 55 *Securities issued in Japan*

(¥ billion)

	1969	1970	1971	1972	1973	1974	1975	1976
Stocks	492·9	688·5	536·4	1,056·4	929·8	539·5	996·3	620·1
Convertible bonds	4·5	96·0	108·1	126·0	526·0	248·8	408·0	59·0
Corporate bonds	504·0	557·5	858·5	652·8	805·2	933·5	1,465·1	1,225·1
Bank debentures:								
Discount bonds	1,524·7	1,906·6	2,273·0	2,815·5	3,426·4	3,947·6	4,982·2	5,798·3
Coupon bonds	906·7	1,061·1	1,684·8	2,190·0	2,047·2	2,316·1	2,869·8	3,174·1
Government bonds (through public offering)	386·0	330·0	720·6	1,810·0	1,505·0	1,570·0	3,302·3	6,749·1
Government-guaranteed bonds	312·2	280·9	325·8	366·5	425·2	405·0	448·4	738·4
Publicly offered special bonds	–	–	–	45·0	66·0	62·0	88·0	165·0
Municipal bonds	81·2	86·7	99·5	114·1	148·1	176·4	239·3	456·5
Foreign stocks	–	–	–	6·5	–	–	–	3·1
Foreign bonds	–	6·0	33·0	85·0	40·0	–	20·0	65·0

redemption. Short-term government bonds are also called short-term government bills. They are issued in discount form and they mature within a period of less than a year. Up to now, the following short-term government bills have been floated: Treasury Bills, Food Bills and Foreign Exchange Fund Bills. These mature in two months. Medium-term government bonds, which are also called "discount government bonds", have been issued since 1977, with a maturity term of five years. Except for special government bonds such as government compensation bonds and subscription certificates, long-term government bonds are divided into those issued under the provisions of the Finance Law (Construction Bonds) and the others floated under the provisions of the Law Concerning Exceptions to the Finance Law (Deficit-covered Bonds). The former expands social overhead capital such as houses, roads and sewerage, and the latter covers the government's ordinary expenses. These bonds usually mature in ten years.

Municipal bonds are issued by prefectures and municipalities for meeting expenditures on public works, for reconstruction and repair of damage caused by natural calamities, for repaying debt, and financing public service companies (tram or bus services, water supply, etc.). However, only 22 major prefectures and municipalities are allowed to float these bonds, which mature in ten years on the public market.

In the category of special bonds, there are bank debentures and bonds issued by government-related organizations under the provisions of relevant legislation. The latter includes Japanese National Railways Bonds, Nippon Telegraph and Telephone Bonds, Japan Highway Public Corporation Bonds, and so on. The government guarantees the payment of both principal and interest on bonds of this kind, which are offered to the public, and they are therefore called "government-guaranteed bonds" and are given credit equivalent to government bonds. (The above organizations may also issue other bonds without the government's guaranty.) Issue of bonds of this type is subject to the permission of the relevant minister, and they can not be issued beyond the limit fixed by Diet resolution.

Bank debentures are divided into the following:

(a) Debentures issued by the Industrial Bank of Japan, the Long-term Credit Bank of Japan, the Nippon Credit Bank and the Bank of Tokyo respectively, under the provisions of relevant laws.

(b) Agriculture and forestry debentures issued by Norin Chukin Bank and industry and commerce debentures issued by Shoko Chukin Bank under the provisions of the reievant legislation.

They are also divided into debentures with coupon (term of redemption one year or five years), and discount bonds on which bearers receive prepayment of interest (term of redemption one year).

There are also bonds issued by special corporations (incorporated under individual special laws) such as Japan Air Lines Co. Ltd and Tohoku District Development Co., as well as those issued by the Japan Broadcasting Corporation and the Teito Rapid Transit Authority under the provisions of the relevant legislation. The issuing terms of the first two, which are guaranteed by the government, are same as those for government-related organization bonds. As the latter do not carry the government's guaranty, their issuing terms are the same as those for corporate bonds described below.

Corporate bonds are issued by private business corporations for raising long-term funds. Their term to maturity is set at ten years in principle. They are divided into unsecured bonds, secured bonds and general mortgage bonds. Unsecured bonds are issued without mortgage. These bonds (except for convertible debentures) so far have not been offered to the public. Secured bonds, or mortgage bonds secured by real mortgage, are issued in conformity with both the Commercial Code and the Mortgage Bond Trust Law. Specific property of the issuer is usually given as a mortgage in order to guarantee interest payment and repayment of principal. Almost all of the corporate bonds so far issued through public offering are of this type. The kinds of property which can be mortgaged are stipulated in the Mortgage Bond Trust Law. In some cases, the whole property of the issuing company is offered as a mortgage. Mortgage bonds are of two types: closed and open-ended. The former type is issued at one time, placing a mortgage on specific property of the issuer, whilst the latter is issued in several instalments, placing the same priority on the mortgage to all issued bonds. Since the latter allows the issuer to issue bonds whenever he requires, almost all outstanding secured bonds are of this type. The issue of general mortgage bonds or legal mortgage bonds is not regulated by the Mortgage Bond Trust Law. Though they are similar to unsecured bonds in form, the relevant special laws give a lien to the holder of these bonds subordinate only to that given by the Civil Code; he is guaranteed the right to receive preferential repayment out of the issuer's property. As to general mortgage bonds, there is no depositary which, as in the case of secured bonds, is given the security in trust and has charge of its management. Up to now, nine electric power companies, Japan Air Lines, Tohoku District Development Co. and so on have issued this type of bond.

In addition to "straight" bonds of the kind already mentioned, there are convertible bonds, which have recently become popular. They are convertible into stock at any holder's request in accordance with the conditions fixed at the time of their issue. They are divided into secured and unsecured bonds and they come to maturity in ten years like straight bonds, but their yield is set at a lower level than the latter. Foreign bonds are issued by non-residents on the Japanese capital market. Starting with the Asian Development Bank Bonds, the World Bank, Australia, Provinces of Quebec and Manitoba in Canada, Mexico, Brazil, Finland, New Zealand, Denmark and Singapore have so far issued bonds in Japan. They are all denominated in yen and almost all of them are listed on the Tokyo Stock Exchange.

5.3 The Structure of the Stock Exchange

5.3.1 OUTLINE

In Japan there are eight stock exchanges. They are located in Tokyo, Osaka, Nagoya, Kyoto, Hiroshima, Fukuoka, Niigata and Sapporo. They play a principal role in stock transaction (bonds are usually traded over the counter). The Tokyo Stock Exchange is the most important, with the trade volume accounting for 84·68% of the total throughout the country in 1976.

TABLE 56 *Stock trade volume by stock exchange (1976)*

	Trade volume (in million shares)	Percentage
Tokyo	69,941	84·68
Osaka	9,553	11·57
Nagoya	2,299	2·78
Kyoto	164	0·20
Hiroshima	280	0·34
Fukuoka	132	0·16
Niigata	175	0·21
Sapporo	56	0·07
Total	82,597	100·00

Stock exchanges are legal persons, organized by securities companies on a membership basis under the Securities and Exchange Law. They take the form of non-profit, autonomous organizations and are expected to maintain their public character and effective management. Member companies are required to be of high quality and credit in order to let the stock exchange with which they are affiliated fully perform its functions. Therefore the articles of incorporation of each stock exchange provide strict supervision of requirements for membership, fix a limit on the number of members and control enrolment of newcomers, with a view to enhancing its members' status.

5.3.2 CLASSIFICATION OF EXCHANGE MEMBERS

Members of a stock exchange are divided into regular and *saitori* members in accordance with the nature of their operation. Regular members are permitted to sell and buy securities on the exchange, either on their own accounts or on the account of clients. Usually, they are called simply "members". *Saitori* are members specializing as intermediaries between two regular members in securities transaction on the exchange. By the nature of their operation, they are found only at the Tokyo, Osaka and Nagoya Exchanges, where trade volume is quite large. Each stock exchange sets a limit to the number of members by its articles of incorporation. The Tokyo Stock

Exchange limits its regular members to 83 and *saitori* members to 12. As of 30 September 1976, the actual number of its members had reached those limits.

5.3.3 QUALIFICATION FOR EXCHANGE MEMBERSHIP
The membership of the stock exchanges is limited to securities companies. (According to the Securities and Exchange Law, any foreign securities company is entitled to claim membership in a stock exchange, if Japanese securities companies are admitted to full membership in any stock exchange in the country where the particular foreign securities company has its head office.) Each stock exchange limits its members to securities companies incorporated under Japanese legislation by its articles of incorporation. They further provide that member companies should not be under the control of a foreigner, a foreign corporation or other organization, or a corporation or other organization under the influence of those enumerated above.

Regular members must be securities companies mainly engaging in the sale and purchase of securities on the exchange. *Saitori* members must be securities companies specializing as intermediaries between two regular members in securities transactions made on the exchange. These qualifications for membership are fixed on the grounds that the similarity of the members in set-up and operation is usually desirable in an organization formed on a membership basis.

The Enforcement Ordinance of the Securities and Exchange Law fixed the minimum amount of capital for the members of each stock exchange as follows:

For regular members of:
    Tokyo and Osaka Stock Exchanges   ¥100 million
    Nagoya Stock Exchange   ¥50 million
    Other stock exchanges   ¥30 million
For *saitori* members of:
    Tokyo and Osaka Stock Exchanges   ¥4 million
    Nagoya Stock Exchange   ¥1 million

In addition, each stock exchange limits the members' debt ratio, that is, the ratio of total liabilities to net worth, at less than ten-fold.

5.3.4 RIGHTS AND OBLIGATIONS OF EXCHANGE MEMBERS
Regular members of a stock exchange have the right to participate in the management of the exchange, in addition to the right to effect transactions on the exchange market. On the other hand, they are obliged to share in the foundation fund of the exchange, to bear its current expenses and to offer a certain amount of deposit to the exchange.

Rights of the Members
The right to effect transactions on the exchange market is the most important among various rights given to the regular members of a stock exchange. The

Securities and Exchange Law stipulates that only the members are allowed to effect transactions on the exchange markets. Therefore, non-member securities companies cannot deal in stocks directly on the exchange markets; they have to perform transactions by placing orders through an intermediary regular member. The *saitori* members are not permitted to buy or sell stocks directly on the exchange markets, as they are special members allowed only to act as intermediaries in securities transactions on the exchange. Members are also given the right to exercise their vote at a general meeting of members, the ultimate decision-making organ of a stock exchange, and at an election of its officers. However, *saitori* members are allowed to exercise their vote only on particular resolutions, such as those concerning dissolution of the exchange and modification of articles of incorporation directly related to them.

Obligations of the Members (of the Tokyo Stock Exchange)

First, members of a stock exchange are obliged to share in the foundation fund of the exchange, which corresponds to the capital of a corporation. Regular members are required to make a contribution of ¥10 million to the fund, and *saitori* members ¥1 million.

Second, in order to cover the current expenses of the exchange, regular members must pay membership fees, composed of a fixed-amount fee and a fee imposed in proportion to the trade volume of each member. However, *saitori* members pay a fixed-amount fee only.

Third, members of a stock exchange must offer a certain amount of deposit to the exchange in compliance with the provisions of the Securities and Exchange Law. This deposit system is to protect clients who entrust transactions of securities to a member. If they have a claim on a member to whom they entrusted transactions, they have priority over other creditors in receiving repayment to be made out of this deposit. The amount of the deposit is fixed at ¥3 million for regular members and ¥20,000 for *saitori* members. (If a regular member firm has offices for receiving orders from clients other than its head office, it must add ¥300,000 to the deposit for each office.)

In principle, trade in listed stocks is made on the floor of the exchange. Members of a stock exchange are obliged to perform all transactions, not only transactions entrusted by their customers but also those carried out on their own account, on the exchange, with a few exceptions.

For this reason, when a client entrusts buying or selling of stocks to a member of an exchange, the transaction is performed on the floor of the exchange, and its contract price is made public as the market price.

Transactions outside the exchange are permitted as exceptions to the above principle in the following cases:

(*a*) Where a member, who is also a member of another stock exchange, effects transactions on that exchange.

(*b*) Where a member makes public an offering of new shares of a listed company or participates in handling such an offering or in buying stocks in response to such an offering.

(c) If a member buys listed stocks as an agent in a takeover bid or sells them in response to such a takeover bid.

(d) With the approval of the exchange, if it admits the necessity of the transaction for the clients, a member may perform transactions of listed stocks for which trading on the exchange is suspended.

(e) If a member effects transactions of stocks in less than the unit number of trading fixed by the exchange (1,000 shares, or if the par value is more than ¥500, 100 shares). Such transactions are called "odd-lot transactions".

(f) Where a member participates in competitive bidding held by the government or a specific financial institution.

5.4 Listing Requirements of the Tokyo Stock Exchange

5.4.1 OUTLINE

As of the end of 1976, stocks of 1,401 Japanese and 17 foreign companies and 411 kinds of bonds were listed on the Tokyo Stock Exchange (TSE). Out of the 1,401 Japanese companies, 914 were listed in the First Section and the remaining 487 in the Second Section. After an initial listing in the Second Section domestic stocks are transferred to the First Section when they satisfy certain conditions.

5.4.2 LISTING EXAMINATION SYSTEM

Japan, like the United States, has adopted a strict system in order to ensure that only securities with high marketability and companies with a sound financial structure are listed on the stock exchange. The process of the listing examination system is as follows. When a company applies for a listing on TSE, the Exchange first examines whether the application fulfills the listing requirements. If it meets all the requirements, TSE asks the Finance Minister to approve the listing.

Listing Requirements for Domestic Stocks

Domestic stocks are listed on the basis of the application by a company. Prior to the listing, TSE conducts a strict examination in order to protect the public interest and future investors. First, TSE examines the application's compatibility with the listing requirements, which are described later. If the application fulfills the requirements, TSE conducts a careful examination of overall trading performance by investigating the company's past financial data, business prospects, and the trends of the industry. TSE also satisfies itself that the company will provide sufficient disclosure of performance and other data to investors after the listing. The TSE is also concerned about the maintenance of a smooth circulation. If such an examination demonstrates that

(a) the company has an excellent business record and therefore will be able to produce stable earnings, (*b*) the company will make full disclosures, and

(*c*) the distribution of the stocks is good, indicating a smooth circulation,

it lists the issue on the Exchange, after approval by the Finance Minister. For indications of smooth circulation after listing, the following conditions must be fulfilled:

(*a*) the total number of shares to be listed must be more than a stipulated amount,

(*b*) the distribution of stocks be good (they are expected to be traded on the market),

(*c*) there be more than a certain volume of stocks with marketability, which is essential to smooth circulation and stock pricing.

The requirements state the minimum standard for the total number of shares to be listed and the standard for the number of stockholders whose holdings range from 500 shares to less than 50,000 shares ("floating stockholders") and their stocks ("floating stocks"). To promote smooth circulation, standards have been established for the transfer agents, the form of stock certificates and free transfer of stock. To judge the financial structure of the issuing company, concrete standards have been established for the value of net assets, the value of net profits, dividends, the length of time since establishment, etc. For a proper disclosure of management activities, there are to be no false reports in the financial statements and other data.

The following are the present stock listing requirements of the Tokyo Stock Exchange:

1. Number of listed shares and the amount of capital:
   (*a*) Companies operating in Tokyo and the surrounding district: not less than 10 million shares and not less than ¥500 million.
   (*b*) Companies operating outside Tokyo and the surrounding district: not less than 20 million shares and not less than ¥1,000 million.
2. Distribution of stocks:
   (*a*) Number of floating stockholders (holdings from 500 shares to less than 50,000 shares): not less than 2,000 by the time of listing.
   (*b*) Number of shares owned by floating stockholders:
      (i) When the number of listed shares is less than 20 million shares: a minimum of 3 million shares or not less than 25% of the listed shares by the time of listing.
      (ii) When the number of listed shares is more than 20 million shares and less than 60 million shares: a million shares + not less than 20% of the listed shares by the time of listing.
      (iii) When the number of listed shares is not less than 60 million shares: 8·2 million shares + not less than 8% of the listed shares up to a maximum 16 million shares by the time of listing.

3. Time elapsed since establishment: not less than 5 years.
4. Net assets: not less than ¥1,500 million and not less than ¥100 per share.
5. Net profits:
   (a) Net profits during the last three years (including taxes):
       (i) First year: not less than ¥200 million
       (ii) Second year: not less than ¥300 million
       (iii) Third year: not less than ¥400 million
   (b) Net profits per share (including taxes): the net profits for each of the last three business years should be not less than ¥15 per share for the average number of issued shares. The net profits for the last year should not be less than ¥20 per share for the number of issued shares as of the end of the last business year.
6. Dividends: the dividends for each of the last three business years should not be less than ¥5 per share per annum. Dividends of not less than ¥5 per share per annum are expected to continue after the listing.
7. Reports in financial statements and other data:
   (a) No false reports should be contained in the financial statements and other data for the last three business years.
   (b) The general report by the certified public accountant or the audit corporation on the audit certificate attached to the financial statements and the similar data for the last business year should be "appropriate", and, in principle, an unqualified report.
8. Maintenance of transfer agents: the affairs concerning stocks are entrusted to a transfer agent authorized by TSE.
9. Form of stock certificates: the form is compatible with that stipulated by TSE.
10. Restriction of stock transfer: there are no restrictions on stock transfer.

   (*Note* The number of listed shares, the distribution of stocks and other standards per share are based on stock with ¥50 par value.)

When the stock listing is finally approved, the company submits to TSE a contract for the stock listing. In this contract, the company promises that:

   (a) it will observe TSE's various regulations, including the operational regulations and the regulations concerning the listing of securities, and
   (b) it will follow TSE's orders, including the delisting and the suspension of stock trading.

The contract becomes effective on the day when the stock concerned is listed on TSE. As a result, the listed company is under control of TSE's various regulations and is obliged to notify TSE of information necessary for TSE's listing administration and to submit various documents to TSE.

Listing Requirements for Foreign Stocks

TSE began listing foreign stocks in December 1973. As of the end of March

1977, 17 foreign companies were listed. They include 14 US companies (AMAX, Borden, Dow Chemical, IBM, Sperry Rand, General Motors, Citicorp, First Chicago, Chase Manhattan, General Telephone & Electronics, IU International, International Telephone & Telegraph, Atlantic Richfield, and Bank America), two French companies (Cie Francaise des Petroles and PARIBAS) and one Dutch company (Robeco). The process of listing foreign stocks is the same as that for domestic stocks, but special qualifications and requirements have been established taking into account unique aspects of foreign stocks.

First, when a foreign company applies for listing on TSE, the company's stock must already be listed on the stock exchange in its home country. TSE also conducts a strict examination of the business performance of the foreign company and the distribution of stocks as in the case of Japanese companies. The listing requirements for foreign stocks have been established under the principle that only the stocks of large companies with stable and favourable performance will be listed for some time, since investors in Japan are generally not familiar with foreign stocks.

The following are the specific listing requirements for foreign stocks:

1. Number of listed shares and the amount of capital: not less than 2 million shares and not less than ¥1,000 million capital.
2. Distribution of stocks:
   (a) Number of floating stockholders in Japan (holdings from 100 shares to less than 10,000 shares): not less than 2,000 by the time of listing.
   (b) Number of shares owned by floating stockholders in Japan: not less than 200,000 shares by the time of listing, and not less than the figure calculated by the following formula (maximum: 9 million shares):

$$9 \text{ million} \div \frac{\text{average price per share for the last six months}}{\substack{\text{simple average price for the last six months of all stocks} \\ \text{listed in the First Section of TSE}}}$$

3. Time elapsed since the establishment: same as domestic stocks.
4. Net assets: not less than ¥20,000 million.
5. Net profits:
   (a) The net profits for each of the last three years should be not less than ¥3,000 million (including taxes).
   (b) The net profit for each of the last three business years (net profits for common stocks on an annual basis, including taxes) should be more than 30% of the amount of the average capital (the average capital for common stocks). If the amount of the average capital exceeds ¥1,000 million, not less than 20% of the surplus should be added. The net profits for the last year should be not less than 40% of the amount of capital as of the end of the last business year.

When the amount of capital exceeds ¥1,000 million, not less than 20% of the surplus should be added.

6. Dividends:
   (a) The foreign company concerned should have offered dividends for common stocks for each of the last two business years. In addition, the dividends for the last business year should have totalled at least 10% of the amount of capital per annum.
   (b) Dividends of at least 10% of the amount of capital per annum are expected to be retained after the listing.
7. False reports in the financial statements and similar data: same as domestic stocks.
8. Designation of the institution responsible for stock affairs and the bank responsible for dividend payment. The foreign company concerned should designate an institution responsible for the affairs concerning stocks (excluding stock transfer and stock issue) and a bank to handle the dividend payments. Both the institution and the bank must have been authorized by TSE.
9. Form of stock certificates: same as domestic stocks.
10. Restriction of stock transfer: same as domestic stocks.

(*Note* The number of listed shares and the distribution of stocks are based on those for the issue with 100 shares as the trading unit.)

Listing Requirements for Straight Bonds

Listing of bonds (excluding convertible bonds) started in April 1956. The 11 issues listed at the outset included: one issue of local government bonds, two issues of government-guaranteed bonds, two issues of financial debentures and six issues of industrial bonds.

Listing of telephone and telegraph subscriber's bonds began in October 1961, that of government bonds in October 1966, and that of yen-denominated foreign bonds in April 1973. The process of bond listing is the same as that of stock listing:

(a) the listing application must be made by a bond issuer;
(b) an examination is conducted on the basis of the listing requirements for straight bonds;
(c) approval by the Finance Minister is required.

However, approval by the Finance Minister is not required for the listing of bonds other than industrial bonds and bonds issued by international organizations. A listing application is not necessary for government bonds.

One issuer cannot list more than one bond issue, except in cases of government bonds, T & T subscriber's bonds and yen-denominated foreign bonds. Because at present the necessity for listing more than one bond issue is small, in view of the state of bond trading, trading aimed at forming a standard price (so-called "trading for bond pricing") is generally conducted on the Tokyo Stock Exchange, while the actual trading is conducted mostly off-market.

For government bonds, T & T subscriber's bonds and yen-denominated foreign bonds, one issuer can list more than one issue. In the case of these, their marketability must be maintained constantly, since these bonds are widely held by individual investors. Also a certain amount of government bonds and yen-denominated foreign bonds must be traded in the market in order to form fair prices based on supply and demand.

In the listing examination of bonds, such items as the total par value of outstanding bonds, the circumstances of the issue of the bond concerned and the individual purchases are examined in order to ensure smooth circulation after the listing. Although the business performance of the issuer is examined as for stock listing, the examination for bond listing is concerned mainly with circulation, because bond issue is limited to the companies which have already been listed on the stock market, to central government, to local government and to public corporations. The specific listing requirements for straight bonds are as follows:

A. Listing requirements for industrial bonds:
  1. Qualifications of the company which plans the listing:
     (a) The amount of capital should be not less than ¥30,000 million.
     (b) The total par value of outstanding bonds should be not less than ¥7,000 million for all the bonds already issued.
     (c) The stock of the company should already be listed on the exchange.
  2. Qualifications of the issue to be listed:
     (a) The total par value of outstanding bonds should be not less than ¥1,000 million.
     (b) The total par value of the non-registered bonds should be not less than 10% of the total par value of outstanding bonds. The bonds concerned should have been widely purchased by individuals.
     (c) Time elapsed since the bond issue should be less than three years.
     (d) The form of the bond certificate to be listed should be compatible with that stipulated by TSE.

B. Listing requirements for other bonds: the listing of government bonds, local government bonds, government-guaranteed bonds, other special bonds, financial debentures, T & T subscriber's bonds and yen-denominated foreign bonds is determined specifically for the issues whose listing is regarded as necessary by TSE, according to the above-mentioned criteria for industrial bonds. As for the yen-denominated foreign bonds, the general conditions of the company which issued the bond is also examined.

Listing Requirements for Convertible Bonds
The listing of convertible bonds began in May 1970. As of the end of 1976, 277 issues of 205 companies were listed, with a total face value of ¥1,020 billion. The process of listing convertible bonds is the same as that for industrial bonds:

(*a*) application by the issuing company;
(*b*) examination based on the listing requirements;
(*c*) approval by the Finance Minister.

Like industrial bonds, the convertible bonds to be listed are limited to those issued by companies whose stocks have already been listed on the exchange.

More than one issue of a company's convertible bonds has generally been listed because the trading prices among these issues differ, since the terms of issue, especially the conversion prices, vary tremendously. The marketability also must be maintained because the subscribers are widely distributed among individual investors. Generally, convertible bonds are listed about two or three months after they are issued in order to ensure smooth circulation. Like industrial bonds, the listing examination for convertible bonds concentrates on the factors relevant to circulation. The specific listing requirements are as follows:

1. The company's qualifications: the company's stock should already have been listed on the exchange.
2. Qualifications of the issue to be listed:
   (*a*) The total par value of the issued bonds should be not less than ¥2,000 million.
   (*b*) The bonds concerned should have been widely purchased by individuals.
   (*c*) The form of the bond certificate to be listed should be compatible with that stipulated by TSE.

5.5 The Dealing System

5.5.1 TYPES OF TRANSACTION
Before the Second World War, transaction of securities in Japan centred on futures transactions. Cash deals played a minor role. After the war, however, futures were prohibited and dealing was limited to cash transactions on the basis of the three principles established upon the reopening of the stock exchanges mentioned at the beginning of this chapter. This change contributed greatly to healthy investment behaviour.

Transactions currently conducted on the stock exchanges are classified into the following four types:

(a) Cash delivery: The delivery is made on the day the transaction is contracted.

(b) Regular way: Delivery is made on the fourth day from the day when transaction is contracted excluding holidays. Most transactions are included in this type.

(c) Seller's option: The delivery is made on a prescribed day within 15 days from the day when transaction is contracted. In principle, this type of transaction can be utilized by clients who intend to sell securities and cannot make the fourth-day delivery since they live at a distance from the stock exchange.

(d) When issued: In the case of an allotment of new shares to stockholders, the transaction begins the day the registration takes effect (in the case of a free offering, the day the capital increase is approved at a meeting of the company's directors). The transactions are made from the day the new shares are issued to a day which the stock exchange designates. The delivery is made within 15 days from the day the transaction is contracted. This is a transaction of unissued stocks which requires a certain amount of margin.

In all types of transactions, the unit of trading for domestic stocks is 1,000 shares for an issue with par value of ¥50 and 100 shares for an issue with par value of ¥500. That for bonds is ¥100,000 of par value. For some issues specially designated by the stock exchange, the transaction can be made in 100 shares in addition to the 1,000-share unit. These special issues must conform to the following conditions:

(a) The average closing price for the last six months is not less than ¥3,000 and the closing price on the day before a designated day is also not less than ¥3,000.

(b) The issued stocks situation is considered to be appropriate for transaction in 100 shares and the 100-share unit transaction is expected to be made in substantial quantity.

The units of trading for foreign stocks are 10, 50, 100 or 1,000 shares, depending on the price. The session for stocks and convertible bonds is held from 9 a.m. to 11 a.m. (morning session) and from 1 p.m. to 3 p.m. (afternoon session). Only the morning session is held on Saturday. The session for bonds (excluding convertible bonds) is provisionally held from 9.30 a.m. to 11 a.m. However, in addition to the morning session, government bonds are traded from 2.30 p.m. to 3 p.m.

5.5.2 MARGIN TRANSACTION

In the cash market, there is a system of margin transaction designed to promote participation in the market by various investors and increase the marketability of stocks. Margin transaction in Japan began on 1 June 1951. on the model of the margin system in the United States. In this system securities firms extend credit to their clients for the issues listed in the First Section of the stock exchange. In this transaction on the stock exchange, delivery is made on the fourth day as a cash transaction. However, clients can trade without holding actual stock certificates or cash, by borrowing stocks (lending stocks or borrowed stocks) or cash from securities companies, after depositing a certain amount of margin at the securities companies.

The margin deposited at the securities companies is, in principle, not less than 30% of the contracted price of the stock traded in the margin transaction. The minimum margin is ¥150,000. Stock certificates and bond certificates can be used as substitutes for margin. The margin requirement changes according to supply and demand of stocks, and measures are taken to prevent the market from overheating.

In principle, the stock certificates sold or cash borrowed in a margin transaction are settled on the day after the date the borrowing occurred. However, the settlement can be postponed for up to six months unless the securities company demands payment. In this case, clients must pay a maintenance fee of ¥0·1 per share per month (minimum ¥100, maximum ¥1,000).

Margin transactions have recently represented about 30% of total transactions. To ensure smooth management and operation of credit and lending stocks by securities companies in margin transactions, three institutions in Japan have been established to handle exclusively the business of credit and lending stocks. They are Japan Securities Company, Osaka Securities Finance and Chubu Securities Financing.

5.6 Indices of the Tokyo Stock Exchange

5.6.1 NIKKEI DOW JONES AVERAGE

Representative of stock indicators on the Tokyo Stock Exchange are the Nikkei Dow Jones Average and the TSE Stock Price Index. The Dow Jones Average has been calculated continuously since the post-war reopening of TSE. The calculation was conducted initially by TSE itself, later by Nihon Shortwave Broadcasting (NSB), and then by Nihon Keizai Shimbun (commonly abbreviated to Nikkei). Accordingly, the name of the index was also changed from TSE Stock Price Average to NSB Dow Jones Average and then to the Nikkei Dow Jones Average.

This index covers 225 major issues listed in TSE's First Section. It is designed to indicate the long-term trend of stock prices by adjusting for a drop in stock prices seen at the time of allotment of new shares to stockholders, in other words, by adjusting ex-rights. In the adjustment, a constant divisor is used. The index is the total market value of the 225 selected issues (the prices of stocks without a ¥50 par value are adjusted on the basis of a ¥50 par value) divided by the constant divisor. When ex-rights occur in the covered issues, the constant divisor is revised and used until the next ex-rights occur.

The formula for obtaining the constant divisor is as follows:

$$\frac{\text{Total market price of 225 issues on the day before ex-rights } (A)}{\text{Current constant divisor (original: 225)}}$$

$$\frac{A - \text{Theoretical amount of stock price drop caused by ex-rights } (B)}{\text{New constant divisor}}$$

$$\text{New constant divisor} = \text{Present constant divisor (original: 225)} \times \frac{A-B}{A}$$

From the investor's point of view, the Dow Jones Average indicates the theoretical change in the assets of an investor who holds the same number of shares of all 225 issues. This index assumes an investor who, if ex-rights occur in an issue, purchases equally all the 225 issues, including the issue experiencing the ex-rights, multiplied by the theoretical amount that the stock price drops.

The importance of the Dow Jones Average is that the calculation is easy and investors have become very familiar with it because of its long history. However, it is not without its problems. The index is affected to a great extent by the movement of high-priced stocks whose prices generally fluctuate widely. Recent figures differ greatly from the actual level of stock prices, since the calculations were begun when the Tokyo Stock Exchange reopened.

5.6.2 TSE STOCK PRICE INDEX

TSE Stock Price Index was established in order to solve the abovementioned problems concerning Nikkei Dow Jones Average. This index is calculated and released by TSE. It is based on the total market value of all the listed issues in the First Section. In order to maintain the continuity of the index, the base market value is revised in accordance with new listing, delisting, ex-rights by capital increase, transfer from the Second Section to the First Section, public offering, allotment of new shares to a third party and conversion of convertible bonds into stocks.

$$\frac{\text{Total market value on the day before revision } (A)}{\text{Base market value on the day before revision } (B)}$$

$$= \frac{A \pm \text{Amount revised}}{\text{New base market value}}$$

$$\text{New base market value} = B \times \frac{A \pm \text{Amount revised}}{A}$$

(*Note* In cases of ex-rights, the total value paid-in is added. In cases of new listing or delisting, the total market value of the issue concerned is added or deducted.)

TSE Stock Price Index was set at 100 for 4 January 1968 but has been computed retrospectively to the post-war reopening of TSE. In addition, there are such subclassifications as the stock price indices by size of capital (large-capital stock, medium-capital stock and small-capital stock), stock price indices by industrial category for the First Section, and the stock price index covering 300 issues listed in the Second Section.

5.7 The Over-the-counter Market

In the over-the-counter market, a wide range of securities, both listed and unlisted, are traded. However, a securities company which is a member of the stock exchange must always trade the orders received for listed stocks within the stock exchange, with some exceptions. Accordingly, the over-the-counter market is not very active as a market for stock trading. However, since bond transaction outside the exchange is widely permitted, the over-the-counter market plays a very important role in circulation.

The Securities Dealers Association of Japan (SDAJ) has taken measures to streamline over-the-counter trading. For unlisted stocks, the issues which securities companies handle are limited to those registered according to the criteria stipulated by SDAJ and the TSE delisted over-the-counter issues. This is necessary to protect investors, since there is a large number of unlisted issues.

The basic requirement for bond trading is that the price formation in the market be correctly and clearly disclosed to investors and securities companies. This serves to bring about effective competition among securities companies as well as fair and smooth over-the-counter trading of issues. To accomplish this, SDAJ has taken the following measures.

(*a*) On Monday, Wednesday and Friday, SDAJ publishes daily over-the-counter quotations of certain indicative stocks based on reports from securities firms.

(*b*) Based on reports from securities firms every Thursday, SDAJ also publishes over-the-counter quotations of issues which are not included in (*a*) but can be regarded as standard issues for trading. They are classified by type, yield and maturity, and are chiefly used as references for individual investors.

(*c*) The trading of less than ¥10 million must be made within a certain range of the median price quotations mentioned in (*b*).

5.8 Commission Rates

TABLE 57 *Current stock exchange commission rates*

Stocks

1. Regular Rates – a percentage of the contracted transaction price (purchase or sale):
   (a) transaction price up to ¥1 m.   1·25%
   (b) transaction price over ¥1 m., less than ¥3 m.   1·05%
   (c) transaction price over ¥3 m., less than ¥5 m.   0·95%
   (d) transaction price over ¥5 m., less than ¥10 m.   0·85%
   (e) transaction price over ¥10 m., less than ¥30 m.   0·75%
   (f) transaction price over ¥30 m., less than ¥50 m.   0·65%
   (g) transaction price over ¥50 m., less than ¥100 m.   0·60%
   (h) transaction price of more than ¥100 m.   0·55%
   (Fractions less than ¥1 are disregarded. The same principle is applied to other cases.)
   (*Note* The rate for a contracted price of less than ¥200,000 is ¥2,500.)

2. When securities companies affiliated with the Securities Dealers Association of Japan or foreign securities companies (i.e. the branches established in Japan by foreign securities companies under Article 3 of the Law concerning Foreign Securities Companies) entrust the transaction, the rate is:
   (a) 50% of the regular rate in cases of entrustment by securities companies which were licensed before 31 October 1971.
   (b) 60% of the regular rate in cases of entrustment by securities companies which were licensed after 1 November 1971.

3. When banks handling trust affairs, in accordance with written orders from clients, entrust the transaction, the rate is 80% of the regular rate.

4. When foreign securities companies and banks entrust the transaction, the rate is 80% of the regular rate.

5. When foreign securities companies in which member companies have made capital participation entrust the transaction to the member companies concerned, the rate is set according to the ratio of the equity capital (the percentage of member companies' holdings of outstanding shares in foreign securities companies).
   (a) The rate is not less than 30% of the regular rate when the ratio is 100%.
   (b) The rate is not less than 40% of the regular rate when the ratio is less than 100% and more than 50%.

Bonds (per ¥100 par value)

	less than ¥5 m.	from ¥5 m. to ¥10 m.	from ¥10 m. to ¥100 m.	more than ¥100 m.
	¥	¥	¥	¥
Govt bonds	0·40	0·35	0·30	0·25
Govt-guaranteed bonds, local govt bonds, foreign govt bonds	0·60	0·50	0·40	0·30
Other bonds	0·80	0·65	0·50	0·35

Convertible bonds

Total par value	
less than ¥1 m.	1·2% of contracted price
from ¥1 m. to ¥5 m.	1·0%
from ¥5 m. to ¥10 m.	0·8%
from ¥10 m. to ¥30 m.	0·7%
more than ¥30 m.	0·6%

When a client entrusts the transaction of listed securities to a member company of the stock exchange and the transaction is actually made, the client must pay a brokerage commission stipulated by the stock exchange to the member company. The commission rate must be set at an appropriate and reasonable level, taking into account various expenses involved in the transaction. The stock exchange must obtain approval from the Finance Minister in stipulating the rate.

The member company is strictly prohibited from discounting or giving a rebate on the commission rate for any reason. The stock exchange intends to encourage sound management of its member companies by preventing excessive competition caused by discounting the commission rate. Such measures consequently protect investors, by ensuring appropriate and fair service.

5.9 Securities Companies

Securities companies are joint-stock companies, licensed by the Finance Minister under the Securities Exchange Law, with sole authorization to conduct securities business. Before the Second World War, financial institutions also conducted securities business, usually by providing underwriting services for securities, while the sales were made chiefly by securities companies. After the war, financial institutions, including banks and trust companies, were prohibited under Article 65 of the Securities Exchange Law to conduct securities business. The functional division between securities companies and financial institutions was ensured by separating the trading and underwriting services from financial institutions. As a result, securities companies came to occupy the central role in the issue and trading markets of securities.

The registration system was adopted for securities business after promulgation of the Securities Exchange Law in 1948. In view of the important function of securities companies, various controls were instituted. Qualifications and business behaviour were regulated through various laws and regulations in order to protect the public interest. Later, through an amendment of the Securities Exchange Law in May 1965, the licence system was adopted on 1 October 1965. The securities companies which had already been registered were permitted to conduct their business without a licence until 31 March 1968. Therefore, the licensing system came into full effect on 1 April 1968. This system was adopted in order to strengthen the management base of the securities companies, enhance their social status, and bring about better protection of investors. This was necessary because the securities business plays a prominent role in the national economy and society.

The licences issued by the Finance Minister are divided into the following four types:

(*a*) sale and purchase of securities;
(*b*) sale and purchase of securities as an intermediary, broke or agent, and commissioning of the sale and purchase orders to be executed on a securities exchange as an intermediary, broker or agent;
(*c*) underwriting and secondary distribution of securities;
(*d*) arrangement for public offering or secondary distribution of securities.

In granting the licence, the Finance Minister is required to examine whether the following standards are met:

(*a*) the applicant has sufficient financial status to carry out its proposed business, and the prospects for profits are satisfactory;
(*b*) the applicant, through its personnel, has sufficient knowledge and experience to carry out its business fairly and adequately and is of good social standing;
(*c*) the proposed securities business is necessary and appropriate according to the existing number of securities transactions, the number of securities companies and their offices, and other economic circumstances in the district where the applicant proposes to carry out its business.

A securities company can be granted more than one of the abovementioned four types of licence simultaneously. Medium-sized and large securities companies are granted all four types of licence.

Securities companies are classified by amount of stated capital. The minimum amount of stated capital is prescribed for each category of securities company, according to the type of licence, the characteristics of business, location of offices and membership.

In recent years progress in the internationalization of the securities market has led to a sharply increasing number of Japanese securities companies expanding their business operations abroad. They play an important role in long-term fund raising for Japanese corporations and for foreign investments in Japanese securities. Meanwhile, there has been a growing trend for foreign securities firms to extend their business to Japan. To cope with this trend, the Law concerning Foreign Securities Companies was established and promulgated in March 1971.

Under this law, each branch in Japan of a foreign securities company has to be licensed by the Finance Minister. The licensed branch is permitted

TABLE 58 *Classification of securities companies*

1. Main underwriter	
(a) Acting as syndicate manager and concurrently engaged in business other than underwriting	¥3 billion
(b) Specializing in underwriting and may act as syndicate manager	¥1 billion
(c) Will not become syndicate manager	¥200 million
2. Regular exchange member company	
(a) Regular member of the Tokyo or Osaka Stock Exchange	¥100 million
(b) Regular member of the Nagoya Stock Exchange	¥50 million
(c) Regular member of any other Stock Exchange	¥30 million
3. Non-member company	
(a) Located in Tokyo or Osaka	¥30 million
(b) Others	¥20 million
4. Company dealing solely with other securities companies (*Saitori*)	
(a) Located in Tokyo or Osaka	¥4 million
(b) Others	¥1 million

to conduct only the securities business prescribed for it. Types of licence, examination criteria and conditions for revocation of licence for foreign securities companies are generally the same as those for the domestic companies. Since foreign securities companies are based in foreign countries, those licensed are obliged to deposit a certain amount of guaranty for each of their branches prior to beginning business in Japan. This measure is taken to protect Japanese investors.

However, taking into consideration business practices in various foreign countries, the foreign securities firms which are not licensed by the Finance Minister can participate in limited activities. With approval of the Finance Minister, they may participate in main underwriting contracts, sign contracts in Japan and then conduct the sales abroad. In addition, foreign business corporations are permitted to conduct securities business by establishing subsidiaries in Japan. These subsidiaries, like Japanese securities firms, must be granted a licence under the Securities Exchange Law. At the end of September 1976 there were 258 securities companies in Japan. In addition, Merrill Lynch and Loeb Rhoades, both of the United States, have set up their respective Tokyo branches.

The "big four" securities companies (Nomura, Nikko, Yamaichi and Daiwa) have an overwhelming share of the Japanese market. The four companies accounted for 18·8% of the total number of offices at the end of September 1976. For the business year ending September 1976, the Big Four represented 45·3% of the total stock transactions in terms of value, 53·6% of the total commissions received and as much as 75·4% of the total after-tax profits. Among the four, Nomura's status is outstanding.

The salesmen of the securities company are required to be registered with the Ministry of Finance under the Securities Exchange Law. They must also qualify as registered representatives as stipulated by the Securities Dealers Association of Japan. In Japan, house-to-house sales activities are permitted and consequently securities salesmen are energetic pursuing new business in this way.

TABLE 59 *Status of major securities firms (September 1976 term)*

| | Commission received | | After-tax profits | |
	¥m.	%	¥m.	%
All securities firms	575,979	(100)	73,228	(100)
"Big four" (total)	308,997	(53·6)	55,244	(75·4)
Nomura	111,405	(19·3)	24,580	(33·6)
Nikko	80,390	(14·0)	17,155	(23·4)
Yamaichi	58,062	(10·1)	5,905	(8·1)
Daiwa	59,141	(10·2)	7,603	(10·4)

5.10 Unit Trusts

5.10.1 BRIEF HISTORY

It is generally said that the first investment trust in Japan was the securities investment union established in July 1937, by Fujimoto Bill Broker Co. This was modelled upon the kind of unit trust which had grown up rapidly at that time in Britain. It was designed to "make investment in a wide range of securities with the funds which are collected through investment of a certain amount of money by many small investors, and thus realize a profitable and secure increase in their assets". However, the management of this securities investment union was suspended in the autumn of 1940 after it was criticized because of its similarity to the joint management trust proscribed in the Trust Law. Later, active management became impossible.

In those days measures were needed to cope with the decline in stock prices caused by public uncertainties. The worsening international situation in wartime, the increase in government control over the economy and the deteriorating performance of private enterprises caused public concern. In addition, the free activities of the securities market were increasingly restricted as the control of fund management was gradually strengthened by the Temporary Fund Adjustment Law and the National Mobilization Law. Accordingly, the inauguration of the investment trust was demanded as a means to expand the business field of securities firms. Under the circumstances, a contractual type of investment trust was launched, in which trust certificates were sold to the general public with a securities firm as manager company and a trust company as trustee company. In November 1941, an investment trust with Nomura Trust as trustee company was established. Then, in November 1942, another investment trust with the five securities firms of Yamaichi,

Koike, Kawashimaya, Kyodo and Fujimoto as manager companies and Nippon Investment Trust as trustee company was started.

Investment trusts on offer until the end of the Second World War were valued at ¥528·5 million. This represented about 30% of the total increase in time deposits at commercial banks (¥1,787 million) during the corresponding period. The offering was suspended at the end of the war and redemption was difficult due to the economic confusion. However, redemption was completed later, due to the upsurge in stock prices in 1948.

The investment trusts established during the war differed from the present investment trusts in the following points:

(a) There was no single basic law governing the investment trust.
(b) There was no regulation concerning partial redemption.
(c) The issuer of the trust certificate was the trustee company.
(d) The name of the holder was printed on the trust certificate.
(e) There were regulations concerning compensation by the manager company for the beneficiary's losses and participation by the manager company in the beneficiary's profits.
(f) The restrictions on management were considerable.

After the war, investment trusts were restored in 1951. At this time the supply of stocks increased as a result of the dissolution of the big financial groups (zaibatsu), the release of stocks held by closed institutions and a series of large capital increases made under the Enterprise Reconstruction Law. In addition, the supply–demand balance of stocks deteriorated as the financial power of large pre-war stockholders was weakened because of the agricultural land reform, increased property tax and serious inflation. The drastic change in the distribution of income, caused by various post-war reforms, led to a decline in the purchasing of stocks. The only effective means to normalize such a weakened supply–demand balance was to introduce the general public's funds into the capital market. These came to play a major new role in capital accumulation. It is interesting that the investment trust was reinstated after the war as a means of stimulating stock prices in the light of the circumstances of their inauguration during the war. The post-war investment trust has been governed by the Securities Investment Trust Law promulgated on 4 June 1951. It has been strengthened substantially compared with the pre-war investment trust.

5.10.2 TYPES OF INVESTMENT

In the Securities Investment Trust Law, a securities investment trust is defined as "a trust for the purpose of operating the trust fund as an investment in specified securities under the direction of a manager company, for the purpose of having unspecified persons acquire fractions of its beneficiary rights and for the purpose of its trustee company acquiring its beneficiary right".

Investment trusts are divided into the company type, organized as a company, and the contractual type, based on the trust system. The definition in the Securities Investment Trust Law, above, indicates clearly that investment trusts in Japan are of the contractual type; nevertheless, their contents are highly varied. They can be subdivided into the open-end type and the closed-end type. The closed-end type has a fixed amount of capital and subscribers cannot ask the issuer to repurchase certificates. Accordingly, the trust period is relatively short – around three years. Meanwhile, the trust period of the open-end type is relatively long – 5, 7, 10, 15 years or for an indefinite period. However, when the outstanding units of an open-end type decrease to less than a fixed percentage of the initially established number of units, it is generally redeemed.

The open-end type is further divided into the additional and the unit type, according to the availability of additional trusts. Once the unit type is established, no additional trusts are offered. Therefore, its initial principal will never increase and is more likely to decrease. With the additional type, offering of additional trusts is possible, depending on the individual case. The outstanding principal is often higher than the initial principal.

As has been stated already, the investment trusts established in Japan are of the contractual type only. The concerned parties are the manager company, the trustee company and the beneficiary. The relationship among the three parties is independent of the general trust system, and their function and scope are prescribed in the Securities Investment Trust Law. In the contractual-type investment trust, the trust contract must first be concluded. A trust contract provides that one party, although having its own rights, is restricted in exercising the right for another party. This right belongs to the trustee company and is established by the manager company. The party who obtains profits from the restriction on the right is the beneficiary.

The manager company, which issues directions concerning the operation of the trust funds, must be a stock company with stated capital of not less than ¥50 million and licensed by the Finance Minister. The Minister is required to ensure that the following standards are met:

(a) the applicant is fully qualified in regard to staff and investment ability;
(b) the applicant has favourable financial prospects in the investment trust business;
(c) the proposed business is necessary and appropriate in the light of the situation of the investment trust and securities market.

At present, nine investment trust management companies have been licensed as manager companies. The Trustee Company plays the role of administering trust funds and must be a trust bank or a trust company.

The beneficiary has the right to receive profits from trust funds (beneficiary rights). Beneficiary rights consist chiefly of receipt of a share of the gains from trust funds, receipt of redemption and request for repurchasing the beneficiary rights. The beneficiary rights are divided equally into a large number of units which are described on the trust certificate.

Securities firms and investment trust sales companies, though they are not legally concerned parties, carry on such business as the offering or trading of trust certificates, payment of the distributed gains and the redemption. At present, there are four investment trust sales companies, whose main business is offering and trading trust certificates.

5.10.3 FOREIGN INVESTMENT TRUSTS

As the overall internationalization of the Japanese securities market progressed and the OECD established standard rules for the management of investment trusts, the Ministerial Ordinance concerning Registration for Public Offering of New or Outstanding Foreign Investment Trust Certificates was promulgated in November 1972. It created the domestic system necessary for the sale of foreign investment trusts. Accordingly, the Board of Directors of the Securities Dealers Association of Japan worked out a series of resolutions. As a result, it became possible, on 1 December 1972, for general Japanese investors to invest freely in foreign investment trusts through domestic securities companies.

When a foreign security is offered publicly in Japan, the issuer of the security must submit a registration statement under the provisions of the Securities Exchange Law. However, in view of the special nature of foreign investment trust certificates referred to in the Ministerial Ordinance, it was necessary to treat them under a different formula. The following requirements were laid down:

(a) the funds must be established for the purpose of investing funds received from a large number of unspecified persons in securities;
(b) the issuer must repurchase the trust certificates, directly or indirectly, upon demand by the holders.

The Ordinance prescribes, for the registration statement of the trust certificate, that a prospectus be filed prior to public offering of the proposed foreign investment trust certificate and that periodic securities reports for continuous disclosure of information follow the public offering. Foreign investment trust certificates which do not meet those requirements are given the same treatment as the liberalized foreign stocks.

5.11 Rules Governing Foreign Investment

Restrictions on investments in Japanese securities by non-residents have been gradually eased since the 1950s. At present, these investments are liberalized in principle, but the following restrictions still apply. When non-residents acquire Japanese stocks through the market, the total foreign acquisition is limited to less than 25% of the total shares outstanding of a

TABLE 60 *Taxes applicable to acquired securities*

Category	1	2	3	4	5	6
	Non-residents without permanent facilities in Japan	Foreign corporations without permanent facilities in Japan	Non-residents with permanent facilities in Japan	Foreign corporations with permanent facilities in Japan	Foreign tax-free corporations	Foreign countries or their agents
Dividend	1. Split taxation 2. Taxation at the source (generally 15%) by the report (form 1) by countries concluding tax agreement 3. Taxation at the source (20%) for other than stipulated in 2	1. Split taxation 2. Taxation at the source (generally 10%) for the report (form 2) by countries concluding tax agreement 3. Taxation at the source (20%) for other than 2	1. Split taxation 2. Taxation at the source (15%) for the report by "certificate for abatement" 3. Taxation at the source (20%) for others than stipulated in 2		1. Split taxation in principle 2. Tax free for cases designated by Finance Minister 3. Same as 2 and 3 of categories (3) and (4) for other cases than 2	1. Split taxation in principle 2. Tax free (exceptional treatment) for sovereign tax exemption 3. Same as 2 and 3 of (4) and (5) for other cases than 2
Division of interests and earnings Investment trusts; interest-bearing bonds	1. Split taxation 2. Taxation at the source (generally 10%) for the report (form 2) by countries concluding tax agreement 3. Taxation at the source (20%) for other than 2				1. Split taxation in principle 2. Tax free for cases designated by Finance Minister 3. Taxation at the source (generally 10%) at "eight rates" for the report (form 2) for countries concluding tax agreement 4. Taxation at the source (20%) for cases other than 3	1. Split taxation in principle 2. Tax free for cases of sovereign tax exemption 3. Taxation at the source (generally 10%) for the report (form 2) for countries concluding tax agreement 4. Taxation at the source (20%) for cases other than 3

Category 1	2	3	4	5	6
Discount bonds: redemption gain					
1. Countries concluding tax agreement		1. Split taxation in principle	1. Tax in principle		Application for refund
(1) Tax free for the report (form 10) – when interest articles include no mention of redemption gain but some other articles		2. Taxation at the source: 10% (12% from Jan 1976 to Dec 1980)	2. Taxation at the source: 10% (12% from Jan 1976 to Dec 1980) Exemption		
(2) Same treatment as interest – when interest articles mention redemption gain and other articles					
(3) Same as residents – when interest articles include no mention of redemption gain and no other articles					
2. Countries having no tax agreement same as residents					
Securities					
Transfer gain	Tax free in principle	1. Tax free in principle	Tax in principle	Tax free in principle	
		2. Tax for continued transactions			

Note Tax at the source is not levied on interests regarding foreign bonds in yen currency possessed by non-residents.

Japanese corporation and not more than 15% for 17 specific industrial categories, including banks and railways. The acquisition is limited to 10% per individual investor. Non-residents can acquire more shares than the regulations prescribe, if the Japanese corporation concerned agrees to it. Table 60 shows the taxes applicable to acquired Japanese securities.

5.12 The Japanese Accounting System

The accounting system practised by Japanese business corporations has the following features:

5.12.1 FISCAL TERM

A six-month accounting system has been long practised in Japan, but today most companies have annual accounting periods, with nearly half of them ending in March. However, they are required to file a six-month interim report. Banks, electric power companies and some others still use the six-month accounting system, and almost all of the fiscal terms end in March and September. Only a few companies, which are listed on the New York Stock Exchanges (*e.g.*, Sony), report earnings on a quarterly basis.

5.12.2 STATEMENTS OF ACCOUNTS

Three major reports on operating results are issued by listed companies:

(*a*) the shareholders' report, based on the commercial code and intended for shareholders;

(*b*) the securities report (*yukashoken hokokusho*), required by the Securities Exchange Law to be filed with the Ministry of Finance (many points of difference from the shareholders' report were eliminated by the revised law of 1974);

(*c*) the corporation tax return prepared, in principle, on the basis of the shareholders' and securities reports. Corporation tax, enterprise tax and real estate tax are levied on the basis of this return. These taxes amount to about a half of pre-tax profits.

5.12.3 AUDITING

In the past, only the securities report was certified by an independent Certified Public Accountant (CPA). However, the revised law of 1974 stipulates that the CPA certify the shareholders' report as well.

5.12.4 CONSOLIDATION

Consolidated financial statements will be officially employed with the term ending in March 1978. About 90 companies issued consolidated statements in 1976, with one-half of them required to do so because of listing on overseas stock markets or the issuing of foreign currency bonds. Many Japanese companies have a number of subsidiaries, most of which do not disclose figures about their operating results to outsiders. Therefore, it was possible to some extent in the past to adjust profits by "managing" transactions among those subsidiaries.

5.12.5 OTHER FEATURES

Reserves

Accounting treatment of reserves differed greatly among companies, partly because of ambiguity in the law. It was possible to adjust reported profits for the period by accumulating or withdrawing reserves and in the long run minimize fluctuations in after-tax profits. However, the revised law of 1974 set more severe standards for accumulation, making it difficult to manage reserves as a means of retaining earnings. Employees' retirement allowances are also unique, in that they are not usually reserved and managed externally but often become an internal source of funds.

Bonuses to Directors

It is customary not to include bonuses to directors in deductible expenses but pay them out of after-tax profits.

Instalment Sales

Instalment sales are booked when the transaction is made, but profits on them are usually recognized only when all proceeds are collected.

5.12.6 COMMENTS

Intentional adjustment of reported profits was possible in the past. However, with the revised law of 1974, the standards for reporting accounts are more unified and stricter. The employment of the consolidated accounting system beginning with fiscal year 1977 will help show a more realistic performance of Japanese companies.

6 REFORMING THE JAPANESE ECONOMY

6.1 Adaptation to Changes in the International Environment

The history of the Japanese economy since 1868 has been characterized by adaptation to the changing international environment. The nation's economy has experienced structural renovation in response to drastic changes approximately every 50 years. 1970 marked the second upheaval since the nation's industrial revolution late in the nineteenth century. Future prospects depend on international economic changes and the Japanese adaptations to them.

Predictions of world economic changes are based on the past development of the world economy. Since the beginning of industrial revolution in the mid-eighteenth century, the international economic system has gone through three upheavals – in the 1810s, in the 1870s and in the 1920s. These upheavals fell in transition periods, as shown in Figure 9. During each of these periods, the world economy experienced raging inflation and economic disorder due to an imbalance between supply and demand. Explosive population growth and the entry of newly-emerged countries into the world economic activity caused the formation of a new international economic order.

A fourth change in the world economy is now occurring. Since 1970, a number of developing nations in Latin America, South-East Asia and the Middle East have entered into the advanced nations' economic sphere. A worldwide supply–demand gap has caused large-scale inflation and has given rise to world economic disorder. A review of the history of modern industrial civilization during the last 200 years illustrates that the future of the international economy depends on when and how an enlarged international economic sphere may be determined. Adjustment of the imbalance among industrially advanced nations, financial aid to non-oil developing countries and large-scale technological innovation in the use of energy and resources seem to be indispensable to surmount the present confusion and to create a fifth stage of prosperity.

178

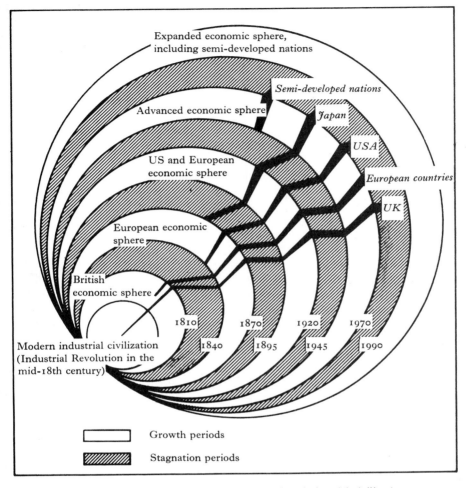

Fig. 9   The development of the world's modern industrial civilization

To adapt itself to such dramatic changes in the international economic situation and to redevelop a dynamic economy of its own, Japan is now undergoing an economic reformation.

6.2 Economic Reformation Using Market Mechanisms

Japan's economic reformation aims to improve efficiency by means of market mechanisms. The economic reformation will be carried out by means of:

(*a*) improved efficiency in the capital and money markets through liberalization of interest rates;

(*b*) increased sophistication of the industrial structure by the effective use of exchange policy;

(*c*) development of economic efficiency through revision of the Act

Concerning the Prohibition of Private Monopoly and Maintenance of Fair Trade (which is generally called the "Anti-Monopoly Act").

6.2.1 LIBERALIZATION OF INTEREST RATES

The post-war Japanese economy has gone through structural changes at intervals of approximately ten years. The post-war rehabilitation and reconstruction of industrial foundations continued until 1954. Increasing sophistication of the industrial structure, and expansion of heavy industries, including the chemical industry, was pushed forward along with trade liberalization during the next decade. During the ten years following accession to GATT in 1955, Japan liberalized its trading patterns and simultaneously expanded its heavy industries.

During the decade from 1965 to 1974, Japan stressed liberalization of capital transactions, strengthening the competitiveness of Japanese corporations.

TABLE 61 *Japan's trade liberalization*

1955	Access to GATT (the beginning of trade liberalization).
1960	Outline of the programme for the liberalization of trade and exchange at a special Cabinet meeting.
1962	The government's changing of its import control announcement method from a positive form to a negative one (*i.e.*, the government stepped up liberalization and publicly announced unliberalized items only).
	Import liberalization included industrial products as well as raw materials and intermediate goods.
	Contribution of import liberalization of raw materials and intermediate goods to corporate rationalization.
1963	Japan recommended to assume an Article VIII status in the IMF.
1964	Japan's assumption of the Article VIII status in the IMF, joining an "open economy" system.
	Japan's admission to the OECD.

Japan is trying to strengthen its economy during the decade from 1975 to 1984, so that it will be able to adapt itself to any drastic changes in the international and domestic economic environments. Liberalization of interest rates and increased efficiency of the capital and money markets will be based on the achievement of the structural reform made during the previous decade. In April 1976, the Committee on Financial System Research, an advisory body to the Finance Minister, proposed more flexible interest rates in its interim report on the role of banks. It has become widely acknowledged that liberalization of interest rates should be put into practice as soon as possible to increase the efficiency of the financial system through market mechanisms.

The Securities and Exchange Council, another advisory body to the Finance Minister, is contemplating reforming the nation's bond market to allow market forces full play, to increase the efficiency of the capital and money markets.

Although difficult to predict exactly, the liberalization process of interest rates will develop steadily with continued floatation of a large number of government and municipal bonds. Internationalization of the capital and money markets will also further this process.

TABLE 62 *Japan's liberalization of capital transactions*

1966	A general plan for liberalizing capital transactions by the Federation of Economic Organizations.
1967	Japan urged by OECD to study the possibility of lifting curbs on its member countries' direct investments in each business sector, as well as simplifying investment procedures.
	The Foreign Investment Council, an advisory organ to the Finance Minister, strengthened by the Ministry of Finance in preparation for liberalization of capital transaction. The Council was consulted about procedures for liberalization centred on direct investment by foreign corporations.
	The problems involved in liberalization of capital transactions studied by the Federation of Economic Organizations' special committee.
	The Federation of Economic Organizations formed subcommittees to study possible effects of liberalization of capital transactions on industrial policy, technology, commodities distribution and securities transactions and finance.
	A programme for liberalization of capital transactions decided by the specially formed Ministerial Council.
	Capital transactions in 50 business sectors liberalized in response to the recommendation of the Foreign Investment Council.
1968	A consensus formed by securities business circles on liberalization of capital transactions.
1969	Lifting of curbs on capital transactions for 55 business sectors (the second-round liberalization of capital transactions).
1970	Lifting of curbs on capital transactions for 323 business sectors (the third-round liberalization of capital transactions).
1971	Complete liberalization of capital transactions with the exception of seven business sectors in response to the recommendation of the Foreign Investment Council.
1972	Various measures announced by the Ministry of Finance for expanding Japanese investment in foreign securities as well as for promoting internationalization of the Japanese capital market.
1973	Liberalization of capital transactions decided in principle.

During the latter part of the 1970s, the liberalization of interest rates will be increased, principally in the bond market. Conditions necessary for liberalization include floatation of large amounts of government bonds, accumulation of corporate surplus funds, increased foreign investments, curbs on large loans, and raising the limits on bond floatation. During the first half of the 1980s, liberalization of interest rates will be accomplished, using market mechanisms along with enlargement of the money market and internationalization of the yen, and a reform of the capital and money markets.

6.2.2 REFORM OF INDUSTRIAL STRUCTURE THROUGH EXCHANGE POLICY

Japan's industrial structure has become more sophisticated and efficient during the past two decades, through progressive liberalization of trade and capital transactions. However, since 1970, restructuring of Japanese industry has been urgently needed, because of dramatic changes in the international economic climate. Increasing cooperation with both advanced and developing nations in international trade has also become necessary. Scrapping of surplus production facilities and encouragement of manufacturers' mergers or changes in trade are now being considered to relieve ailing industries. The industries faced with prolonged structural slumps are steelmaking with open-hearth and electric furnaces, aluminium smelting, chemical fertilizers, machine tools, textiles, corrugated cardboard and polyvinyl chloride.

At the same time, internationally competitive industries are required to become less aggressive in trade with advanced nations. Japanese industries will be gradually restructured from their present all-embracing framework to more narrow and selective ones aimed at international cooperation. This will be accomplished by an effective use of exchange policy – that is to say, by leaving the rate of exchange to market forces.

6.2.3 REVISION OF THE ANTI-MONOPOLY ACT

An amendment of the Anti-Monopoly Act was enacted on 27 June 1977 to take effect from December of that year. The major revisions were divestiture

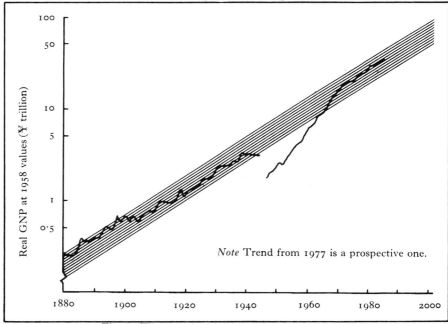

Fig. 10 The growth trend of the Japanese economy

of monopolistic corporations, measures against collusion on price increases, penalties on corporations forming illegal cartels, curbs on excessive equity holdings by monetary institutions and big businesses, as well as improvement of the Fair Trade Commission's investigation and hearing procedure. The amendment of the Anti-Monopoly Act, which was drawn up after two-and-a-half years of heated discussion, will chart the future course of the Japanese economy. It will operate as a kind of constitution of the free economy, influencing the nation's future economic activity. It is notable that the Japanese people by consensus chose to reinforce the capitalist economy through the free functioning of market mechanisms, in the face of probable restrictions to be imposed on market forces.

To sum up, the reformation of the Japanese economy will be based on improved efficiency of the capital and money markets, reform of the industrial structure by an effective exchange policy and increased economic efficiency through revision of the Anti-Monopoly Act. Japan's economic reform seeks full use of market mechanisms which will contribute to the stabilization as well as the revitalization of the Japanese economy in an unstable world economic environment.

6.3 The Medium-term Outlook for the Japanese Economy

6.3.1 5% GROWTH

A review of the Japanese economy on a basis of real GNP shows a 5% growth trend in the pre-war years and 10% growth in the post-war age. The 10% growth pattern for 25 years after the Second World War was attributable to an abundant supply of low-priced resources, stable international trade and monetary systems, and revolution of labour productivity by a rapid shift to heavy and chemical industries. Rapid expansion of latent consumer demand with increasing income and the relatively light fiscal burden on the Japanese people also contributed to the high growth from Japan's post-war economic position.

Around 1970, these favourable post-war conditions began to change. Due to dramatic changes in the international economic climate, the Japanese economy was forced to slow down, and its average growth rate from 1971 to 1976 came down to 5·6%, similar to its pre-war growth.

Average annual growth rate of the Japanese economy on a basis of real GNP for the next ten years is likely to remain at 5%. The present supply and demand position of energy and other resources, international trade and monetary relations and the North–South relationship are international constraints on growth. Domestic conditions in the social and economic fields and the actual growth potential of the Japanese economy will also restrain the level of growth.

6.3.2 INFLATION

In the wake of the oil crisis, 1973 consumer and wholesale price indices shot up to 127·4 and 156·8 respectively, based on 1970 as 100. However, prices showed signs of levelling off thereafter, owing to the completion of the round of increases in prices of finished goods as a result of increased resource prices. Progress in energy and resources saving, appreciation of the yen, stepping up of labour–management reconciliation in wage bargaining and monetary policies have also slowed inflation. Even during the business upturn from 1975 to 1977, both consumer and wholesale prices remained stable (*see* Figure 3, p. 37).

Although future price trends (for instance, resource price trends) depend largely on the development of the international economy, the average GNP deflater for the decade from 1976 to 1985 is expected to be 4%. This is similar to that for the decade prior to the oil crisis (1963–72), which was 4·9%.

6.3.3 THE TREND IN INTEREST RATES

As inflation subsides, interest rates will decline, after staying at an abnormally high level between 1973–75.

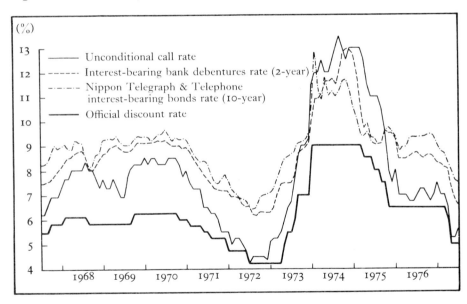

Fig. 11 Changes in interest rates

From March to April 1977, the second round reducing the official discount rate was made after a previous lowering between April and October 1975. There were only two precedents for such a two-stage rate cut within an interval of more than one year in the history of bank rate policy in Japan. These occurred in the period 1925–30 and in 1932–36. These periods were similar, in that normalization of extraordinarily high interest rates caused by worldwide inflation in 1920 was occurring. The present situation can be considered a process of adjustment of abnormally high interest rates caused by worldwide inflation after the oil crisis.

At present, Japan has a low official discount rate, second only to that of West Germany. Interest rates in Japan are expected to decline in the foreseeable future with the slowing inflation, although they will fluctuate slightly with the business cycle.

6.4 The Rapid Growth of the Capital Market

Among foreseeable changes in the economic environment, special attention should be paid to the prospective rapid growth of the capital market, especially from such viewpoints as corporate finance, public bond floatation, individual and institutional investors.

6.4.1 CHANGES IN THE NATURE OF CORPORATE FINANCE

The structural change of the Japanese economy is affecting corporate finance. Corporate demand is likely to slacken because of sluggish capital spending, adjustment of inventory investment, and shrinkage of inter-company credit. On the other hand, corporate capacity for self-financing is expected to increase considerably with the accumulation of corporate profits. According to the Ministry of Finance's survey of 170,000 corporations in various industries, the ratio of self-financing to total corporate demand is expected to rise from 39% in 1975 to 56% in 1980 and to 83% in 1985. In particular, the ratio of cash flow to capital outlay is expected to rise from 62% in 1975 to 84% in 1980 and to reach 120% in 1985. When the ratio tops 100%, the nature of corporate financing will have completely changed, and corporate behaviour in the financial market will also have changed. This tendency to decrease the financial burden started with the repayment of debts by some of the more successful businesses in 1976. It is expected to develop gradually over the years ahead and to be in full swing in the 1980s.

Along with expansion of corporate self-financing capacity, there will be more stress on floatation of bonds to meet an increasing need to shift to long-term financing. The ratio of funds raised by bond floatation to the total amount of those raised from the outside is likely to rise from 5% for 1971–75 to 14% for 1976–80. The ratio for 1981–85 is expected to top the 20% level.

There is, therefore, a growing tendency among corporations to increase their self-financing capacity, to step up repayment of their debts and to invest surplus funds in securities. The total of the nation's corporate working capital, which amounted to approximately $94 billion at the end of 1976, is expected to exceed $200 billion in 1985. This increase in corporate working capital seems certain to promote corporate investment in securities.

6.4.2 LARGE-SCALE FLOATATION OF PUBLIC BONDS

It is expected that large-scale floatation of public bonds will continue as the Japanese economy shifts to a government-led one. In Japan, the ratio of the total amount of outstanding long-term government bonds to GNP stood at 16·6% in 1976 compared with 27·1% in the United States and 42·8% in Great Britain (in 1975). However, the ratio is expected to rise gradually, approaching the US and British levels during the 1980s. With the increase in outstanding government bonds, promotion of policies for their control, as well as the improvement of the bond trading market, can be expected.

6.4.3 SOPHISTICATION OF PERSONAL FINANCIAL ASSETS

The total amount of personal financial assets exceeded $700 billion at the end of 1976, and is expected to top $1,700 billion in 1985. Along with the quantitative expansion, the quality of personal assets will improve, reflecting a sluggish increase in individual disposable income and a fall of the rate of savings. There are also signs of increased sensitivity on the part of individual investors to interest rates and a preference for investment in securities. Securities accounted for 17·6% of the total personal financial assets at the end of 1976, but the rate will rise in the future.

6.4.4 GROWTH OF PENSION FUNDS

At present, public and private pension funds are estimated at $100 billion and $10 billion respectively. The ratio of pension funds to GNP is 19% and is increasing. Due to a rapid increase in private pension funds, the total amount is expected to reach $220 billion in 1980, and $350 billion in 1985. Its importance is better understood when compared with Japan's aggregate stock market value of $200 billion and outstanding bonds of $330 billion.

Pension funds' investments in securities are likely to expand as in the United States and Europe, where investments by pension funds play an important role in the capital market. With sluggish corporate investment in plant and equipment, such institutional investors as life insurance companies and trust banks will emphasize investments in securities.

The ratio of securities to the total working assets of other monetary institutions is also rising, and the average ratio of securities to total deposits of all city banks is expected to rise to 30% in 1985 from 20% in 1975.

6.4.5 INTERNATIONALIZATION OF THE CAPITAL MARKET

These changes in the domestic situation will be coupled with a rapid internationalization of the capital market. This will merit special attention as Japan's position in the world economy improves, as changes occur in the international monetary system (with a shift to floating exchange rates), and as world flow of capital is accelerated. Investment in Japanese securities by non-residents, and in foreign securities by Japanese institutional investors, along with the internationalization of capital and an increase in yen-denominated foreign bonds, are expected to be fully realized with the decontrol of foreign exchange. Internationalization of the yen will also accelerate this trend.

Internationalization of the capital market is related to that of the currency market. When examining the cases of the New York and London markets, internationalization of the currency interacts with the capital market, which depends on funds from the short-term money market.

Internationalization of the yen will have the following effects on the Japanese capital market:

Development of the Short-term Money Markets

Internationalization of the yen will accelerate the growth of the short-term money market, including the government bill and discount markets.

Internationalization of the Bond Market

The internationalization of the capital market has preceded that of the short-term money market, since stricter curbs are placed on the flow of short-term capital. However, exchange decontrol has been stepped up since the beginning of 1977. Regulations on conversion of dollars into yen have been eased, and floatation of yen-denominated foreign bonds have been further increased. Curbs on remittances of money acquired by non-residents by selling of Japanese bonds within six months after their purchase were lifted. Thus, decontrol on the flow of short-term funds has progressed. This will trigger a rapid increase of foreign investments in Japanese bonds.

Foreign examples have shown that expansion of bond transactions by non-residents contributes to the internationalization of the capital market. In the New York market, for instance, the annual volume of long-term bonds traded by non-residents normally exceeds the market's turnover for stock transactions and even in lean years does not fall much below 50% of stock transactions. In European markets, the bond market is more developed than the stock market. Since internationalization of the yen is inseparable from exchange decontrol, and because it will stimulate the functioning of interest rates in the bond market, expansion of the bond market and internationalization of the capital market will make remarkable progress.

Yen-denominated Foreign Bonds

Outstanding yen-denominated foreign bonds reached $9 billion at the end of 1976. At present, issuers of these bonds are limited to international organizations such as the World Bank and the Asian Development Bank, as well as central and local governments of advanced nations. The following changes are expected:

(a) These bonds will be issued more frequently, although the Ministry of Finance will continue to retain control of their floatation.

(b) In addition to international organizations and governments of advanced nations, a larger variety of organizations such as large corporations of advanced countries and governments of developing nations will be allowed to float bonds.

Floatation of Foreign Currency Bonds

The total outstanding foreign currency bonds floated by Japanese issuers reached $6 billion at the end of 1976. According to Morgan Guaranty, the ratio of foreign currency bonds floated by Japanese issuers to the total has gradually increased from 3·5% in 1974 to 9·2% in 1975 but dropped to 6·4% in 1976. A further increase is expected with progressive internationalization of Japanese corporate activity.

By opening its doors to overseas issuers, the Tokyo capital market took a step towards internationalization, by acting as a recycling market to adjust the uneven distribution of funds in the world. The Tokyo capital market is expected to expand as one of the international markets not only in trading but also in floatation.

As stated above, the Japanese capital market is expected to grow rapidly under these changing circumstances. The value of outstanding bonds will rise to $1 trillion in 1985 from $330 billion in 1976. The aggregate market value of stocks is also likely to increase from $200 billion in 1976 depending on the expansion of the Japanese economy. Along with such quantitative expansion, the Japanese capital market is expected to become more sophisticated, by the active investment of domestic and foreign investors. Expansion of the bond market through liberalization of interest rates, and internationalization stepped up not only by exchange decontrol but by internationalization of the yen, will bring the Japanese capital market to a stage of full growth.

6.5 Conclusion

The Japanese economy is increasing its efficiency through market mechanisms whilst maintaining its stability, the yen is accepted as a strong currency and the Tokyo capital market is taking on an international character. It is now an appropriate time to attach more weight to investment in Japanese stocks and bonds in the management of portfolios.

The Tokyo market is coming of age. It reflects not only the strength of the well developed industrial economy of Japan but also the financial sophistication and understanding resulting from its dealings with the more advanced capital markets of the United States and Europe.

INDEX

accounting system 176–177
administrative capacity of political
    parties 29
age of population 16–17, 20
agricultural cooperative associations
    124–125
agriculture and fisheries 15
    financial institutions 124–125
    labour force 15
agriculture and forestry debentures
    125, 150
agriculture-, forestry- and fishery-
    related financial institutions
    124–125
Anti-Monopoly Law
    history 48–49
    revision 182–183
audio equipment industry 99–103
auditing requirements 176
automobile industry 6–7, 41, 74,
    89–93

balance of payments 9, 40–43
    see also foreign trade; trade balance
bank debentures 150
Bank of Japan 48
    monetary policy control by 132–135
banks 118–128
basic industries 73–76
bond floatation
    foreign currency bonds 187–188
    public bonds 185–186
bond market
    development 143
    internationalization 143, 187
bonds 143, 148–152

listing requirements, Tokyo Stock
    Exchange 159–161
trading for pricing 159–160

call and bill discount markets 136–138
    control by authorities 132
call brokers 128, 136
capital market
    growth 185
    internationalization 186–187
    liberalization 181
    see also financial market
Central Bank of Commercial and
    Industrial Cooperatives (Shoko
    Chukin Bank) 129
Central Cooperative Bank of
    Agriculture and Forestry 125
chain stores 112–117
chemical industry 6–7, 44, 49
city banks 118–119
climate 1
commercial banks 118–120
Commercial Code 151
Commercial Law, provisions on stocks
    148
commission rates on stock exchange
    transactions 166–167
Committee on Financial System
    Research 180
commodity imports 9–11, 14
companies
    decision-making 62
    differences from Western companies
    58–62
    management 52–54
    profit ratios 59–61
    training 18

zaibatsu origins 51
 see also ringi system
company accounts 176–177
consensus system of management 53
conservatism (politics) 19, 23–25
consolidation of company accounts
  176–177
construction industry 74–75, 86–89
convertible bonds 151
 listing requirements, Tokyo Stock
  Exchange 161
corporate bonds 151
corporate finance, changes in 185
corporate growth 58–59
corporate investment in securities 141
credit associations 124

Daimyo 2
dealing system on Tokyo Stock
  Exchange 161–163
decision-making in business 53, 61, 62
defence industry 4–6
Democratic Socialist Party 27–28
demographic structure 15–16, 20–21
department stores 112–117
Depression era (1930s) 6–7, 51
Diet (Parliament) 19–20
directors 52–53
discount regulation, Bank of Japan *see*
  window operation
Dodge Mission 8
Domei (Japanese Confederation of
  Labour) 28

economy
 adaptation of 178–179
 growth 183
 policy 35, 46–48
 reform of 179–183
 size and characteristics 30–31
education 3, 17–19
electrical equipment industry 5, 75,
  93–99
electronics industry 93–99
 see also audio equipment industry
emperor 2
employment *see* labour; lifetime
  employment system;
  unemployment
energy consumption 11–14, 45
environmental problems 23, 45
exporting industries 75–77
exports 35, 40–41, 75–77
 electrical equipment 75, 95
 electronic equipment 95

motor vehicles 75
steel 75
synthetic fibres 105, 106
 see also foreign trade; balance of
  payments

Federation of Agricultural Credit
  Cooperative Unions 125
fibre production 104–105
financial institutions 118–131
financial market 118–131, 135–139
 outlook 142–143
 structural changes 139–143
 see also capital market
First World War 5
fiscal policy 46–48
fisheries
 financial institutions 124–125
 labour force 15
food resources 15
foreign bonds, yen-dominated 147,
  151–152, 187
foreign-capital firms in Japan 62–65
 see also foreign investment in
  Japan; joint ventures
foreign currency bonds floatation 187–
  188
foreign investment in Japan 5, 62–65
 easing of restrictions on 173, 176
 taxes applicable 174–175
foreign investment trusts in Japan 173
foreign stocks, listing requirements on
  Tokyo Stock Exchange 157–159
foreign trade 40–43
 see also balance of payments; trade
  balance
forestry, financial institutions 124–125
futures trading in securities 144, 145

geography 1
government bonds 148–150
government expenditure 34–35
 as policy instrument 46
government-guaranteed bonds 150
government-related financial
  institutions 128
Great Depression (1930s) *see*
  Depression era
groupism 53–55
growth rates of industries 67–73

hi-fi manufacturers *see* audio
  equipment industry
high-growth industries 72–73
history 1–9

Housing Loan Public Corporation   48,
     128, 129

imports of resources 9–11, 14, 40
     steel industry 79
income equality 23, 25
indices of Tokyo Stock Exchange
     163–165
industrial development, history 3–9
industrial policy 48–50
industrial revolution 4–5, 179
industrial structure 44–45
     reform 182–183
industry
     basic industries 73–76
     forecasts 67–77
     growth rates 68–72
     high-growth industries 72–73
inflation
     effect on economic policy 46
     outlook 183–184
institutional investors, increasing role
     of 141
insurance companies 125, 128
interest rates
     changes 184
     liberalization 180–182
     trends 184–185
internationalization of the capital
     market 187
investment see foreign investment in
     Japan; Japanese investment
     abroad; plant and equipment
     investment; private investment
investment trusts 170–173
invisibles deficits 43

Japan Communist Party 25, 28
Japan Development Bank 128, 129
Japan Export–Import Bank 128, 129
Japan Socialist Party 20, 25, 27, 28
Japanese Confederation of Labour
     (Domei) 28
Japanese investment abroad, 11, 65–66
Japanese–Western relations, history 2,
     3, 5
joint ventures 3, 5, 62–66

key industries 77–117
Komeito 25, 27, 28
Korean War 8

labour
     age 17
     educational level 17–19
     financial institutions for 125
     history 5
     Japanese Confederation of Labour
          28
     occupational composition 22–23
     unemployment 37–38
     see also lifetime employment system;
          unions
Liberal Democratic Party 19–20, 26,
     28–29
liberalization
     capital transactions 181
     interest rates 142–143, 180–182
     securities investment 147
     trade 180
lifetime employment system 38,
     55–56, 61–62
listing requirements, Tokyo Stock
     Exchange 155–161
living standards see standard of living
local banks 119–120
long-term credit banks 120–121
long-term financial assets, increasing
     weight of 141
long-term financial institutions 120–
     121

macro-economic policy 45–48
management of companies 52–54,
     55–58, 61–62
mass production, economics of 7, 58
Meiji era 3–4, 51
middle classes 9, 23, 25
military development of industry 3,
     4–6
monetary policy 46–48
     instruments of 132–135
money market see capital market,
     financial market
money supply 135
moneylenders 128
mortgage bonds 151
motor industry see automobile
     industry
municipal bonds 150
mutual banks 121, 124

national expenditure 32–35
National Federation of Credit
     Associations 124
national income 30–31
National Income Doubling Plan 9
nationalization of businesses 25
natural resources see resources
New Liberal Club 20, 26

Nikkei Dow Jones Average 163–164

official discount rate 132, 133
oil crisis (1973), effect on corporate growth 62

pension funds, growth of 186
People's Finance Corporation 129
personal consumption 32–33
personal financial assets 186
    see also private investment, private savings
plant and equipment investment 3–9, 31–32, 33–34, 40
political parties 20, 25–30
political system 19
politics 19–30
population 2, 15–17
    age 16–17, 20
prices 35–37
private investment 33–34
private savings 31–32
product divisions (management organization) 53–54
profit ratios 59–61
progressives (politics) 25
promotion 56–58, 62
public bond floatation 185–186

reform of the Japanese economy 179–183
religion 15
repurchase market 138–139
reserve ratio adjustment 132, 133
residential investment 33
    Housing Loan Public Corporation 48, 128, 129
resources 9–15, 45
    imports 9–11, 14, 40
restrictive trade practices 48–49
retail industry 112–117
ringi system 53, 61
Russo-Japanese War 5

saitori members of stock exchanges 152, 153–154
Second World War 6–7, 145
securities
    commission rates on transactions 166–167
    corporate investment in 141
    over-the-counter market 165
Securities and Exchange Law 145, 146, 152, 153–154, 167–169
securities companies 169–170

Securities Dealers Association of Japan 165
securities market, history 144–148
seniority system of promotion 56–58, 62
shipbuilding industry 82–86
    history 4–8
Shogun 2
Shoko Chukin Bank (Central Bank of Industrial and Commercial Cooperatives) 129
short-term government bonds (bills) 148–150
short-term money market 135–136
Showa era 144
Sino-Japanese War 4, 144
Small Business Finance Corporation 128, 129
small businesses, financial institutions for 121, 124, 128, 129
social equality 23
special bonds 148, 150
spot trading in securities 144
standard of living 2, 20–24
steel industry 8, 45, 74, 77–81
    structural depression of 49
stimulative financial policies 46–48
stock exchanges 152–155
    commission rates 166–167
    history 144–146
    listing on 155–159
    members 152–155
stocks 148
    listing requirements on Tokyo Stock Exchange 155–159
synthetic fibre industry 9, 103–107

TSE Stock Price Index 164–165
Taisho era 144
tendering for construction work, methods of 87
textile industry 4, 6, 8
    structural depression of 49
    see also synthetic fibre industry

Tokugawa period 1–2
Tokyo Stock Exchange 144, 147, 152–167
trade balance 40–43
    see also balance of payments; foreign trade
trade liberalization 180
trading companies 107–112
Treasury Investment and Loan Plans 128–129, 130–131

trust banks 121

unemployment 37–38
unions 39
    Japanese Confederation of Labour
        28
unit trusts 170–173
urbanization 15–16

wages 39–40
    effect on prices 36–37
    negotiations 54–55
Western countries' relations with
    Japan, history 2, 3, 5

wholesale prices 37
window operation 48, 132, 133–135
workers' credit unions 125
workforce *see* labour; population
world economic changes 178–179

yen-denominated foreign bonds 147,
    151–152
    internationalization 187

zaibatsu 51–52, 54, 144
    dissolution of 145, 171